WORDS At PLAY

Quips, Quirks & Oddities

O. V. Michaelsen

Sterling Publishing Co., Inc.
New York

Edited and arranged by Jeanette Green
Designed by Judy Morgan

Library of Congress Cataloging-in-Publication Data

Michaelsen, O. V.
  Words at play : quips, quirks & oddities / O. V. Michaelsen.
    p.   cm.
  Includes index.
  ISBN 0-8069-9791-5
  1. American wit and humor.   I. Title
PN 162.M84 1997
398.8—dc21   97-23519

1   3   5   7   9   10   8   6   4   2

Published by Sterling Publishing Company, Inc.
387 Park Avenue South, New York, N. Y. 10016
© 1997 by O. V. Michaelsen
Distributed in Canada by Sterling Publishing
% Canadian Manda Group, One Atlantic Avenue, Suite 105
Toronto, Ontario, Canada M6K 3E7
Distributed in Great Britain and Europe by Cassell PLC
Wellington House, 125 Strand, London WC2R 0BB, England
Distributed in Australia by Capricorn Link (Australia) Pty Ltd.
P.O. Box 6651, Baulkham Hills, Business Centre, NSW 2153, Australia
Manufactured in the United States of America

Sterling ISBN 0-8069-9791-5

Yo de todo te doy.
"I give you a bit of everything."

CONTENTS

4 WORD
FOR WORDS
FOREWORD

Welcome to a bounding, abounding playground of words. Step right through the gate and frolic with some of our most nimble and whimsical words as they clamber over jungle gyms, bounce up and down see-saws, swing on rings, ring on swings, careen down sliding boards, and merrily whirl around on merry-go-rounds.

This wordplayground isn't just for children. There is nothing immature or regressive about messing around with words. Around the age of six, children in just about every society on earth start pushing the envelope and enveloping the push of their native languages. We see this creativity in the six-year-old who climbed onto the kitchen sink in his home and cackled, "I'm sink-ing!" We see it in the eight-year-old experiencing her first day at school. A woman came up and introduced herself by saying, "I'm the principal here." The girl replied: "No, you're not. You're the princessipal!"

Sure, we human beings have acquired language to help us survive the demands of our whirled world:

"Please pass the ice water." "How much does this cost?" and "How do I get to Carnegie Hall?" But there is another gene ration that makes us generate the likes of "A waist is a terrible thing to mind," and "How do you get to Carnegie Hall?—Practice, practice."

We are the only creatures on this planet who employ language recreationally and *re*-creationally. We glorify the punderful humanity of language in four primary ways.

◆ *We fiddle around with meaning.* *Jumbo shrimp* is a punny oxymoron.

◆ *We explore the bounds of sound.* *Expediency* is composed of five letters pronounced "XPDNC."

◆ *We laugh at loopy logic.* Groucho Marx, in a letter to the Friars Club, wrote: "Please accept my resignation. I don't want to belong to any club that would have me as a member."

◆ *Or we make the alphabet dance.* Toss all the letters in *O. V. Michaelsen* up into the air and down comes the anagram "Manic, he loves."

This book celebrates all these tour-de-farces. Anyone who has ever chuckled at a clever verbal quip will treasure this pleasury of the best in sprightly wordplay. The author has obviously lived his life as a genuine, certified, authentic wordaholic, logolept, and verbivore. He has poured that life into this miscellany of verbal shenanigans. *Words at Play* is a party of life. Imbibe its witticisms, and you will become the life of any party.

—RICHARD LEDERER

ACKNOWLEDGMENTS

◇ ◇ ◇

I am especially indebted to the National Puzzlers' League, in which I used the pseudonym Rom Dos; Sheila Anne Barry; my editor, Jeanette Green, for her outstanding work; book designer Judy Morgan; Newton B. Lovejoy; Frank W. Elwell for many puzzle columns and journals he collected from 1879 to the early 1900s; Howard W. Bergerson, former editor of *Word Ways: The Journal of Recreational Linguistics,* for permission to reprint material from his book *Palindromes & Anagrams* (1973); and Dmitri A. Borgmann, the father of modern "logology" (recreational linguistics), founding editor of *Word Ways,* and author of *Curious Crosswords* (1970), *Beyond Language: Adventures in Word & Thought* (1967), and *Language on Vacation: An Olio of Orthographical Oddities* (1965).

Thanks to my wife, Lois Marin Fischer, for proofreading, suggestions, and technical assistance; author Willard R. Espy for planting the seed and for permission to reprint material from his books; puzzlemeister Will Shortz for his invaluable resources, exceptional consideration, and support; Dr. A. Ross Eckler, author of *Making the Alphabet Dance* (1996) and former editor of *The Enigma,* for kindly helping with puzzle sources and dates and for his generous permission to reprint material from *Word Ways;* David Morice, editor and illustrator of "Kickshaws" in *Word Ways* and author of *Alphabet Avenue* (1997); Ken Elrod for permission to reprint quotes from his Mensa SIG newsletter, *Word Fun*; Kent L. Aldershof, puzzle editor of *Word Fun*; Chris Long for his word squares; Eric Albert for his many contributions, corrections, and comments; Murray R. Pearce for his helpful insight; Trip Payne for permission to reprint the truncated inverted pyramid form puzzle from his newsletter *The Former*; Emily Cox and Henry Rathvon for permission to reprint palindromes from their "Word Games" column in *Atlantic Unbound* (*The Atlantic Monthly* on-line); Tony Augarde for supplying me with the sources of some of the anagrams quoted in his book *The Oxford Guide to Word Games* (1984); Professor John E. Connett for permission to include his palindromes; Barbara Sindriglis for sending me "Reverse Parallelisms"; Wendy Maruyama for passing along to me some "Poor Translations"; Joseph J. Adamski; Wilder Bentley; Herbert Pfeiffer; Mark Saltveit; Jouko Valta; Kim Walker-Daniels, former editor of the *Mensa International Journal*; to authors Paul Dickson and Richard Lederer for their thoughtful suggestions, and to Martin Gardner for his key role in making this book a reality.

Quotes from *The Enigma* are reprinted by permission from the National Puzzlers' League.

"Famous Last Words" come from a variety of sources: William Emmette Coleman's articles in *Queries*, 1888; Edward S. Le Comte's *Last Words* (1955); Gyles Brandreth's *The Last Word* (1979); Scott Slater's *Exits* (1980); and Espy's *Another Almanac of Words at Play* (1980).

A fan of the rock group The Doors called my attention to the fact that reshuffling the letters in the words "Mr. Mojo risin'" from the song "L. A. Woman" reveals the name JIM MORRISON. While browsing through dictionaries I found rhymes for *orange*, *silver*, and *purple*. Discoveries like these piqued my interest in word curiosities.

In my research, I perused more than forty puzzle columns in periodicals published in the United States and the United Kingdom since 1866, including privately issued puzzle journals, broadsides, and newsletters.

Wordplay and puzzles have been among my favorite pastimes as long as I remember, but I must give credit (or blame) to author Willard R. Espy for being a major source of my early inspiration. Through his books I discovered the National Puzzlers' League, *Word Ways* magazine, works of Dmitri A. Borgmann, and those of other wordsmiths.

Much of the material and most of sources collected here have not been previously published in book form.

—O. V. MICHAELSEN

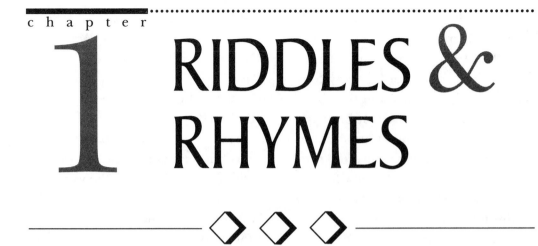

RIDDLES & RHYMES

THE BEST OF RHYMES, THE WORST OF RHYMES

Colorful Rhymes

Although it has been said that there are no rhymes for *purple, orange,* and *silver,* there are these.

PURPLE
hirple   (British) walk lamely or hobble
curple   hindquarters, especially of a horse

ORANGE
blorenge   a hill near Abergavenny, Wales
sporange   a sac in which spores are produced; sporangium

An anonymous 19th century poet in a London weekly, *Athenaeum,* 1865, wrote this orange ditty.

The second James a daughter had,
Too fine to lick a porringer;
He sought her out a noble lad,
And gave the Prince of Orange her.

And here's one from Willard Espy's *The Game of Words* (1972).

The four eng-
ineers
wear orange
brassieres.

SILVER
Wilver   "Willie" Stargell, coach for the Atlanta Braves
chilver   a ewe lamb

And here is Stephen Sondheim's solution, first published in *Time* magazine, but also in Willard Espy's *An Almanac of Words at Play* (1975).

To find a rhyme for silver,
Or any "rhymeless" rhyme
Requires only will, ver-
bosity and time.

TRIPARTITE COLOR RHYMES
In this poem by David Morice, *WW*,
May 1993, all three colors merge into
an anecdote about the favorite drink
of one of the Wild West's most color-
ful figures.

Wyatt Earp'll
Shoot till he's purple,
Then carefully chill ver-
mouth in a silver
Cup, which he'll pour, inj-
ecting an orange.

Other Stubborn Rhymes

VELOCITY
Having once gained the summit,
and managed to cross it, he
Rolls down the side with uncommon
velocity.—Richard Harris Barham (1788–1845)

PELICAN
Dixon Lanier Merritt was the author
of this familiar limerick.

A wonderful bird is the pelican,
His bill can hold more than his
  belican.
He can take in his beak
Enough food for a week,
I'm darned if I know how the helican.

Stock Rhymes in Popular Songs

the way you walk, the way you talk

glance, chance, dance, romance

love, dove, thinkin' of, the moon/the
  stars/the Lord above

Hold me tight, all through the night,
  till the morning light, it'll be all right.

bought, brought, caught, (for)got,
  hot, not, fought, a lot

strong, (be)long, wrong, song

low, dough, slow, flow, owe, grow, no, go

living without you, thinking about you

(I'm) down on my knees, (I'm) beg-
  ging you, "Please!"

all alone, telephone

hurtin', for certain

lonely, only

lazy, crazy

drinkin', thinkin'

dreaming, scheming

make a change, rearrange

June, tune, moon, soon

maybe, baby

reelin', feelin'

hand in hand, along the sand

your charms, in my arms

tease me, squeeze me, please me,
  frees me

stranger, danger

warning, morning

illusion, confusion

years, tears

the rain, the train, the pain, again

wife, strife, knife, life

worry, hurry

jail, bail

money, honey

highways, byways

double, trouble

sorrow, tomorrow

try, cry, die, good-bye

RIDDLES, RELATIVES & DUBIOUS PRAISES

Riddled Praises

An 1800s newspaper reported that a clever young writer composed riddles and other puzzles to entertain female admirers. Because they had become expert in guessing the answers, they asked him for a more challenging puzzle. He sent them this.

When you ask a harder question,
To unriddle your suggestion,
I am sure, itself suggests the answer
  plain,
It has puzzled many sages
Of many lands and ages,
But no doubt you will tackle it in vain.

By taking the first letter of the first line, the second letter of the next, and so on down to the fifth, you will find the word *woman*. The girls deciphered the puzzle and also found, to his surprise and regret, that the letters immediately following form the word *hussy*.

The "–gry" Riddle

Contrary to what many believe, there are only two "common" words which end in "-gry": *angry* and *hungry*. The puzzler Nightowl mentioned the old "-gry" words riddle in her Rochester, New York, newsletter *The Ag Mine*, Mar. 1997: "A local newspaper columnist found the first logical explanation I have seen of that so-called riddle. The correct version of the riddle is 'Think of words ending in '-gry'. *Angry* and *hungry* are two of them. There are only three words in the English language. What is the third word? The word is something we use every day.

   If you have listened carefully, I have already told you what it is.' The answer is *language*, which is the third word in 'the English language.' Most versions of the riddle change the wording and make it insoluble. Let's hope this puts that 'riddle' to rest."

A Genealogical Riddle

This riddle by Mabel Poete appeared in the puzzle column "Odd Knots" in *The Independent*, a New York weekly, Dec. 19, 1894. The theme was later used in the song "I'm My Own Grandpa/Grandma," credited to Dwight Latham and Moe Jaffe, and recorded by many since the 1940s, including Guy Lombardo, Lonzo & Oscar, Homer & Jethro, and Ray Stevens. It was based on a story called "Singular Intermarriages," printed in Charles Bombaugh's *Gleanings* (1870).

'Twas long ago, in the days of witches and the "Bible Laws," that a mysterious old woman took up her abode in a cabin on the outskirts of a New England town. She was regarded with some curiosity and suspicion by her neighbors, and their questions concerning her family elicited such strange replies that she was finally conceived to be a witch, and brought before a magistrate on that charge.

"Who was your mother?" the judge inquired first.

"My daughter-in-law was my mother," the woman replied.

"And your father?"

"My stepson was my father."

"Have you no children?"

"My aunt was my daughter," she answered sadly, "and my only child, but she is long dead."

"And your grandfather?"

"My husband was my grandfather, but he is also dead."

"Well, your grandmother, who was she?"

"Alas," said the woman weeping, "I am my own grandmother and only living relative!"

"Now, by good Mather's shade," cried the exasperated judge, "either thou mockest me or thou art indeed a daughter of the Evil One, and thou shalt burn this day in the public square!" But the old woman said: "I speak only truth, and can explain the mystery if thou wilt but hear me!"

A little later she was dismissed, and the judge was giving to the public her explanation, which he declared to be quite simple and satisfactory.

The woman said: "My mother married the second time a man much her junior—the son of a widower. Curiously enough, I later married the widower. My mother then became my daughter-in-law, since she was the wife of my step-son; my step-son became my father, since he was the husband of my mother; I had a daughter, and she was also my aunt, being the sister of my father; my husband was my grandfather, because he was the father of my father; and, as the wife of one's grandfather is one's grandmother, I became, of course, my own grandmother."

2 WHEN WORDS GO AWRY

◇ ◇ ◇

THE BEST OF THE WORST, FICTIVE MUSES

These excerpts were selected from unsolicited manuscripts sent to a prominent editor of (serious) fiction, who chose to be anonymous. They were recorded in "From the Slush Pile" in *The National Lampoon* in 1981 and 1989.

✍ "The man wore a charcoal-gray, three-piece suit and sported a diamond ring on his pinky that Sergeant Miller exaggerated to himself as being the size of a hamburger."

✍ "From the moment he crushed Cora's skull, he knew it was going to be a rotten Monday."

✍ "Catherine awoke in a panic that she was going blind, then she realized that her eyes were shut tight."

✍ "Martin knew that under Jeannie's thin veneer of outward convention she was totally naked."

✍ "He snorted mentally."

✍ "My day at work had been rather hectic for me, as it had been for the past several days, and I came home exhausted and angry at the world, and at Mr. Whipple in general."

✍ "Dale was not one to mince words and came directly to the point. 'Hi,' he said."

✍ "'Os swoh skcirt?' Jack asked when I arrived at the office. 'I'm fine, Jack,' I said. 'But you know I hate it when you talk backwards.'"

PUNS & MALAPROPISMS

A *malapropism* is an absurd misuse of a word, especially by the confusion with a word similar in sound. Here's a famous example from Mistress Malaprop, a character in Richard Sheridan's *The Rivals* (1775): "As headlong as an 'allegory' on the banks of the Nile." Malapropisms are uttered almost as often as the intended words, and sometimes they are more interesting. A woman applying for a divorce was asked by the clerk whether she wanted the form for "disillusion (dissolution) of marriage." Here are more malapropisms, puns, and offbeat phrases.

"The cookbook is being compiled. Please submit your favorite recipe and a helpful antidote concerning it."
—**Richard Lederer,** *Anguished English* **(1987)**

"Dyslexics of the wolrd, untie!"—**graffito**

"If people don't want to come, you can't stop them."—**Sol Hurok**

"Posterity is just around the corner."
—**George S. Kaufman**

"Beauty is only sin deep."—**Saki**

"The driver swerved to avoid missing the jaywalker."—**Leo Rosten in Joseph Shipley,** *Playing with Words* **(1960)**

"Life's a bleach, and then you dry."
—**sign in a Chapel Hill, North Carolina, laundromat**

"Wagner's music is better than it sounds."

This quote about Wagner was not the words of Mark Twain, as many believe, though he often quoted it. According to John George and Paul F. Boller, Jr., in *They Never Said It* (1989), the line belongs to American humorist Edgar Wilson ("Bill") Nye.

Bill Peterson (1920-1993), Florida State Football Coach

"Pair off in groups of threes."

"I'm the football coach around here, and don't you remember it!"

"Line up alphabetically by height." **(also credited to Casey Stengel)**

After being inducted into the Florida Sports Hall of Fame: "They gave me a standing observation."

Samuel Goldwyn (1879-1974)

The motion picture mogul Samuel Goldwyn was said to have uttered these gems.

"Withering heights"

"Tell me, how did you love the picture?"

"We have all passed a lot of water since then." He intended to say: "A lot of water has passed under the bridge."

"No, thanks; coffee isn't my cup of tea."

On color television: "I won't believe it until I see it in black and white."

"When I want your opinion, I'll give it to you."

"We're overpaying him, but he's worth it."

"I had a monumental idea last night, but I didn't like it."

> **❝** *I never put on a pair of shoes until I've worn them five years.* **❞**

"I never liked you, and I always will."

"I may not always be right, but I'm never wrong."

"For your information, I would like to ask you a question."

"Going to call him William? What kind of a name is that? Every Tom, Dick, and Harry's called William. Why don't you call him Bill?"

"Let's have some new clichés."

"The scene is dull. Tell him to put more life into his dying."

"If I could drop dead right now, I'd be the happiest man alive."

And Not Goldwyn

According to Paul F. Boller, Jr., and John George in *They Never Said It* (1989), Samuel Goldwyn *never* said these lines.

"Include me out."

"I read part of it all the way through."

"Our comedies are not to be laughed at."

"An oral contract isn't worth the paper it's written on." What he actually said was: "His verbal contract is worth more than the paper it's written on," referring to film executive Joseph M. Schenk.

And Goldwyn denies having said: "Anyone who goes to a psychiatrist ought to have his head examined!"

Yogi Berra (b. 1925)

These Yogi Berra jewels come from Phil Pepe's *The Wit & Wisdom of Yogi Berra* (1974) and other sources.

On the shadows cast on Yankee Stadium's left field in the fall: "It gets late early out there."

To a friend, while working as a head-waiter at a St. Louis restaurant: "Nobody comes to this restaurant—it's always too crowded."

Referring to Yankees manager Miller Huggins: "If Miller was alive today, he'd be turning over in his grave."

When asked about his disputes with Yankees owner George Steinbrenner: "Oh, George is all right—we just agree different."

About baseball: "Baseball is ninety percent mental. The other half is physical."

 *You should go to your friend's funeral; otherwise, he might not come to yours.*

"You can observe a lot by watching."

"A nickel ain't worth a dime anymore."

"(It's) *déjà vu* all over again."

On being quoted: "I didn't really say half the things I said."

Dale Berra, when asked to compare himself to his father: "Our similarities are different."

Famous Fumbles & Witty Quotes

"The climate of the Sahara is such that its inhabitants have to live elsewhere."—**Antony Lake in Joseph Shipley,** *Playing with Words* **(1960)**

"All I want out of you is silence, and damn little of that!"—**a judge in Joseph Shipley,** *Playing with Words* **(1960)**

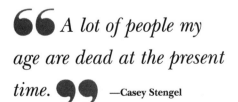 *A lot of people my age are dead at the present time.* —**Casey Stengel**

During a trial in Salisbury, Rhodesia (now Zimbabwe), a witness was asked if the accused was conscious or unconscious at the scene of the crime. "He was pretending to be conscious, but he wasn't," replied the witness.

MONDEGREENS
(Aural Malapropisms)

A *mondegreen* is an aural malapropism—a mishearing of a word or phrase. The term, not yet officially recognized, was coined by writer Sylvia Wright. A word or phrase which sounds the same as another has been referred to as an *oronym*, similar to a charade or *redivider*. Columnist Jon Carroll of the *San Francisco Chronicle* explains that she had heard the Scottish ballad "The Bonny Earl of Murray" as a child and thought one stanza read like this.

Ye highlands and ye lowlands
Oh, where hae you been?
Thou hae slay the Earl of Murray
And Lady Mondegreen.

"Poor Lady Mondegreen, thought Silvia Wright—a tragic heroine dying with her liege. How poetic. When she learned years later that what they had actually done was slay the Earl of Murray and 'laid him on the green,' Wright was so distraught by the sudden disappearance of her heroine that she memorialized her with the neologism."

Jon Carroll also supplied these mishearings of song lyrics. Of course, with wine and song, words easily run into each other.

"'Scuse me while I kiss this guy." ("'Scuse me while I kiss the sky," from "Purple Haze.") Jimi Hendrix would actually kiss a guy after singing the line in concert.

"We risked our lives in traffic." ("We tripped the light fantastic," from "Sidewalks of New York.")

"Midnight after you're wasted . . . " ("Midnight at the Oasis").

"There's a bathroom on the right." (There's a bad moon on the rise," from "Bad Moon Rising.")

PERSONAL PLEDGE

Here is a mangled version of our beloved "Pledge of Allegiance" from Jon Carroll's collection.

"I pledge a lesion to the flag of the united state of America, and to the republic for Richard Stans, one naked individual, with liver, tea, and just this, for all."

In 1950, Congressman George Smathers defeated incumbent Senator Claude Pepper in the Florida Democratic Senatorial Primary by circulating, in rural communities of northern Florida, literature stating that the senator had "matriculated" with young women. Smathers also accused Pepper's sister of being a "thespian" and his brother of being a "practicing 'homo sapien.'" As if that wasn't enough, Smathers used McCarthyism as leverage against his opponent by referring to him as "Red" Pepper.

SILVER SPOONERISMS

A *spoonerism* is (usually) an unintentional transposition of letters or syllables in words. A subtle example I found is (Baltimore) Orioles—(Houston) Oilers, if spoken with a Midwestern accent.

The term *spoonerism* was named after the Reverend William Archibald Spooner, warden of New College in Oxford, England, from 1903 to 1924, holder of the first honorary degree in *orthinology*—word botching. Before Spooner, this form of metathesis was sometimes called a "marrowsky," after a Polish count who supposedly suffered from the disorder. These, like malapropisms, can be more interesting than the intended phrases. These spoonerisms were attributed to the clergyman, though few, if any, were actually uttered by him.

To a woman in church: "Mardan me, padom, but you are occupewing my pie. Allow me to sew you to another sheet."

To one of his students: "You have hissed my mystery classes; you have tasted two worms!"

To a group of farmers: "I have never addressed so many 'tons of soil.'"

"I have in my bosom a half-warmed fish" (half-formed wish).

To a bridegroom: "It is kisstomary to cuss the bride."

"He is a 'newted nose' analyst."

"His sin twister"

"Is the bean dizzy?"

"Our 'queer old Dean'" (dear old Queen [Victoria]).

More Spoonerisms

Lowell Thomas presented British statesman Sir (Richard) Stafford Cripps as "Sir Stifford Craps."

Another documented example is this gem by a newscaster: "Rumor that the President would veto the bill came from a high 'White Horse souse.'" The White Horse is a famous New York tavern where Dylan Thomas is said to have drunk himself to death.
—**Kermit Schafer's "Pardon My Blooper," an LP of broadcast blunders**

"Now missen, lister, all I had was tee marthroonis. So I theem under the affluence of inkahol, I am not palf as hickled as thinkle peep I am."
—**Martin Gardner, O&C (1961)**

"I'd rather have a (free) bottle in front o' me than a (pre)frontal lobotomy."—**credited to both Dorothy Parker and Fred Allen**

"Work is the curse of the drinking classes."—**Oscar Wilde**

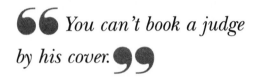 *You can't book a judge by his cover.*

"A drama critic is a man who leaves no turn unstoned."—**George Bernard Shaw**

"I am a conscientious man./ When I throw rocks at birds/ I leave no tern unstoned. /I am a meticulous man/ and when I portray baboons/ I leave no stern untoned."—**Ogden Nash**

"It's tired and I'm getting late."—**from the late 1960s song "Home to You"**

"I remember your name, but I just can't think of your face."

"Time wounds all heels."—**Groucho Marx**

"A waist is a terrible thing to mind."—**Ron Naftal, WF, Dec. 1994**

On the wall of a Seattle coffeehouse, an anonymous philosopher penned: "I am, therefore I think," and was answered with: "Aren't you putting Descartes before the horse?"

George S. Kaufman's response to his daughter after she told him that a friend of hers had eloped from college: "Ah! She put her heart before the course!"

In 1960, while campaigning in St. Paul, Minnesota, Adlai Stevenson was offended by a political remark made by clergyman Norman Vincent Peale. When questioned by the press about his visit, Stevenson said he found St. Paul "appealing" and Peale "appalling."—**Martin Gardner,** *Scientific American,* **Sept. 1964**

Spoonerhymes & Spoonergrams

In *The Enigma*, Mar. 1945, puzzler Emmo W. introduced the *spoonergram,* and David Silverman in *WW*, Feb. 1970, gave us the *spoonerhyme.* Other variations of the spoonerism are the "spannergroom," "spammergroon," and "groonerspam." Most examples here were published in *The Enigma* between 1945 and 1960; others are from *John O'London's Weekly* and *WW*, as noted.

optimistically   misty optically—**Allez, July 1951**

facsimiles   sick families—**O'London's, Dec. 28, 1929**

Pretty verse!   Witty! Terse!—**Eric Albert**

rebuff   Be rough.—**Quirk, July 1959**

visitation   'Tis evasion.—**Emmo W., Apr. 1947**

butterfly   flutter by (*old term*)

Ban the toys!   Tan the boys! (Don't!) —**Mrs. Ev, Mar. 1959**

high flyer   Fly higher.—**Plantina, Dec. 1947**

cats in a rage   (like) rats in a cage —**O'London's, May 24, 1930**

Tiny shoe!   Shiny, too!—**Arty Ess, Sept. 1959**

gin, ale   in jail—**Emmo W., Apr. 1946**

letting go   getting low—**Macropod, Aug. 1954**

run wild   one riled—**Alouette, Nov. 1956**

Would she?   Should we?

parking space   sparking pace—**Boo Jee-Kay, Sept. 1954**

Holy Grail   Glory! Hail!—**Ab Struse, June 1940**

ill-fed   Fill Ed.

running cat   cunning rat—**X. Spellary, Feb. 1949**

Drink tequila shooters.   Shoot tequila drinkers!—**"The Tonight Show," Mar. 23, 1993**

Beer nigh?   Nearby.—**J. A. Lindon,** *WW*

In casks?   Kin asks.—**Mary J. Hazard,** *WW*

OPPOSITES

backing losers   lacking boozers —**Y. Knott, Apr. 1960**

charred hills   hard chills—**Mrs. Ev, Oct. 1959**

free rein   refrain—**O'London's, May 24, 1930**

DOUBLE SPOONS

Here is a spoonerhyme by K. F. Ross, from the *Mensa Bulletin*, Apr. 1969.

Ill wit.

Will it

Die out?

I doubt.

SYLVAN SPRING

Alfred Kohn's poem "Sylvan Spring," from Willard Espy's *The Word's Gotten Out* (1989), contains *spoonerhymes* and near-spoonerhymes.

The snowdrops push through soggy
  grounds;
The she-bear senses spring is here.
Her mate still mumbles groggy
  sounds;
She wheezes softly in his ear.
Outside the den, a doe and fawn
Are hiding from their foe at dawn.
Amid bare trees a dreary lake
Is harboring a leery drake.
Two robins gather reed for nest,
And later they have need for rest.
A frog is eyeing a blue fly,
(It missed the one that just flew by).
A chipmunk, furried little ball,
Digs nuts it buried in the fall.
So there are creatures, weak and mild,
And others meek, and others wild.

POOR TRANSLATIONS

Executives of Coca-Cola were puzzled as to why sales of their product were doing poorly in mainland China until they discovered that the Chinese symbols CO CA CO LA translate literally to "bite the wax tadpole," or "female horse stuffed with wax." The Chinese translation of the Kentucky Fried Chicken slogan "finger licking good" was given as "eat your fingers off." In Taiwan, the Pepsi-Cola Company was told that its slogan, "Come Alive with the Pepsi Generation," was translated as "Pepsi brings back your dead ancestors."

Electrolux, a Scandinavian vacuum-cleaner manufacturer, advertised its product in the United States with the slogan: "Nothing sucks like an Electrolux."

Perdue's slogan, "It takes a tough man to make a tender chicken," was translated in Spanish as "It takes a hard man to make a chicken aroused." The translation appeared on billboards all over Mexico, showing him with one of his hens.

Batman was a movie box-office hit in 1989 in the United States, but it did not fare so well in Scandinavia. Perhaps one reason was the difficulty in translating the title. In Norway, for instance, it appeared on theatre marquees as *Flaggermous Man* ("Flying Mouse Man").

According to actor-comedian Billy Crystal, in France the title of the film *City Slickers* (1991), in which he co-starred, was changed to *Life, Love & Cows*. (There is no French word equivalent to *slickers*.)

Former U.S. President John Kennedy, in his 1963 speech at the Berlin Wall, intending to say "*Ich bin*

Berliner!" (I am a Berliner!), proudly proclaimed, "*Ich bin ein Berliner!*" (I am a jelly doughnut!).

General Motors found to its embarrassment that, in Spanish, Nova ("*no va*") means "It won't go"; and Ford discovered that *pinto* is Brazilian slang for "tiny male genitals."

During a tour of Poland, former U.S. President Jimmy Carter (around the time of his famous confession in *Playboy* to lusting in his heart) delivered a speech in which he expressed his "strong desire to know the Polish people." Through an inept translator, his message was heard as "I have a carnal desire for the Polish people."

Foreign Menus & Products You Can't Get at Home

From the Menu
In honor of the visiting Pope John Paul II, a hotel in Wroclaw, Poland, printed a special menu in three languages—Polish, German, and English: "Limp red beet soup with cheesy dumplings in the form of a finger; sirloin in clotted cream; a slice of bovine meat; beef rashers, beaten up in the country people fashion; ham below the knee, pickled and cooked; and roasted duck let loose."

Europe   garlic coffee, sweat from the trolley
Vietnam   pork with fresh garbage
Bali   toes with butter and jam
Spain   goose barnacles

China   cold shredded children and sea blubber in spicy sauce
Japan   strawberry crap, fried fishermen, buttered saucepans, and fried hormones

Brand-Name Products
Netherlands   Superglans (car wax)
Canada   Catch-It (kitty litter)
Greece   Zit (soft drink)
China   Ass Glue (as opposed to cow or horse-hide glue), Swine (chocolates)

Made in Japan

Junior Poison
My Fanny
(bathroom tissue)
Pocket Wetty
(moist towelettes)
Shot Vision (television sets)
Fingernail Remover
(fingernail cleaner)
Trim Pecker (jeans)
Green Piles
(lawn fertilizer)
Cow Brand (shampoo)
Dew-Dew (candy)
Kolic (mineral water)
Nasal ("for stuffed nose and snot")
I'm Dripper
(instant coffee)
Squid-Flavored Peanuts
Chocolate Colon (candy)
Last Climax (tissues)

Japanglish T.V.

Here are some English translations of actual Japanese television programs, as listed in *Japan Times*.

"Babbling Music Hall"

"Welfare Sumo"

"Quiz Time Shock"

"Music Tomato Japan"

"Young Oh Oh"

"It's Laughing"

"Joyful Map Variety"

"Unknown World: 'Toilet Seats of the World'"

Special: "Naked Clans of the World"

"Surprise World #1: 'Fried Ants'"

BRITISH BROADCAST BLUNDERS

Here are "Outtakes of the Year" (1986–1991) found in *Listener* magazine, London.

"He's got a fresh pair of legs up his sleeve."—**soccer reporter on "Good Morning Scotland" (BBC Radio, Scotland)**

"Clearly the Prime Minister's devious hand is afoot."—**John Smith, referring to a cabinet reshuffle; "The World Tonight" (Radio 4)**

"The reason he is struggling to bowl straight is because his head is in the wrong place."—**Fred Trueman, referring to Greg Thomas, "Test Match Special" (Radio 3)**

"I'll come back to the free interchange of needles for drug addicts if anyone's interested in pushing that point."—**Raymond Kendal, secretary-general of Interpol, "Call Nick Ross" (Radio 4)**

"No one would go to Hitler's funeral if he were alive today."—**Ron Brown, Labor MP, "News" (LBC)**

❝ *Most dreams are about everyday things—falling, flying, walking naked down the street.* ❞

—**Russ Parker, "Dreaming" (Radio 4)**

"They'd spent the weekend in a ditch waiting for a duck to fly over with a shotgun."—**Peter Benson, novelist, "Kaleidoscope" (Radio 4)**

"The chief dietician at Crew Hospital had only a skeleton staff."—**"The Food Program" (Radio 4)**

"The banks have to watch their backs on that front."—**"The Financial World Tonight" (Radio 4), Oct. 1990**

"This reminds me of last week's 'Farming Today,' which, of course, starts tomorrow."—**"Farming Today" (Radio 4, London)**

REDUNDANCIES

add on to

advanced reservation/warning

and plus

aquamarine

at least (*choose your number*) or more

ATM machine

attack bomber

bare naked

basic/necessary essentials

betwixt and between

bits and pieces

Blanco White   the given name of a
   minister and of a 1920s author

both/two alike

bought and paid for

brand name

brotherhood of man

cease and desist

close proximity

coalesce/combine/merge (*etc.*)
   into one

complete(ly), absolute(ly),
   and total(ly)

consensus of opinion

continue to persevere

crammed/stuffed full

crazy in the head

(in this) day and age

down below

downfall

dive/drop/fall down

each and every

empty gap/space

end result

a/every single one

eyesight

eyewink

fair and just

false illusion(s)/pretense(s)

fast/high rate of speed

fill up

final conclusion/result

fine and dandy

First, let's begin with . . .

foot pedal

forever and ever

forewarn

free and clear

free gift/giveaway

fuller

gone away

G.O.P. party   Grand Old Party is an
   epithet of the Republican party
   (1880).

hale and hearty

head butt

head honcho

great big

he-man

hot water heater

I, myself

increasingly more

individual person

integral part

irregardless

ISBN number

join/link/gather/collide (*etc.*)
   together

just merely

kicked his feet

leaps and bounds

leave go

leave of absence

left or right of center

like another

little bit

live concert

lo and behold

look and see

lower down

manual dexterity

mean average

meet together

model example

move to another location

name brand

Needless to say . . .

(set a) new record

new recruit

now/currently/presently/is/are/am
  (*verb*)-ing

old geezer

NO PARKING AT ANY TIME

orbit around

nooks and crannies

null and void

one hundred percent pure

OPEC countries   Organization of
  Petroleum Exporting Countries

optimistic about the future

Ouija   This trademark combines *oui*,
  French for "yes," and *ja*, German for
  "yes."

outward/physical appearance

over and above/done

over-exaggerate

overwhelm

past experience

past/previous/prior history   as
  opposed to the oxymoron
  current history

per each

pick and choose

PIN number

plan ahead

pre-/arranged/planned/recorded/
scheduled/screened/tested, *etc.*

quagmire   "marsh-marsh"

refer back to

reflect back on

reindeer   *Rein* is from *hrien*, Old
  Norse for "reindeer," and *deer* is from
  dyr, Old Norse for "deer."

reiterate

a relic of the past

Remembrance of Things Past   Marcel
  Proust's novel, mistranslated title

rest and relaxation

retrospective hindsight—former Virginia
Governor Douglas Wilder

rice paddy

rise/lift up

round circle

rules and regulations

sad and blue

scheduled appointment

skin rash

SNAFU   Situation Normal: All
  Fouled Up

so on and so forth

still continuing/remaining

sum total

survival of the fittest

temper tantrum

ties that bind

time clock

time period/period of time

time schedule

together with

too excessive

true fact

the truth, the whole truth, and
  nothing but the truth

twelve o'clock midnight/noon

underneath

unexpected surprise

up above

vast majority

very/somewhat/quite/relatively
  unique
vim and vigor
VIN number   Vehicle Identification
  Number
warn in advance/warn ahead of time
White Anglo-Saxon Protestant
whys and wherefores
wrack and ruin
young child

More Redundancies

Wesley Price collected these redundancies, recorded in Willard Espy's *Another Almanac of Words at Play* (1980).

future plans
prior notice
He nodded his head.
skirted around
mutual cooperation
thought to himself
personal friend
wall mural

Redundant Quotes

"careful caution"—advised by former U.S. Secretary of State Alexander Haig

The Department of Redundancy Department—from a skit by the comedy troupe The Firesign Theatre

"A hypothetical situation that does not now exist."—Henry Kissinger

"I'm abolishing and doing away with redundancy."—J. Curtis May, Wisconsin State Elections Board, in Tom Burnam, *Dictionary of Misinformation* (1976)

"I will try not to repeat myself, as I said . . . "—David Dimbleby (BBC1)

"Money is better than poverty, if only for financial reasons."—Woody Allen

"overdestroy"—former Secretary of Defense Robert McNamara

"I have reiterated over and over again what I have said before."—former New York Mayor Robert Wagner

3 UNUSUAL
NAMES & TITLES

In matters of naming people, places, and things, we seem to have infinite resources. We tolerate and even celebrate the bizarre, unusual, suggestive, and uncannily appropriate. We begin where Adam left off, conjuring up creatures of our own, mapping new territories, and singing or writing about the experience.

◇ ◇ ◇

PEOPLE

This list of unusual names was collected from many sources. Col. Clarence Clapsaddle, Katz Meow, I. C. Shivers, and Justin Tune were in John Train's *Remarkable Names of Real People* (1977). Genghis Cohen appears in *Even More Remarkable Names* (1979), Groaner Digger in *Most Remarkable Names* (1985), and Judge Law and Judge Judge in Gyles Brandeth's *The Joy of Lex* (1980). Mark Johnson, *WF*, Feb. 1992, discovered Dr. Cheek and Justin Brown, and *WF*, Aug. 1994, the dangerous-sounding Dr. Hatchet.

Constant Agony   former resident of Chazy Lake, New York

Itis Akin   former resident of Atlanta, Georgia

Dr. Bonebrake   there are five, including a dentist and a chiropractor

Dr. Carver   surgeon in Bartlesville, Oklahoma

Dr. Cheek   facial cosmetic surgeon in Jackson, Mississippi

Col. Clarence Clapsaddle   in the U.S. Army (West Point, class of 1940)

Lorraine Cocaine   Murrieta, California

Genghis Cohen   Orewa, New Zealand

Groaner Digger   Houston undertaker

G. Zippidy Duda   North Atlanta, Georgia

Bob Dunker   lifeguard from Capitola, California, known for heroism

Lotta Dust   a tombstone in Roselawn Cemetery in Detroit, Michigan, reads: "Here lies Lotta Dust"

Dr. Hatchet   surgeon in Bartlesville, Oklahoma

Ima Hogg   Houston; daughter of Texas governor; Ura Hogg is apocryphal

Judge Law and Judge Judge   dispensed justice in Santa Ana, California

Judge Lawless   unfortunately, there are several

Mayor Lawless   Port Lucie, Florida

Captain Mariner   Rosemary Mariner, current officer in the U.S. Navy

Katz Meow   former resident of Hoquiam, Washington

A. Moron   Randolph, New Jersey

Noyes   "no" "yes" might well succeed as a politician

Judge Outlaw

Warren Peace   there are many

Purvy Purviance   former executive director, Crime Stoppers International

I. C. Shivers   John Hancock Life Insurance Company

Cardinal Sin   archbishop, Manila, Philippines

Chip Splinter   cosmetic surgeon in La Mesa, California

A. Swindler   Xenia, Ohio, and many other locales

William L. Toothaker   dentist in Pomona, California

Justin Tune   chorister, class of 1947, Princeton, New Jersey

James Weirdo   Dublin, Pennsylvania

Unflattering Origins of English Given Names

Male

Caleb	(Hebrew)	dog
Calvin	(Latin)	bald
Cameron	(Celtic)	crooked nose
Ichabod	(Hebrew)	without honor
Seth	(Hebrew)	substitute

Female

Alta	(Germanic)	old
Deirdre	(Irish)	sorrow
Hedda	(Germanic)	strife
Leah	(Hebrew)	weary
Mary	(Hebrew)	bitter

Famous People & Their Original Names

Famous Name	Original Name
Albert Brooks	Albert Einstein
Michael Caine	Maurice Joseph Mickelwhite
Kim Darby	Derby Zerby
Bobby Darin	Walden Robert Cassotto
John Denver	Henry John Deutschendorf, Jr.
Stewart Granger	James Stewart
Michael Keaton	Michael Douglas
Lorrie Morgan	Lorretta Lynn
Hugh O'Brian	Hugh Krampe
Roy Rogers	Leonard Slye
"Jersey" Joe Walcott	Arnold Raymond Cream
Jerry Jeff Walker	Ronald Crosby
John Wayne	Marion Michael Morrison
Stevie Wonder	Steveland Judkins Morris
Tammy Wynette	Wynette Pugh

What If . . .

Swoosie Kurtz married Patrick Swayze
. . . —**Wanda Shelton,** *WF*

Tuesday Weld married Fredric March
II . . .

Alison Eastwood married Stevie
Wonder, then married Edwin Land . . .
—**Richard Lederer,** *WF*

More Names

A Mr. Death named his sons Jolly and
Sudden, and a man named Sykes
named his sons Lovewell, Dowell,
Diewell, and Farewell.—**William Walsh,**
Handy-Book (1892)

The first whiskey bottle was designed
by a Kentuckian named E. G. Booze.

Major-league baseball
has had its share of
interesting names:
Ty Pickup, Tony Suck,
Shadow Pyle,
Clay Touchstone,
Urban Shocker, and
Van Lingle Mungo.

BUSINESS AS USUAL

Curl Up & Dye   beauty salon, New
Berlin, Wisconsin

Hannah & Her Scissors   beauty salon
in Miami Beach, Florida

Nukem   now defunct producer of
fuel for atomic parts in the former
West Germany

The Grill from Ipanema   Brazilian
restaurant in Washington, D.C.

PLACE-NAMES

These place-names, it would seem,
variously comment on character, dis-
position, or place, and even tell you
where to go.

Bland, Missouri and Virginia

Boring, Maryland and Oregon

Eros, Louisiana

French Lick, Indiana

Ha! Ha! (River and Lake), Quebec

Hell, Michigan and Norway

Humptulips, Washington

Joe Batt's Arm, Newfoundland

Nutsville, Virginia

Peculiar, Missouri

Silly, Belgium

Spread Eagle, Wisconsin

Stab, Kentucky

Why, Arizona

Redundant Place Names

Avon (a river in England)   *Avon,*
from Celtic, means "river."

Table Mesa (Mesa, Arizona)   *Mesa* is
Spanish for "table."

Greenwich Village (New York, New

York) *Greenwich* means "green village."

Torpenhow Hill (near Plymouth, England) and How Hill (Ripon, England) *Tor* is Saxon for "hill," *pen* is Celtic for "hill," *how* comes from the Scandinavian *hau(g)r* for "hill," and if that were not enough, *hill* is Middle English for "hill."

Murderkill (a river in Delaware) Although it sounds like double murder, *kill* here, means "creek" or "stream."

Street Names

In Williamson County, near Austin, Texas, you'll find a Nameless Road, in a Nameless Valley. Various contributors to *Word Fun* found these other street names.

In Ventura, California, there is a North Street that runs east and west, so it is possible to walk east on the south side of West North Street.—**Ken Elrod**

In Lima, Ohio, there is also a North Street that runs east and west, and a West Street that runs north and south. North Street is, of course, divided into East North Street and West North Street. West Street is divided into North West Street and South West Street. It only gets confusing when West North Street and North West Street intersect, but no one there seems to mind.—**Julia Strawn**

In Jackson, Mississippi, North, West, and East streets run north and south, and South runs east and west. South intersects South West, but North runs out before it can cross South, and East is southwest of South, West, and North.—**Mark Johnson**

WHAT'S IN A NAME?

French King Charles the Mad (VI) was formerly known as Charles the Well Beloved.

Before Stephen Foster decided to title his song "Old Folks at Home," he considered calling it "Way Down Upon the Yazoo River" or "Way Down Upon the Pee Dee River."

In Feb. 1986, a county in Washington state was changed from King, for former U.S. Vice President William Rufus de Vane King, under Franklin Pierce, to King, for Martin Luther King, Jr.

In Jan. 1992, David Powers entered the race for Governor of Washington state as Nobody.

Dissatisfied with mainstream choices of candidates offered to voters in the 1979 Louisiana gubernatorial election, Luther Knox entered the race under his legally changed name, None of the Above. Despite his devotion to the cause, he never made it to the ballot.

According to Ken Elrod in *Word Fun*, Texan Gary Eugene Duda had his middle name legally changed to Zippidy and now answers to G. Zippidy Duda.

A Mrs. Dorsey, who had been widowed for several years, decided to have the name on her bank card changed from (the late) Mr. Dorsey to Mrs. Dorsey. On the form, for "husband's name," she wrote "deceased." Two weeks later, the card arrived in the mail addressed to Mr. Deceased.

Rock stars Grace Slick and Paul Kantner named their daughter god, using a lower-case "g," for modesty. They renamed her China, with a capital "C."

In 1994, 17-year-old Peter Eastman, Jr., of Carpinteria, California, had his name legally changed to Trout Fishing in America, as a tribute to the 1967 book by Richard Brautigan.

Boxer Marvin Hagler had his first name legally changed to Marvelous.

In 1991, Patrick Allen, a white-bearded gentleman of Harrisburg, Pennsylvania, had his name legally changed to Santa A. Clause.

A lacertiliaphile had his name legally changed to Henry Lizardlover.

Until 1796, the state of Tennessee was named Franklin, after Benjamin Franklin; before 1847, San Francisco was called Yerba Buena; and until 1882, Regina, capital of the province of Saskatchewan, Canada, was named Pile O'Bones.

Other Curiosities

Is it a mere coincidence that the letters in Hal, the name given to the computer in the film *2001: A Space Odyssey* (1968), are the letters of the alphabet that precede I-B-M? The director of the film claimed that the name is a hybrid of the two principal learning systems, Heuristic and Algorithmic.

In the name Harry S. Truman, the period after the "S" is optional.

A resident of Tangier, Morocco, is called a Tangerine.

BOOKS & AUTHORS

Pen Names of Famous Authors

English poet Robert Southey also signed himself Abel Shufflebottom; Geoffrey Crayon was one of at least three pseudonyms used by Washington Irving; and William Makepeace Thackeray was also known as Michael Angelo Titmarsh.

More Literary Curiosities

Russell Ash and Brian Lake collected these Odd Book Titles and these Aptly Named Authors in *Bizarre Books* (1985).

ODD BOOK TITLES
New Guinea Tapeworms & Jewish Grandmothers (1981) by Robert S. Desowitz

Favorite Flies & Their Histories (1955) by Mary Orvis Marbury

How to Cook Husbands (1899) by Elizabeth Strong Worthington

APTLY NAMED AUTHORS

Art of Editing (1982) by Jack Sissors and Floyd Baskette

Diseases of the Nervous System (1933) by Baron Brain

Motorcycling for Beginners (1980) by Geoff Carless

Land Speed Record (1971) by Cyril Posthumus

Running Duck (1979) by Paula Gosling

COUNTRY SONG TITLES

"You're the Hangnail in My Life"
" . . . and I can't bite you off"

"My Uncle Used to Love Me, but She Died"

"Not Tonight, I've Got a Heartache"

"You Can't Get Love from an Artificial Heart"

"She Got the Gold Mine, I Got the Shaft"

"Heaven's Just a Sin Away"

"If You're Going to Do Me Wrong, Do It Right"

"I Don't Know Whether to Kill Myself or Go Bowling"

"Where Were You When the Ship Hit the Sand?"

"Thanks to the Cat House, I'm in the Dog House with You"

"I Meant Every Word That He Said"

"I Still Miss You, Baby, but My Aim's Gettin' Better"

"If the Jukebox Took Teardrops, I'd Cry All Night Long"

"Been Roped and Thrown by Jesus in the Holy Ghost Corral"

"Thank God and Greyhound (You're Gone)"

Proposed Song Titles

These would-be song titles appeared in the "Wordplay" column of the *Mensa Bulletin*, Nov. 1987.

"I've Got a Strong Right to Love You with a Week Left to Live"—**Wayne Silka**

"I'm a Rabbit in the Headlights of Your Love"—**Chris Blunt**

FICTITIOUS FILM SEQUELS

These imaginary film sequel titles appeared in the May 1990 issue of the *Mensa Bulletin* in the column "Wordplay." The film trilogies appeared in the Sept. 1990 issue.

Death on the Nile   Five Graves to Cairo —**Miriam Kiss**

September Affair   Born on the Fourth of July (Conceivable)—**C. Caldwell**

Dial M for Murder   Sorry, Wrong Number —**several were submitted**

Eating Raoul   Heartburn—**Pat Tricamo**

The World's Greatest Lover   The Big Sleep—Loyd Dillon

Jaws   A Farewell to Arms—Chris King

Jealousy + The Fuller Brush Man = Death of a Salesman—David Hambley

Dr. Jekyll & Mr. Hyde + Cyrano de Bergerac = The Good, the Bad & the Ugly—Paul Dudey

Red Dust + Blue Skies = Purple Haze—Kerry Kaszak

The Birds + The Bees = The Facts of Life—Ellen Skagerberg

A Man & A Woman + The Secret Partner = I Want a Divorce

The Electric Horseman + The Rain Must Fall = Blazing Saddles (or *Short Circuit*)

LUDICROUS ACRONYMS

Sources for these lists of ludicrous acronyms and other peculiar acronyms include Jennifer Mossman's *The Acronyms, Initialisms & Abbreviations Dictionary* (1996), Ralph De Sola's *The Abbreviations Dictionary* (1986), and Paul Hellweg's *The Insomniac's Dictionary* (1986).

BANANA   Build Absolutely Nothing Anywhere Near Anybody; a revision of NIMBY—Not In My Back Yard

BEAVER   Better End All Vicious Erotic Repression   Canada's first association of prostitutes

CINCUS   Commander-In-Chief, U.S. fleet   This acronym was created by the Navy during World War II but dropped after the attack on Pearl Harbor.

CLAP   Citizens Lobbying Against Prostitution

CRAP   Committee to Resist Acronym Proliferation

CRAP   Constructive Republican Alternative Programs   These were position papers on legislative issues prepared for Republican House leaders during former U.S. President Lyndon B. Johnson's administration.

CREEP   Committee to Re-Elect the President (Richard Nixon)   This fund-raising organization was run by many government officials later convicted for involvement in Watergate.

DAM   Mothers Against Dyslexia—comedian and actor Max Alexander

FOE   Females Opposed to Equality

FRUMPIE   Formerly Radical Upwardly Mobile Professional—California Assemblyman Tom Hayden

FUCM   Full Utility Cruise Missile

G.O.D.   Guaranteed Overnight Delivery   This New Jersey trucking firm's telephone is 1-800-DIAL GOD.

MADD   Manufacture of Artificial Dog Dung

MOM/WOW   Men Our Masters/ Women Our Wonders

MUFFIE   Middle-aged Urban Failure

OINK   One Income, No Kids

PAL   Prisoner At Large

PEEK   People for the Enjoyment of Eyeballing Knees   1970s group opposing below-the-knee skirts

POETS   Phooey/Pee On Everything,

Tomorrow's Saturday

SAHAND   Society Against "Have A Nice Day"

SCUM   Society for Cutting Up Men   This radical feminist group, conceived by Valerie Solanas in the late 1960s, had the purported intention of eliminating, via sabotage, every facet of society that did not pertain to women.

SWAG   Scientific Wild-Assed Guess

SWALCAKWS   Sealed With A Lick, 'Cause A Kiss Wouldn't Stick

WIMPS   Weakly Interactive Massive Particles   remnants of the Big Bang

WOOPIES   Well-Off Older People

XYZ   Examine Your Zipper

YUMMIES   Young Upwardly Mobile Marxists   Soviet lawyers in the United States.

YUPPIE   Young Urban Professional   Columnist Alice Kahn reportedly coined this familiar and useful acronym in 1983.

Other Peculiar Acronyms

ACORN   Acronym-Oriented Nut
—quoted in William Safire's column "On Language" in *NY Times Magazine*

BITCH   Black Intelligence Test of Cultural Homogeneity, or Black Intelligence Test to Counter Honkyism

CAVE   Communities Against Virtually Everything

DIED   Department of Industrial and Economic Development   This Ohio department is now defunct.

EGADS   Electronics Ground Automatic Destruct Sequencer   U.S. Air Force system for destroying malfunctioning or approaching missiles

LIE   Long Island "Expressway"

LORD   Let Oral Roberts Die   This was the punch line of George Bush's joke about "a new fundamentalist group," told to an unappreciative audience of staunch conservatives in Lansing, Michigan, in Feb. 1987. It referred to Roberts's claim that if his church failed to receive enough donations, the Lord would take him home.

NASA   Not Another Shuttle Aborted?

PTL   Praise The Lord   This televised ministry, headed by Jim Bakker, was nicknamed Pass The Loot by less-than-faithful viewers, and because of his 1989 conviction for bilking parishioners of over $150 million, the acronym was reinterpreted as Prison Term Long. Bakker's original 45-year sentence was reduced to 18 years, and then to eight. The televangelist was released from federal prison in 1994 after serving just five years.

Would-Be Acronyms

The "Wordplay" column in the *Mensa Bulletin*, June 1988, provided these less whimsical samples.

CONDOM Can't Overlook New Date's Old Mates—Richard Guttman

KAYPRO Keeps All Yuppies' Personal Records Organized—Sarah Bandes

MASSACHUSETTS INSTITUTE OF TECHNOLOGY Many A Science Student At Cambridge Hoped, Unless Stopped Educationally by Terrible Test Scores, to Initiate Noteworthy Scientific and Technological Inquiries, To Uncover Truths, Explain Observations and Facts, and To Examine Critical Hypotheses, but Never Once to Linger Over the Glories of Yesterday—Tom Delaney

TOSHIBA Trade Our Secrets? Heavens! I'm Buying American.—John Coe

4 OXYMORONS

An *oxymoron* (from *oxymoros,* meaning "pointedly foolish"), which combines the Greek words *oxys* ("sharp or keen") and *moros* ("dull"), is a combination of contradictory or incongruous words. These words, like John Milton's "darkness visible," are often used for literary effect. Some examples in this chapter do not fit the strict definition, but do suggest amusing contradictions.

◇ ◇ ◇

CLASSIC OXYMORONS

Act natural.
Advanced BASIC   Advanced
  Beginner's All-purpose Symbolic
  Instruction Code
alone together
Anarchy rules!
athletic scholarship
authentic reproduction/replica
awfully good/kind
a back door front   meteorological
  term
black light
blues festival
building down   referring to nuclear
  disarmament
business ethics
chicken-fried steak
civil war
Congressional leadership

cruel kindness
deciding not to decide
dimwit
down escalator
drag race
dress pants
drink yourself sober
elevated subway
false truth
farewell reception
final draft
free with purchase
fresh frozen
full of holes
God-awful
Good grief!
graduate student
green orange(s)
historical fiction
holy war

home office

Internal Revenue "Service"

It's bad luck to be superstitious.

killed alive

Labor Day holiday

laborious idleness

lay professional

light or friendly casualties   Vietnam War terms

light heavyweight

a little (bit) big/much

living end

maxi brief

MiniMax   trade name of a portable exercise machine

a miss hit   table tennis term

modern classical

Moral Majority   changed in Jan. 1986 to The Liberty Foundation

much/a lot less

negative growth

neoclassical/neo-/Gothic/traditionalist

never, ever

Now, then . . .

numb feeling

old news

open secret

original copy

paid volunteer

peacekeeping force/missiles

(*chose your number*) percent pure

permanent loan

plastic silverware/glass(es)

pretty ugly

pygmy mammoth   found in a 1994 archaeological dig

random order

Reagan memoirs

religious science

rolling stop

same difference

science fiction

scientific creationism

Scottish Danish   a pastry sold at 7-Eleven stores

a sharp and blunt speech

shirtless and shoeless, with trousers to match

sight unseen

small fortune

SMALL   musician Baby Gramps

sophomore   from the Greek *sophos*, meaning "wise," and *moros*, "foolish"

Still waters run deep.

super flyweight

terribly pleased

There are no absolutes.

thunderous silence

unsalted saltines

unscented incense

well-preserved ruins

whole piece

wintergreen

Quotable Oxymorons

"Clichés are a dime a dozen: avoid them like the plague."

"I'd give my right arm to be ambidextrous."

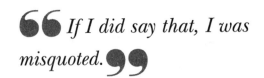 **If I did say that, I was misquoted.**

—Lord Hanson, "The World at One" (Radio 4, London)

"If you fall and break your legs, don't come running to me."

66 *Give me the luxuries of life and I will gladly do without the necessities.* 99

—Frank Lloyd Wright

"May I ask you a question?"

"The more I think of you, the less I think of you."

"perfectly wrong"—**NASA official referring to a defective mirror of the Hubble telescope in 1989**

My Favorites

at this time in history
buying them like they were going out
  of style
current history
drive-in exit
express line
extra low (*price*)
extraordinary
history in the making
hypo-manic
ivory black
marine airmen   anagrammatic
"No comment."
objective opinion
pop culture
preventive medicine
sunshade
tomboyish girl   redundant

turn(ed) straight
twelve o'clock in the afternoon
wireless cable

Word Ways Oxymoron Collection

by reason of insanity
a closet claustrophobic
dimwit
dry lake
even odds
monopoly—**Marjorie Friedman**
novantique
objective journalism
Positively no!
spendthrift
split union
standard deviation
sure bet
turn up missing
underoverlooker   in Webster's second
  unabridged dictionary—**Tom Pulliam**

STAGE & SCREEN
Film Titles

Advance to the Rear (1964)   comedy

Death Benefit (1996)   starring Peter Horton

Dead Alive (1993)   horror film starring Timothy Balme and Diana Penalver

Faraway, So Close (1993)   fantasy starring Otto Sander

Hide in Plain Sight (1980)   crime drama starring James Caan

Little Big Man (1970)   novel by Thomas Berger (1964); film starring Dustin Hoffman

Little Giants (1994)   Duwayne Dunham film starring Rick Moranis

True Lies (1994)   starring Arnold Schwarzenegger and Jamie Lee Curtis

And Now Tomorrow (1944)   drama starring Loretta Young

About Place

Hill Valley was the name of the town in the film *Back to the Future* (1986), and changed to Hilldale in *Back to the Future, Part III* (1990). Hilldale was also the town in the television series "The Donna Reed Show." The home of "Dennis the Menace" was Hillsdale.

Quotes from Stage & Screen

On the army: "What other job lets you die for a living?"—**Hawkeye Pierce, "M*A*S*H*," in Jack Mingo and John Javna's** *Prime Time Proverbs* **(1989)**

"I'm an atheist. Thank God I've always been one."—**Spanish surrealist filmmaker Luis Buñuel**

"In film, the best sound of all is silence."—**Faye Dunaway**

"When I'm good, I'm really good; but when I'm bad, I'm better."—**Mae West**

"Everything I've ever told you has been a lie, including that."—**Peter Cook in the film** *Bedazzled* **(1967)**

"caught in the act of being themselves"—**Allen Funt, from the television show "Candid Camera"**

"There's a broad with her future behind her."—**Constance Bennett on Marilyn Monroe**

"I knew her before she was a virgin." —**Oscar Levant on Doris Day**

"ruthful butchery"

"I must be cruel, only to be kind." —**William Shakespeare's** *Hamlet*

"undisputed boxing champion"

"jumbo shrimp"—**George Carlin**

"Last week I blew $5,000 on a reincarnation seminar. I figured, what the hell—you only live once."—**comedian Ronnie Shakes**

"Don't miss it if you can."—**traffic reporter Brian Ward, KKOB, Albuquerque, New Mexico**

"It costs a lot to look this cheap." —**Dolly Parton**

"It takes a smart man to know he's stupid."—**"Lou Grant" television series, in Jack Mingo and John Javna's** *Prime Time Proverbs* **(1989)**

POLITICS & DIPLOMACY

The language of politics and diplomacy is always a rich source for oxymorons, circumlocutions, chop logic, and double-speak.

"I intend to open this country up to democracy, and anyone who is against that, I will jail, I will crush!"—**1979 presidential speech by Brazil's General João Baptista Figueiredo**

"Capital punishment is our society's recognition of the sanctity of human life."—**Utah Senator Orrin Hatch, 1988**

 *We must allow our soldiers to fight this war in peace.* "

"We had to destroy the village in order to save it."—**explanation during the Vietnam War**

"violent peace"—**U.S. Navy reference to a limited armed conflict**

"permanent pre-hostility"—**the Pentagon referring to peace**

"peacekeeper"—**former U.S. President Ronald Reagan referring to the MX missile in a televised speech, Nov. 22, 1982**

"Organize spontaneous cheering." —**former U.S. President Jimmy Carter's public-relations manual for his 1976 campaign**

"an incomplete success" Former U.S. President Jimmy Carter used this term when referring to the attempted rescue of American hostages in Iran.

"I believe that this country's policies should be heavily biased in favor of nondiscrimination."—**U.S. President Bill Clinton**

Progressive Conservative one of Canada's three major political parties

Revolutionary Institutional Party (Mexico)

LITERARY OXYMORONS

"The coldest winter I've ever spent was a summer in San Francisco."—**Mark Twain**

"It usually takes more than three weeks to prepare a good impromptu speech."—**Mark Twain**

" . . . His honor rooted in dishonor stood, and faith unfaithful kept him falsely true."—**"Lancelot and Elaine" from Alfred, Lord Tennyson's** *Idylls of the King* **(1885)**

"faultily faultless"—**Alfred, Lord Tennyson**

"His only fault is that he has no fault." —**Pliny the Elder**

Benjamin Disraeli said that William Gladstone had "no redeeming defects."

"He hasn't a single redeeming vice." —**Oscar Wilde**

"To be natural is such a very difficult thing to keep up."—**Oscar Wilde**

"Life is much too important a thing to ever talk seriously about it."—**Oscar Wilde**

"Nature, to be commanded, must be obeyed."—**Francis Bacon**

"scalding coolness"—**Ernest Hemingway**

"melancholy merriment"—**George Gordon, Lord Byron**

"proud humility"—**Edmund Spenser**

"hateful good"—**Geoffrey Chaucer**

"There is nothing in this world constant, but inconstancy."—**Jonathan Swift, "A Critical Essay upon the Faculties of the Mind" (1707)**

"What the crowd requires is mediocrity of the highest order."—**Auguste Préault, 19th century French writer**

By Definition

These oxymoronic definitions are found in Ambrose Bierce's *The Devil's Dictionary* (1911).

habit "a shackle for the free"
Hades "the place where the dead live"
recollect "to recall with additions something not previously known"

In Quotes

ANDY WARHOL
"I always run into strong women who are looking for weak men to dominate them."

"I am a deeply superficial person."

WOODY ALLEN
On life and death: "Eternal nothingness is OK if you're dressed for it."

"I'm not afraid to die; I just don't want to be there when it happens."

GROUCHO MARX
"'Military intelligence' is a contradiction in terms."

In a letter to the Friars Club: "Please accept my resignation. I don't want to belong to any club that would have me as a member."

Lederer's Oxymoron Collection

These treasures were found by Richard Lederer, author of *Crazy English* (1989) and other amusing books on the discrepancies of our language. Lederer also comments on the triple oxymoron "permanent guest hosts," NBC's term for Joan Rivers, then Jay Leno, on television's "The Tonight Show."

baby grand
ballpoint
bridegroom
building wrecking
conspicuously absent
divorce court
flat busted
light heavyweight
loose tights
mandatory option
many fewer
nonworking mother
pianoforte (soft–loud)
preposterous (before–after)
press release
someone
speech writing
student teacher
superette (big–small)
wholesome
working vacation

"It takes about ten years to get used to your age."

"Your anner, I was sober enough to know I was dhrunk."

OXYMORONS IN NAME, TITLE & SONG

Dome Valley (Arizona)

Eden Industrial Park (near Salinas, California)

Hilldale (Utah)

Little Bighorn River (Wyoming, Montana)

Little Big Man   American Indian leader who rode with Crazy Horse

Mediterranean Sea   *mediterranean* is Latin for "middle of the land"

Montvale ("mountain valley") (New Jersey and Virginia)

The National State Bank   (based in New Jersey)

Santa Monica Synagogue—**Garrison Keillor discovered**

Silence Bellows   editor of *The Christian Science Monitor*

MEMORABLE BOOK TITLES

Memories of the Future   original title of Erich Von Däniken's *Chariots of the Gods?* (1983)

Oscar Levant's *Memoirs of an Amnesiac* (1989)

Elliot Richardson's *Reflections of a Radical Moderate* (1994)

SONG TITLES

"Glad to Be Unhappy"—**Richard Rodgers and Lorenz Hart**

"Happy with the Blues"—**lyrics by Peggy Lee**

"If You Won't Leave Me Alone, I'll Find Someone Who Will"—**Delbert and Glen**

"I Forgot to Remember to Forget" —**Stan A. Kesler and Charlie Feathers**

"That-a-Boy, Girl!"—**Roger Miller**

"The Sound of Silence"—**Paul Simon**

"Earth Angel"—**a 1955 hit by The Penguins**

"Something Must Be Wrong Because Everything Is Going Right"—**Dr. Jazz**

SONG LYRICS

"Now they know how many holes it takes to fill the Albert Hall."—**John Lennon and Paul McCartney's "A Day in the Life"**

"I can't forget that I don't remember what . . ."—**Leonard Cohen's "I Can't Forget"**

"To live outside the law you must be honest."—**Bob Dylan's "Absolutely Sweet Marie"**

"I was so much older then; I'm younger than that now."—**(redundant oxymoron) Bob Dylan's "My Back Pages"**

"Close your eyes and look at me." —**King Crimson's "Walking On Air"**

"With his hair cut long"—**"Where Has My Little Dog Gone?"**

Loving You Drove Me Mad
The Oxymoron Song

Here are the lyrics to my 1979 song "Loving You Drove Me Mad: The Oxymoron Song." It contains ten oxymorons.

I lost my mind to win your heart,

Knowing well we were off to a finishing start.

I can't get into getting out

'Cause I'm certain about my doubt.

I'm happy feeling sad,

Loving you drove me mad.

I turned you on, then you turned on me,

When it came my turn, you turned away.

I could never get used to getting used

To do the things that you refused to.

It's the blues, if I keep or lose you;

Loving you drove me mad.

Well, it takes a lot of the little I've got;

I'm more confused the more I give it thought.

I lost it all on one "sure bet,"

Now I can't recall what I ought to forget.

Let's just forget we've never met;

Loving you drove me mad.

Now, bad is good, and cold is hot,

It's a contradiction, then again, it's not.

I've given up all o' my sanity,

In search of some sweet memory,

But nostalgia ain't what it used to be;

Loving you drove me mad.

You're the best I've never had;

Loving you drove me mad.

5 PROVERBS & ADVICE

◇ ◇ ◇

CONTRADICTORY PROVERBS

Look before you leap.
He who hesitates is lost.

It's better to be safe than sorry.
Nothing ventured, nothing gained.

If at first you don't succeed, try, try again.
Don't beat your head against a stone wall.

Silence is golden.
The squeaky wheel gets the grease.

Actions speak louder than words.
The pen is mightier than the sword.

Many hands make light work.
Too many cooks spoil the broth.

Two is company, three is a crowd.
The more the merrier.

Clothes make the man.
Don't judge a book by its cover.

You're never too old to learn.
You can't teach an old dog new tricks.

Never send a boy to do a man's job.
" . . . and a little child shall lead them."

Absence makes the heart grow fonder.
Out of sight, out of mind.

Good things come in small packages.
The bigger, the better.

Like attracts like.
Opposites attract.

Great minds think alike.
Fools never differ.

When in Rome, do as the Romans.
Above all, to thine own self be true.

Do unto others as you would have others do unto you.
Nice guys finish last.

   The proverb "He who hesitates is lost" comes from Joseph Addison's play *Cato* (1713): "The woman that deliberates is lost." More contemporary journalists have revised it: "He who hesitates is lunch." Proverbs, like all folklore, continue to have a lively history.

The saying "Nice guys finish last" was credited to Leo Durocher, who had referred to baseball player Mel Ott as "one of the nice guys who finishes last" (1948). Stanley Kelley has revised the saying: "Last guys don't finish nice."—**Paul Dixon, *The Official Rules* (1978)**

REVISED PROVERBS

A schoolteacher asked her seven-year-old students to fill in words she omitted from proverbs. Here are some of the surprises.

"You can't have your cake and still be hungry."

"Too many cooks cook."

"Better late than last."

"A miss is as good as a mister."

Of course, adults, though lacking children's innocence, modify proverbs, too.

❝ *Imitation is the sincerest form of television.* ❞
—**Fred Allen**

"Where there's a will, there's a relative."—**George Carlin**

"One good turn gets all the blankets."

"The shortest route to a man's heart is through his chest."

A child's lament: "Cleanliness is next to impossible."

"I cried because I had no shoes, until I met a man who had no class."

Reconstructing Glass Houses

Here are some variations on a familiar proverb,"People who live in glass houses shouldn't throw stones."

"People who live in grass houses shouldn't stow thrones."

"People who live in fur houses shouldn't throw stoles."

"People who live in doghouses shouldn't throw bones."—**Al Roker**

Quips & Quotables

Jazz musician Paul Desmond, admiring California palms and a friend's aquarium allegedly said: "With fronds like these, who needs anemones?"

In the late 1960s, an anti-Reagan activist referred to the California governor as "the fascist gun in the West."

When Richard Nixon, from a Quaker family, welcomed the support of evangelist Billy Graham in his 1968 presidential campaign, a columnist referred to him as a "Graham Quaker."

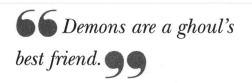

Demons are a ghoul's best friend.

Garrison Keillor, "Prairie Home Companion" radio raconteur, explains: "In America, cows don't get 'mad,' they get eaten."

Old Standards

Here are some revised old standards; the last three are my inventions.

"A fool and his money are some party."

"He's a wolf in cheap (or chic) clothing."

"He's rusting on his laurels."

"All's fear in love and war."

"Abstinence makes the heart grow fonder."

"He always ends a sentence with a proposition."

"He drank himself to Bolivia."

"He's waiting for the right girl to come alone."

"He sees all women as sequels."

"He's dead and married."

"A man cannot live in bed alone."

"It takes two to tangle."

ORIGINAL APHORISMS

Since proverbs and aphorisms are the stuff of poets and common men alike, I thought I'd include a few of mine.

"Life is too short to rush through."

"I'm a contradiction, then again I'm not."

"One problem with old age is that it's hard to reminisce about."

"Tongue-in-cheek and foot-in-mouth go hand in hand."

"Show them the road, not the mountain."

In the Game

"The game is fixed! All right . . . deal me in."—*"The Game," from Dory Previn's LP Mythical Kings & Iguanas* (1971)

6 SHAKE A SPEAR

◇ ◇ ◇

COINED BY SHAKESPEARE?

William Shakespeare is credited with coining well over 1,700 words (one in every ten he wrote), although many of these had been used regularly in speech before they were recorded on paper in the earliest folios or used in plays. Many of these "coined words" were gleaned from other languages.

The term *zany*, for example, first appeared in English in *Love's Labour's Lost* (1594) in the line "some slight zanie." According to *Webster's Word Histories* (1989), the English word is thought to have been derived from the 16th century Italian word *zanni* for "a stock comedy character" or "clown," found in improvised comedies. Here are other words attributed to the Bard that are still in use today.

Words

accommodation	clangor	eventful	housekeeping
aerial	compunctious	exposure	hurry
amazement	countless	fitful	illumine
apostrophe	courtship	foppish	impartial
assassination	critic	fretful	indistinguish-
auspicious	critical	frugal	able
barefaced	denote	generous	invulnerable
baseless	dexterously	gloomy	lackluster
bump	disheartened	gnarled	lapse
castigate	dislocate	heartsick	laughable
changeful	dwindle	hoodwinked	leapfrog

lonely	obscene	premeditated	seamy
majestic	pedant	radiance	sportive
misplaced	perusal	road	submerged
monumental	pious	sanctimonious	suspicious
multitudinous			

Expressions

These expressions have been credited to Shakespeare.

more in sorrow than in anger
lie low
an eyesore
laughed yourself to stitches
a tower of strength
long-haired
break the ice
the long and short of it
keep a civil tongue
one fell swoop
cold comfort
playing fast and loose
a matter of fair play
salad days
be that as it may
if the truth were known
the devil incarnate
make short shrift
eat out of house and home
the game is up
fair play
strange bedfellows
fancy free
suspect foul play
a foregone conclusion
the crack of doom
for goodness' sake
tongue-tied
good riddance

too much of a good thing
a stony-hearted villain
'twas Greek to me
green-eyed jealousy
it's ('tis) all one to me
heart of gold
a virtue of necessity
high time
we've seen better days
hot-blooded
now what the dickens
your own flesh and blood
more sinned against than sinning
there's the rub
the wish is father to the thought
vanished into thin air
something (is) rotten in (the state of) Denmark
foul play
a laughing stock

More Expressions

The expression "without rhyme or reason," from Shakespeare's *The Comedy of Errors* (1592), *As You Like It* (1599), and *The Merry Wives of Windsor* (1600), first appeared in Blanchet's (1459–1519) French farce *L'Avocat Pierre Patelin*, quoted by William Tyndale in English in 1530. Here are lines from Edmund Spenser's "Lines on His Promised Pension," published posthumously in Thomas Fuller's *Worthies of England* (1662).

I was promised on a time
To have reason for my rhyme;
From that time unto this season,
I received no rhyme nor reason.

The expression "budge an inch," from Miguel de Cervantes's *Don Quixote de la Mancha* (1615), also appeared in print years before Shakespeare used it in *The Taming of the Shrew* (1593). Other common expressions that we usually recognize as Shakespeare's, which are also echoed in *Don Quixote*—like "dead as a doornail," "to be in a pickle," "give the devil his due," and "I have not slept a wink"—from *Henry IV*, Part 1(1590), had been in popular circulation or printed in texts before Shakespeare used them.

Willard Espy's book *The Word's Gotten Out* (1989) includes a list of expressions that Shakespeare had been mistakenly credited with coining, along with the titles, acts, and lines of the plays in which the phrases were used. Robert McCrum, William Cran, and Robert MacNeil in *The Story of English* (1986) also reveal other non-Shakespearean expressions.

SHAKESPEARE & THE 46th PSALM

Rev. Arthur Pearson, in *The Twentieth-Century Standard Puzzle Book* (1907), related these peculiar facts about Shakespeare and the 46th Psalm (paraphrased).

Quite as cryptic and convincing as any of the curious Shakespeare–Bacon ciphers is the evidence which connects the great English poet with the 46th Psalm of the King James Bible.

Shakespear, as he sometimes spelled it, contains four vowels and six consonants. This is the key to the position. If, guided by these figures, we turn to the 46th Psalm and count from the beginning, we find the 46th word is *shake*. Then, counting from the end (disregarding *Selah*, a Hebrew word of uncertain meaning, and not part of the actual psalm), we find the 46th word is *spear;* hence "Shakespear."

The King James Bible was said to have been completed in early 1610, when Shakespeare was 46, and published the following year. Although the date of his birth is unknown, it is celebrated on April 23rd. Church documents show he was baptized on April 26, 1564. Shakespeare's death is observed on April 23rd, but records indicate it was several days later, in 1616.

Richard Lederer in "Hidden Bard" in *WW*, May 1994, credits Missy Clinebell and Barbie Henderson for another discovery. "If you count down from the first word to the 14th, the word *will* appears. If you then count up from the ending, *selah*, to the 32nd word, you land on the words 'I am.' 14 + 32 equals 46."

J. Karl Franson in "A Myth about the Bard," in *WW*, Aug. 1994, explained that Richard Taverner's

1539 version of Psalm 46, printed many years before Shakespeare's birth, has *shake* and *spear* in the same positions as in the King James Bible and that the words appear in nearly the same positions in other versions published before 1611. He also stated that *will*, *I*, and *am* are also in Taverner's version of the psalm—*will* as the 14th word and "I am" as the 32nd and 31st words.

Another curious coincidence that Rev. Pearson pointed out, is that the letters in the name William Shakespere (one of at least 13 spellings he used of his name) form the anagrammatic sentence: "We are like his Psalm."

LIVE & DIE

Shakespeare made use of this truism in *Henry VI, Part III* (act 5, scene 2, line 28) (1590), keeping to one-syllable words: "And, live we how we can, yet die we must."

SHAKESPEARE WITH HONOR, HOLD THE BACON

The 27-letter nonsense word *honorificabilitudinitatibus*, from medieval Latin, translated "with honorablenesses," is the longest word in Shakespeare's writings and appears in *Love's Labor's Lost* (act 5, scene 1, line 44) (1594). Many Baconians were pleased when it was found that the word can be transposed into the Latin "*Hi ludi F. Baconis nati tuiti orbi.*" Translated: "These plays, F. Bacon's offspring, are preserved for the world." Bailey's *Dictionary* (1721) cited *honorificabilitudinity* as the longest word in English. It was certainly the longest word containing an uninterrupted alternation of consonants and vowels.

7 WORDS TO FEAR

You're probably familiar with the usual phobias, like agoraphobia or claustrophobia. Here are a few "other phobias" psychologists credit that may not be in your vocabulary. And beyond those already in the unusual scientific lexicon, here are more phobias we readily recognize and could usefully add—some everyday, others suggesting rare talent or suffering.

OTHER PHOBIAS

These phobia words were compiled from many sources, including Paul Hellweg's *The Insomniac's Dictionary* (1986). Alfred Hitchcock had *policophobia*. He never drove a car for fear of being ticketed by the police. Dweezil Zappa reportedly has *levophobia* while driving, and J. Edgar Hoover suffered from the same affliction. Hoover forbade his chauffeurs to make left turns. Natalie Wood, who feared water, died by drowning.

Ritchie Valens, singer of the hit "La Bamba," suffered from *aerophobia*, fear of flying. He died in a plane crash with Buddy Holly and the Big Bopper in 1959.

The term *hydrophobia* is both "the fear of water" and the medical term for "rabies." There are two definitions of *lyssophobia*, "the fear of water" and "the fear of becoming hydrophobic," but, to my knowledge, there is no term for "the fear of lyssophobia." Here are some of the other lesser-known phobias.

alektorophobia chickens
apeirophobia infinity
aulophobia flutes
aurophobia gold
barophobia gravity
carnophobia meat
cherophobia gaiety
chronophobia time
dextrophobia things to the right
dikephobia justice
eleutherophobia freedom
euphophobia good news
gelophobia laughter
geniophobia chins
hedonophobia pleasure
heliophobia sunlight
hellenophobia cumbersome Greek or Latin words
homilophobia sermons
hygrophobia, dampness or liquids, especially wine or water
ideophobia ideas
levophobia *or* **sinistrophobia** things to the left
linonophobia string
medectophobia penis contour revealed through clothing
melophobia music
metrophobia poetry
odontophobia teeth
oneirogmophobia wet dreams
optophobia opening one's eyes
panophobia fears
papaphobia the Pope
pentheraphobia mother-in-law
philophobia love
phronemophobia thinking
prosophobia progress
pteronophobia feathers

rhinophobia noses
selenophobia the moon
siderophobia stars
sinistrophobia *or* **levophobia** things to the left
sophophobia learning
teratophobia monsters or giving birth to a monster
uranophobia heaven
venustaphobia beautiful women
vestiophobia clothing

WOULD-BE PHOBIAS WORDS

We have lots more in the world to fear than in the annals of psychologists and medical practitioners. Consider these.

aibohphobia palindromes
arachibutyrophobia peanut butter sticking to the roof of the mouth— *People's Almanac* (1975)
cacophonophobia bad music
corpulophobia, diametrophobia, expansophobia, radiaphobia widths
lunaediesophobia Mondays
omophagiaphobia, omositiaphobia eating raw flesh
paronomasiaphobia puns
phlebophobia blood tests
phobologophobia phobia words—**Paul Hellweg**
profundophobia depth
vacansopapurosophobia blank paper

8 BRITSPEAK, AMERISPEAK & WHAT?

◇ ◇ ◇

COMMONLY MISPRONOUNCED WORDS

These words all have common non-standard or erroneous pronunciations. The peculiar preferences of Britspeak and Amerispeak—or indeed Aussie, New Zealand, Indian, Continental, Canadian, and French-Canadian English—account for some differences, but certainly not all. And if we were to factor in all the regional accents or dialects, broadcast- and movie-speak, it quickly becomes mumble-jumble. Hybrid speech and bilingualism often introduce odd, humorous, or puzzling inflections, too.

asterisk   AS-ter-ik, AS-trik
athlete   ATH-eh-leet, ATH-uh-leet
bacterium (*singular*)   bak-TEER-ee-uh (bacteria [*plural*])

barbiturate   bar-BICH-oo-et
biathlon, decathlon   by-ATH-eh-lahn, de-KATH-eh-lahn, etc.
criterion (*singular*)   cry-TEER-ee-uh (criteria [*plural*])
deteriorate   de-TEER-ee-ayt
drowned, drowning   drounded, drounding
escalate   ES-keuh-layt
escape   ex-SCAYP
excerpt   EK-sert, EK-zert, EK-serp, EK-zerp
foliage   FO-lij, FOI-lij
heinous   HAY-nee-us
immune   em-YOONd, ihm-YOOND (immuned)
intravenous   intra-VEE-nee-us
jewelry   JOO-ler-ee, JOO-luh-ree
larynx   LAIR-nex, LAIR-eh-nex
medium (*singular*)   MEE-dee-uh (media [*plural*])
memento   moh-MEN-toh

mischievous mis-CHEE-vee-us
NASA NA-sah (Nassau)
nuclear NOO-kyuh-ler
paraplegic, quadriplegic pair-uh-puh-LEE-jik
phenomenon (*singular*) feh-NAHM-eh-nuh (phenomena [*plural*])
peripheral per-IF-ee-uhl
perspiration pres-per-AY-shun
prostate PROSS-trayt
pumpkin PUNG-ken
Realtor REEL-eh-ter
similar SIM-yuh-ler, SIM-yoo-ler
Social Security so-sha kyer-ih-tee, soh-suhl seh-kyer . . .
stole stold (stoled)
supposedly suh-POH-ziv-lee, suh-POH-zub-lee
surprise suh-PRYZ
valentine, Valentine's Day VAL-en-tym ('s day)
Venezuela ven-zoo-AY-luh
veterinarian vet-n-AIR-ee-en, vet-NAIR-ee-en
Wimbledon WIM-bl-ten

MISNOMERS

Guinea pigs are not pigs and do not come from Guinea; *blindworms* are legless lizards that can see; a *dressed chicken* is undressed; the *French phone* was invented by Robert Brown, an American; a *mosquito bite* is a puncture; *caraway seed* is not a seed, but a dried fruit; a *silkworm* is a caterpillar; in *dry cleaning*, all articles are thoroughly saturated in a wet solution; the *jackrabbit* is a hare; the *Jerusalem arti-choke* is a sunflower (*Helianthus tuberosus*); the *Pennsylvania Dutch* (really Deutsch) are German; *catgut* strings are made from sheep intestines; *bedstraw* is not straw, but an herb, formerly used to stuff mattresses; the sides of *Old Ironsides* were made of wood; *hay fever* is not caused by hay, but by pollen; a *peanut* is neither a pea nor a nut, but a leguminous herb; *Arabic numerals*, also called Arabic figures (the numbers 1 to 9), are not Arabic—they were invented in India; *India ink* comes from China and did not originate in India. The country of India, by the way, is officially known by its Hindu name, Bharat.

WORDS WE SHOULD COIN

affluential affluent and influential

Amereconomics the ultimate in capitalism

classive pertaining to class

crosstume a cross-dress costume

fileophile a lover of files

mediacracy government controlled by the media

parapsychosis the state in which a delusion is perceived by the subject as paranormal, or a disabling devotion to the supernatural; similar to *entheomania*: religious insanity

platinym a platitude synonymous with another, like "appearances can be deceiving" and "you can't judge a book by its cover"

realitize   face reality; make real— carry out a plan or an idea; live out a fantasy

ACCIDENTAL INJURY
Moving Violations

These are alleged personal accounts from auto accident reports. All except the last three come from William G. Espy's collection in Willard R. Espy's *Another Almanac of Words at Play* (1980).

"An invisible car came out of nowhere, struck my vehicle, and vanished."

"The guy was all over the road. I had to swerve a number of times before I hit him."

"Coming home, I drove into the wrong house and collided with a tree I don't have."

"The pedestrian had no idea which direction to go, so I ran over him."

"I had been driving my car for forty years, when I fell asleep at the wheel and had an accident."

"A pedestrian hit me and went under my car."

❝ *The indirect cause of the accident was a little guy in a small car with a big mouth.* **❞**

"I saw the slow-moving, sad-faced old gentleman as he bounced off the hood of my car."

"I pulled away from the side of the road, glanced at my mother-in-law, and headed over the embankment."

AS I WAS SAYING . . .

"If you aren't fired with enthusiasm, you'll be fired with enthusiasm."—Vince Lombardi

"We are all in this alone."—Peg Tuppeny in Paul Dickson's *The New Official Rules* (1989); also attributed to Lily Tomlin

"We must believe in free will; we have no choice."—novelist Isaac Bashevis Singer in his acceptance speech for the Nobel Prize for Literature in 1978

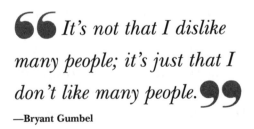

❝ *It's not that I dislike many people; it's just that I don't like many people.* **❞**
—Bryant Gumbel

"You've no idea what a poor opinion I have of myself, and how little I deserve it."—Gilbert & Sullivan

"I'm simply complex."—Barbra Streisand, "60 Minutes" interview

"This report is filled with omissions."—John Henrick, *Omni* magazine

"Be nostalgic for the future."—Maxwell Maltz

66 *I'm not a snob. Ask anybody. Well, anybody that matters.* 99 —Simon LeBon of the rock group Duran Duran

"That's what show business is—sincere insincerity."—British comedian Benny Hill

"I think of myself as a 'resident out-of-towner.'"—Calvin Trillin

MISINTRODUCTIONS

Actress Jean Harlow, boldly introducing herself to Lady Asquith at a Hollywood party, addressed her by her first name, Margot, pronouncing it "mar-got." Lady Asquith coolly replied: "My dear, the *t* is silent, as in Harlow.'"

KIDSPEAK

Better than Alice's hot buttered toast? When hearing that adults around the breakfast table were having boysenberry syrup on their waffles, 8-year-old Mariah Green asked: "Could I have some poison berries on my awful?"

Ariel Silva, age 5, declared that she likes her eggs "sunny side out."

A boy explained that his faithful family dog is a "damnation" (dalmation).

Fourteen-year-old Noah Deneau appears to be a natural palindromist: "Egad, nab a bandage!" he advised.

IMMACULATE MISCONCEPTION
At age 8 or 9, influenced by 1960s television-commercial jingles, Judy Morgan thought the Immaculate Conception referred to pristine kitchen floors waxed by perfect housewives.

TRAVELERS' ADVISORY

Sign Language

This collection, touted on the Internet, reportedly first took flight in *Air France Bulletin*, Dec. 1989.

In a Paris hotel elevator: "Please leave your values at the door."
On a menu at a Swiss restaurant: "Our wines leave you nothing to hope for."
In a Japanese hotel: "You are invited to take advantage of the chambermaid."
At a Bangkok dry cleaner: "Drop your trousers here for best results."

Services Available

A newspaper ad by a Hong Kong dentist: "Teeth extracted by the latest Methodists."

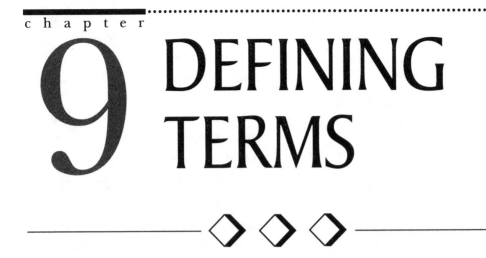

9 DEFINING TERMS

THE DEVIL'S DICTIONARY

Ambrose Gwinett Bierce, born in 1842, was the youngest in a large family that lived in the rural settlement of Horse Cave, Ohio. He educated himself in his father's library and left home at age 15. After years of aimless drifting, he settled in San Francisco and became a highly acclaimed journalist, writing articles and short stories for local weeklies. On Christmas, 1871, he married and the couple moved to England. It was there that he established himself as a humorist, and his articles appeared regularly in the monthly journal, *Fun.* In November 1913, at age 71, he left for Mexico on an undisclosed mission—presumably to join or write about Pancho Villa's army. What became of him after he crossed the border remains a mystery.

His best-known work was *The Devil's Dictionary* (1911). It was a collection of definitions from his popular column, variously identified as "Webster's Improved Dictionary," "The Demon's Dictionary," and "The Devil's Dictionary." It ran in several newspapers from 1881 to 1906. Here are definitions selected from his book.

accordion an instrument in harmony with the sentiments of an assassin

barometer an ingenious instrument which indicates what kind of weather we are having

bigot one who is obstinately and zealously attached to an opinion that you do not entertain

bride a woman with a fine prospect of happiness behind her

congratulation the civility of envy

cynic a blackguard whose faulty vision sees things as they are, not as they ought to be

egotist a person of low taste, more interested in himself than in me

faith belief without evidence in what is told by one who speaks without knowledge, of things without parallel

hers his

ocean a body of water occupying about two-thirds of a world made for man, who has no gills

philosophy a route of many roads leading from nowhere to nothing

rear in American military matters, that exposed part of the army that is nearest to Congress

saint a dead sinner, revised and edited

selfish devoid of consideration for the selfishness of others

BAILEY'S ODD DEFINITIONS

(Nathan) *Bailey's Universal Etymological English Dictionary: An Interpreter of Hard Words* was first published in London in 1721. Most of its definitions are eccentric, and some of them incredibly so. Very little is known about the author of this dictionary, other than the fact that he was a schoolmaster at Stepney, England, and died in 1742, according to Arty Fishel, editor of "Puzzledom," in a Sept. 1902 *Golden Days* issue.

Here are some samples of Nathan Bailey's definitions.

balloon a football; also a great ball which noblemen and princes use to play

cow a beast well known

eye an instrument of light

lightning a meteor

man a creature endowed with reason

medlar a fruit which is grateful to the stomach, but is not ripe till it be rotten

milk a food well known

mouth part of the body of a living creature

peacock a fine bird

rainbow a meteor of diverse colors

sea-unicorn, or **unicorn whale** a fish eighteen foot long, having a head like a horse, and scales as big as a crown-piece, six large fins like the end of a galley oar, and a horn issuing out of the forehead nine foot long, so sharp as to pierce the hardest bodies

snow a meteor well known in northerly and southerly climates, especially beyond the tropics

thunder a noise known by persons not deaf

MELLO-LINGO LEXICON

Here are some definitions from my short "Mello-Lingo Dictionary" (1984), updated. *Mello-lingo* is pop jargon that evolved from the 1960s subculture and has been adopted by the modern middle class.

centered   SELF-centered

cokehead   snowflake

color therapy   one of the safest alternatives to effective medical treatment
—O. V. Michaelsen and Eric Albert

crashing   falling asleep in the fast lane

"Fer shurrr!"   I totally agree, but could you run that by me again?

free spirits   nuts

ganja   holy smoke

generation X   too young to conform, too old to rebel

groovy   a beautiful time in a Nehru jacket

G-spot   a thousand-dollar bill

heavy metal (music)   rock bottom

"I like you as a person."   I don't find you physically attractive; let's be friends instead.

jam session   a loud and often drug-induced battle of blues scales played out of tune at innocent bystanders

klutz   a stutterer in body language

low rider   parked at full speed

metaphysics   out of body, out of mind, and out of touch

mod   an archaic abbreviation of "modern"

numerology   adding up to one more thing that one can't count on

open marriage   more often than not, an arrangement proposed by a *man* who got caught

peace movement   war against aggression

pop psychology   fast food for thought

quickie   Wham, bam! "Thank you, ma'am!" and the rare response: "Whimper, whirrr . . . Thank you, sir!"

recession   omni-pittance

sensuality   willingness to try anything once; sometimes mistaken for *stupidity*, willingness to try everything twice

skin flicks   elbows and knees out of focus

snow   a determining factor between the fast lane and the skids

spaced(-out)   on a transcendental excursion; expected back after lunch

subculture   the econo-classed

transactional analysis (TA)   "I'm OK and you're OK," despite my honest opinion.

transcendental meditation (TM)
enlightenment for the indolent—**David Bradley**

DEFINITIONS & OPINIONS

The definitions for *flood, pollution-free car,* and *sandstorm* are from Norm Dvostkin in *Farmer's Almanac,* 1990; those for *drunkard* and *mistake* are from "Literary Competitions" in *John O'London's Weekly,* Sept. 21, 1929; and those for *pessimist* (first definition) and *potboiler* are from *John O'London's Weekly,* Feb. 14, 1941. The left-handed definitions for the terms *highbrow* and *lowbrow* come from Leonard Louis Levinson's *The Left-Handed Dictionary* (1963). Other credits follow definitions; those uncredited are mine.

adolescence a stage between infancy and adultery—**H. L. Mencken,** *Dictionary of Quotations* **(1942)**

B.C. before computers—**Lois Fischer**

capitalist one who has everything and wants to share nothing—as opposed to a *socialist,* who has nothing and wants to share everything
—**anonymous**

capital punishment killing the violent

change the forever endeavor

Christianity a blessing in the skies

contras Banana Republicans

convention a workaholic's vacation
—**Lois Fischer**

deluxe the poor man's top of the line

diplomacy a lie for a lie, a truth for a truth

dream house surreal estate

drunkard one who lets well alone—**B. P.**

flood a river that's too big for its bridges

the flow We went with it all that time and *still* don't know where it goes.—**David Bradley**

free agent unemployed

highbrow the kind of person who looks at a sausage and thinks of Picasso—**A. P. Herbert**

hooker a fisher of men—**Gordon Bowker**

hookers When they say "love," they mean business.

jogging an exercise performed by those who don't need it—**anonymous**

Los Angeles New York lying down
—**Quentin Crisp**

lowbrow the kind of person who looks at a Picasso and thinks of baloney

minimum wage fiscal abuse

mistake an error that begins in mist and ends in an ache—**A.D.**

network anything reticulated or decussated at equal distances, with interstices between the intersections
—**Dr. Samuel Johnson,** *Johnson's Dictionary* **(1755)**

optimist an accordion player with a business card—Jay Leno

pessimist (1) a person who thinks things should be worse than they are; (2) someone who once financed an optimist—Jake Cunix, *WF*

pollution-free car emission impossible

potboiler (1) an author's admission that a person must eat; (2) an attempt by an author to earn sufficient money to write; (3) a cheap article for a quick market in time for dinner; (4) temperament doing what it can to live to do what it likes

preppy tight shoes, loose shorts, and a warm place to shop—Lois Fischer

pulp novels illiterature

sandstorm the great terrain robbery

San Francisco There's no "no" there.

self-centeredness It takes one to no one.

sinner the next best thing to a saint

tabloid news a void in the issues

utopia no-man's-land

vampire a hemogoblin—film critic Gene Shalit

weirdo an eccentric who's not an artist

white lie aversion of the truth
—F. G. Lewis

yoga chakra therapy

yogi a karmakhanic—Susan Fischer Smith

EARLIEST CITATIONS OF TERMS

According to *Merriam-Webster's Collegiate Dictionary*, 10th edition (1995), the word *gunslinger* first appeared in print in 1928, *gunslinging* in 1944, and *shoot-out* in 1948. *Groovy* (meaning "wonderful") dates at least as far back as 1937. *Hip* ("keenly informed or involved in the newest styles") was published by 1904 and *hep* by 1908. The phrase *out of sight* ("wonderful") was in print by 1893, *spaced-out* by 1937, *teen-age* by 1921, and *OK* (the abbreviation of "oll korrect") by 1841.

William Safire has stated that the term *politically correct* was traced to Mao Tse-tung in the 1960s, and that, to his knowledge, the earliest printed source of *politically incorrect* was Vladimir Nabokov's novel *Bend Sinister* (1947).

Many words, such as *television*, were coined long before the actual inventions; others are not as old as one might assume. Merriam-Webster dated the term *pizza* at 1935, *sexy* at 1925, *contact lens* at 1888, and *fortune cookie* at 1962. The *microwave oven* was invented in 1953, but the term was not published until ten years later. Merriam-Webster dates *lipstick* and *cryptogram* at 1880, but the term *cryptogram* was used in American puzzle columns by 1875. Although the first telephone book was printed in New

Haven, Connecticut, in 1878, the term first appeared in 1915.

Here are more terms and the earliest years they are known to have appeared in print.

aeroplane   1873
automobile   1883; as a motor vehicle: ca. 1889
baseball   1815
fax   1948
fiber optics   1956
microchip   1969
one on one   1967
photograph, **photographic**, and **photography**   1839; the first photo was taken in 1826
photographer   1847
pro-life   1961
respirator   1836
sleeping pill   1664
taco   1934
telegram   1852
telegraph   1794
telephone   1849
telephone book   1915
telephone number   1885
televise   1927
television   1907
wordplay   1855

FROM UGLY TO BEAUTIFUL, BY DEFINITION

By using dictionary definitions, it is possible to transform *ugly* into *beautiful*, as demonstrated by Dmitri Borgmann in *Beyond Language: Adventures in Word & Thought* (1967).

UGLY—OFFENSIVE
OFFENSIVE—INSULTING
INSULTING—INSOLENT
INSOLENT—PROUD
PROUD—LORDLY
LORDLY—STATELY
STATELY—GRAND
GRAND—GORGEOUS
GORGEOUS—BEAUTIFUL

chapter

10 WHERE'S YOUR GRAMMAR?

◇ ◇ ◇

FIVE TIPS TO BETTER GRAMMAR

Here are some takes on grammar rules you thought you knew.

1. Dangling from a sentence, one should always avoid leaving a participle.

2. Double negatives are no-nos.—**Bob Johnston in Paul Dickson,** *The New Official Rules* **(1989)**

3. Don't verbify nouns.—**David Means,** *Mensa Bulletin,* **Dec. 1995**

4. Don't use a preposition to end a sentence with.

5. And never start a sentence with a conjunction.

About rule 4, there really is no such grammar rule, but most writers and teachers avoid breaking it. When criticized for ending a sentence with a preposition, Sir Winston Churchill replied: "This is the type of arrant pedantry up with which I will not put!" Berton Braley in "No Rule to Be Afraid of" mused: "The grammar has a rule absurd/ Which I would call an outworn myth:/ 'A preposition is a word/ You mustn't end a sentence with.'" Rule 5 also does not exist in any reliable grammar guide.

JOAN RIVERS, ON GRAMMAR

Joan Rivers, in a commencement speech she gave in 1989 at her daughter Melissa's graduation from the University of Pennsylvania, said:

"You're college graduates now, so use your education. Remember—it isn't who you know, it's whom."

JUNIOR PREPOSITION

Junior yells downstairs to ask his father to bring up a certain book and read it to him. Dad appears with the wrong book. Junior says: "Aw, whaddya bring that thing I don't wanna be read to out of up for?"—**Martin Gardner, O&C (1961)**

WRITE ADVICE

"Never say 'never,' and always avoid 'always.'"—**John M. Hazlitt in Paul Dickson, *The New Official Rules* (1989)**

"Be obscure clearly."—**E. B. White**

66 *'Free verse' is like 'free love'; it is a contradiction in terms.* **99** —**G. K. Chesterton**

RIDE & WALK

Leigh Mercer in Martin Gardner's *Oddities & Curiosities* (1961) provides this confusing sentence.

"How much better it is to ride in a car and think 'How much better it is to ride in a car than it is to walk' than it is to walk and to think 'How much better it is to ride in a car than it is to walk.'"

MISDEMEANORS

Many former grammatical felonies have been reduced to minor misdemeanors, or even decriminalized, in today's vernacular. A few ungrammatical phrases that have become common usage include "healthy diet" ("healthful diet"), "different than" ("different from"), "anxious to" ("anxious about" or "eager to"), "like I said" ("as I said"), and "like it is" ("as it is"). Other expressions that have crept into everyday speech are "hopefully" ("I am hopeful that . . ."), "more importantly" ("more important"), and the ever-present suffix "-wise," as in "temperature-wise" and "time-wise."

11 SPELLCHECK

VOWEL SEARCH

English Words without Vowels

sh *or* shh

tsktsk(s)

nth

The Longest English Word without an "E"

Floccinaucinihilipilification, the longest English word without an "e," means "the action or habit of estimating a thing or an idea, etc., worthless" (*OED*).

Vowels in Alphabetical Order

Words in current use containing the six vowels (*a, e, i, o, u,* and *y*) in alphabetical order include *abstemiously, affectiously, facetiously, half-seriously,* and *pareciously*. The words in this list contain the regular five vowels (*a, e, i, o,* and *u*) in order.

abstentious

atenisodus

acheilous (same as *achilous*)

acheirous

aerious (the shortest)

annelidous

arsenious (alternate spelling of *arsenous*)

arterious

atenisodus

bacterious

caesious

fracedinous

lamelligomphus (the longest)

lateriporus

parepitoxus

More Ordered Vowels in Phrases

In the word *adventitious*, the letter "i" is repeated. The longest terms containing the regular vowels in order seem to be *lawn tennis court* and *watering trough*. Willard Espy in *Another Almanac* (1980) provides a sentence containing all the vowels in order: "Ann's bed is old but dry."

CHEMICAL SYMBOLS & ELEMENTS

Twelve chemical elements can be spelled using only elemental symbols. Puzzler Nightowl supplied this list in her puzzle newsletter *The Ag Mine*, quoted from *Chemical & Engineering News* (1993).

ArSeNiC	KrYPtON
AsTaTiNe	NeON
BiSmUTh	PHOsPHORuS
CArBON	SiLiCoN
CoPPEr	TiN
IrON	XeNon

WORDS IN NUMBERS

I00204I80 translated into words reads: "I ought not to owe for I ate nothing."

280? Too weighty.

NUMBERS IN WORDS

This fabricated ad first appeared in a 1968 Mensa publication, with numbers one through nine in order.

"Want a wooden overcoat? Buy h*one*st John Whi*two*rth's heal*th-re-e*nergizing sul*fo-u*ranyl-impregnated 'Com*fi*-V*es*t' with its unique qua*si-x*yloid fibers—obtainable only from the Paradi*se* V*en*ding Company, Harpurville H*eigh*ts, Nin*eve*h, New York."

WORDS IN NUMBERS & LETTERS

Simple, but perfect examples of the "letter rebus" are IV (ivy), NV, SA, FND (effendi), SKP, NME, XLNC, and XPDNC.

Rebuses and other riddles were very popular in the 18th and 19th centuries. *The Youth's Companion*, Sept. 25, 1879, featured an "illustrated" or "pictorial" rebus of a man in a tent, lying tied to the top of the letters "X" and "L." Below the picture were these questions.

Why is this man likely to succeed in life? (He is bound to XL.)

Why do we know he has reached middle life? (He is over forty.)

How does the picture indicate his occupation? (He is in tent on letters.)

WORDS & LETTERS IN WORDS

Wordsmith Mark Saltveit refers to the *charades* in the right column as "redividers," a more descriptive term. "Barm aid," "is a belle," "on us," and "Reform a Tory" could be considered *oronyms*, words which sound like others.

1. abalone—a "B" alone

2. alkaline—Al Kaline

3. amiable together—Am I able to get her?

4. "An 'A' to my—anatomy," said Adonis.

5. attendances—at ten dances
—John Newton, *Merry's Puzzles* (1860)

6. barmaid—barm aid

7. beauties—beau ties (bow ties)

8. a caravan—a car, a van

9. generations—gene rations

10. handled—hand-led

11. Isabelle—is a belle

12. island—is land

13. manslaughter—man's laughter

14. mendicant—Mend, I can't.

15. nowhere—now here

16. onus—on us

17. rampant—ram, pant

18. reformatory—Reform a Tory.

19. (psycho)therapist—(psycho,) the rapist

20. Wasted—was Ted!

More Charades

A reversal charade: Leno—One "l"

A *toreador* who had never learned *to read or* to write, when asked for his signature, gave this *significant* reply: "How can I *sign if I can't* write?"
—Dmitri Borgmann, *On Vacation* (1965)

English bibliographer William Oldys (1687–1761) wrote of himself: "In word and *will I am* a friend to you,/ And one friend *old is* worth a hundred new."

SOUND SPELLING

HOMONYMS, HOMOPHONES & HOMOGRAPHS

The homonym *chase* means both "to pursue" and "to ornament metal." And then we have homophones, words with the same sound but different spellings. Consider *heir* and *air*; and, if you feel fanciful, *compassion* and *come, passion.* These homonyms and homophones should not be confused with homographs, words spelled alike with different origins and meanings, whether they are pronounced alike or not. Examples are *homer,* "home run" or "unit of measure"; and *Polish (polish),* "from Poland" or "to make smooth and glossy."

HETERONYMS

The words *refuse* (re-FUSE) and *refuse* (REF-use) are spelled alike, but pronounced differently, have different meanings, and are derived from different roots. Another example of a *heteronym,* as this is called, found by Darryl Francis (*WW,* Aug. 1979), is *union-ized* and *un-ionized.*

12 CONTRA-dictory TERMS

◇ ◇ ◇

LOVELY LYRICS

The meaning of these song titles and lyrics can be made more interesting by stressing a different word in each.

What is this thing called LOVE?
What IS this thing called, love?
What is THIS thing called, love?
What is this THING called, love?
What is this thing CALLED, love?

You DO something to me.
You do something to ME.

It's all OVER, my friend.
It's all over my FRIEND.

What's that on the ROAD ahead?
What's that on the road, a HEAD?

"THE PERFECT COUNTRY SONG TITLE"

These lyrics are to my tune called "The Perfect Country Song Title."

Cheatin' and Drinkin',
The Lord and Mama,
Blue Jeans, Honky-Tonks,
Trains and Trucks.

PRO & CON

An observant 19th century wordsmith pointed out the prefixes of opposite meaning in the words *progress* and *Congress.*

CONTRANYMS

A *contranym* or *contronym,* which is a recently coined term, means a word or an expression having two or more opposite meanings. This has also been called a Janus-faced word, and the dictionary refers to it as an *antilogy.* Two homonymous contranyms are *raise—lift* and *raze* or *rase—tear down.* Here are classic examples of ordinary contranyms.

aloha   Hawaiian for "love," used as "hello" and "farewell"

bimonthly   every two months—twice a month (semimonthly)

bolt   secure in place—dart away

bound   restrained—to spring

buckle   fasten—come undone

cheerio   "hello"—"good-bye"

cleave   adhere to—split or divide by force

commencement   beginning—conclusion

dust   remove fine particles from—sprinkle fine particles on

fast   speedy—fixed firmly in place

give out   produce—stop producing

handicap   advantage—disadvantage

hold up   support—hinder

impregnable   invulnerable—able to be impregnated

left   departed from—remaining

overlook   fail to notice—examine

put out   generate—extinguish

ravel   entangle—disentangle

root   implant firmly—remove completely

scan   examine carefully—glance at or read hastily

screen   view—conceal

seed   remove seeds from—add seeds to

shank   the latter part of a period of time—the early part

temper   soften—strengthen

trim   add to—cut away

vital   lively; necessary to life—deadly; destructive to life

weather   withstand—wear away

wind up   start—end

PSEUDO-ANTONYMS

Word Ways collectors have discovered some of these. David Silverman found *catwalk, lowlands, maternity dress,* and *nighthawk* (Feb. 1970); Murray Pearce, *hereafter* and *undergo* (Aug. 1970); and Leslie Card, *hotheads* (Aug. 1970).

catwalk—dogtrot
give in—take out
give off/put off—take on
give up/put up—take down
hereafter—therefore
hotheads—cold feet
inning—outing
input—outtake
layout—stand-in
left off—Right on!
lowlands—high seas
maternity dress—paternity suit
nighthawk—mourning dove
overlay—understand
sit(-)in—stand out/standout
undergo—overcome
walk-on—run off/runoff
walkout—run(-)in
walk-up—run(-)down

QUASI-ANTONYMS

These *quasi-antonyms*, some from Tom Pulliam and Dmitri Borgmann in *WW*, have the same or similar meanings. Some dictionaries list *noninflammable*, a self-contained quasi-antonym.

barred—debarred
bone—debone
burn up—burn down
fat chance—slim chance
fill in—fill out
flammable—inflammable
irregardless—regardless
loosen—unloosen
ravel—unravel
restive—restless
slow up—slow down
unremorseless—remorseless

PSEUDO-SYNONYMS

British wordsmith Peter Newby introduced *pseudo-synonyms* in *WW*, Feb. 1995, and Susan Thorpe provided these examples.

wind power—air force

raindrop—waterfall
Central Time—Middle Ages
tall order—high command

SEEING DOUBLE

Mirror Words

Turn this page upside down before a mirror and read these words.

HIDE OXIDE CHOICE COD

Latin & Greek
It is said that President James Garfield was able to write in Greek with his left hand and Latin with his right, simultaneously.

13 A MISCELLANY

WHAT'S YOUR SIGN?

This anonymous satire, of questionable taste, has appeared in many versions in many newspapers since the mid-1970s, including *The Arizona Republic* (1980) and Emmett Watson's column in the *Seattle Post-Intelligencer* (1978).

 ARIES (Mar. 21–Apr. 19)   You are the pioneer type and hold most people in contempt. You are quick-tempered, impatient, and scornful of advice. You are not very nice.

 TAURUS (Apr. 20–May 20)   You are practical and persistent. You have a dogged determination and work like hell. Most people think you are stubborn and bull-headed. You are a Communist.

 GEMINI (May 21–June 21)   You are a quick and intelligent thinker, but are inclined to expect too much for too little. In other words, you are cheap.

 CANCER (June 22–July 22)   You are sympathetic and understanding of other people's problems. They think you are a sucker. You are always putting things off; that's why you'll never amount to anything. Most welfare recipients are Cancerians.

LEO (July 23–July 22)   You consider yourself a born leader. Others think you are pushy. You are vain and dislike honest criticism. Your arrogance is disgusting. Leo people are bullies.

 VIRGO (Aug. 23–Sept. 22)   You are the logical type and hate disorder. This nitpicking is sickening to your friends. You are cold and unemotional, and sometimes fall asleep while making love. Virgos make good bus drivers.

 LIBRA (Sept. 23–Oct. 23)   You are the artistic type and have a difficult time with reality. If you are a male, you were probably born the wrong sex. Chances for employment and monetary gains are excellent. Libra women make good hookers.

 SCORPIO (Oct. 24–Nov. 22)   You are shrewd in business and cannot be trusted. You will achieve the pinnacle of success because of your total lack of ethics. Most Scorpios are Republicans.

 SAGITTARIUS (Nov. 23–Dec. 21)   You are optimistic and enthusiastic. You have a reckless tendency to rely on luck, since you lack talent. No one really knows what goes on in the mind of a Sagittarian, but people laugh at you a great deal.

 CAPRICORN (Dec. 22–Jan. 19)   You are conservative and afraid of taking risks. You don't do much of anything and are lazy. There has never been a Capricorn of any importance. Capricorns should avoid standing still for too long, as they take root and become trees.

 AQUARIUS (Jan. 20–Feb. 18)   You have an inventive mind and are jealous and possessive. You lie a great deal. On the other hand, you are inclined to be reckless and impractical; therefore, you make the same mistakes over and over. People think you are stupid. Aquarians actually believe in astrology.

 PISCES (Feb. 19–Mar. 20)   You have a vivid imagination and often think you are being followed by the CIA or FBI. You have minor influence over your associates and people resent you for flaunting your power. You lack confidence and are generally a coward. Pisceans do terrible things to small animals.

FAMOUS LAST WORDS

Hiram ("Hank") Williams, singer-songwriter, was 29 years old when he died from a mixture of alcohol, morphine, and chloral hydrate on New Year's Day, 1953, en route to a show in West Virginia. When he died, his song "I'll Never Get Out of This World Alive" was a hit. According to writer John Javna, he was found seated in the back of his Cadillac holding a piece of paper with these handwritten words.

We met, we lived,
And dear, we loved,
Then comes that fatal day,
The love that felt so dear fades far
  away.
Tonight love hath one alone and
  lonesome,
I you you [sic] still
And always will,
But that's the poison we have to pay.

Dominique Bonheurs, French grammarian: "I am about to—or am going to—die. Either expression is correct."

Herman Mankiewicz, producer and screenwriter: "Well, that finishes everything I've got to take care of before I go to meet my Maker. Or in my case, should I say 'Co-Maker?'"

Major-General John Sedgwick, in the Battle of Spotsylvania (Virginia): "They couldn't hit an elephant at this dist . . . "

Nathan Hale, American Revolutionary hero, was thought to have said: "I only regret that I have but one life to lose for my country." Tom Burnam in his *Dictionary of Misinformation* (1975) stated that, according to a diary by Captain Frederick Macenzie, a British officer who was with Hale in his final hours, his dying words really were: "It is the duty of every good officer to obey any orders given him by his commander-in-chief." The famous line attributed to Hale, born 1755 and died 1776, was a misquote from Joseph Addison's tragedy *Cato*, act 1, scene 4 (1713): "What pity is it that we can die but once to serve our country."

Leonardo da Vinci, Italian painter, architect, and engineer: "I have offended God and mankind because my work didn't reach the quality it should have."

(Desiderius) Erasmus, Dutch scholar: "Lord, make an end."

Matthew Prior, English poet: "The end."

W(illiam). Somerset Maugham, English novelist and dramatist: "Dying is a very dull, dreary affair. And my advice to you is to have nothing whatever to do with it."

George Sanders, English actor, in a suicide note: "I'm bored."

St. John Philby, Arabic scholar: "God, I'm bored."

Sir Winston Churchill, British statesman and prime minister: "Oh, I am so bored with it all."

Giovanni Giacomo Casanova of Seingalt, Italian adventurer: "I have lived as a philosopher; I die as a Christian."

Daniel Defoe, English writer: "I do not know which is the more difficult in a Christian life, to live well or to die well."

John Adams, second U.S. president: "Thomas Jefferson still survives." He was unaware that Jefferson had died earlier that day, July 4, 1826.

Neil Cream, convicted poisoner: "I am Jack (the Ripper?)."

James W. Rodgers, murderer, before a firing squad, when asked if he had a final request: "Why, yes—a bullet-proof vest."

Lytton Strachey, English biographer: "If this is dying, then I don't think much of it."

Anna Pavlova, Russian prima ballerina: "Get my swan costume ready."

Elizabeth I, Queen of England: "All my possessions for a moment of time."

Karl Marx, German political philosopher: "Go on, get out! Last words are for fools who haven't said enough."

Johann Wolfgang von Goethe, German poet and dramatist: "Let the light enter."

Augustus Bozzi Granville, Italian sailor, doctor, and patriot: "Light. All light."

Victor Hugo, French novelist: "I see black light."

O. Henry (William Sydney Porter), American writer: "Turn up the lights; I don't want to go home in the dark."

Thomas Hobbes, English philosopher: "I am taking that fearful leap in the dark."

Stephen Crane, American author of *The Red Badge of Courage* (1895): "Robert, when you come to the hedge—that we all must go over—it isn't so bad. You feel sleepy—and you don't care. Just a little dreamy anxiety—which world you're really in—that's all."

Elizabeth Barrett Browning, English poet, asked how she was feeling: "Beautiful."

Thomas Edison, American inventor, briefly recovering from a coma: "It is very beautiful over there."

Jean Corot, French landscape painter: "How beautiful it is! I have never seen such beautiful landscapes."

Jean Paul Richter, German author: "My beautiful flowers! My lovely flowers!"

Solomon Foot, Vermont senator: "What, can this be death? So easy? It is come already? . . . I see it! I see it! The gates are wide open! Beautiful!"

William Allingham, Irish poet: "I am seeing things that you know nothing of."

J(ohann). C(hristoph). Friedrich von Schiller, German poet, dramatist, and historian: "Many things are growing clear to me."

Sir Walter Scott, Scottish poet and novelist: "I feel as if I were to be myself again."

Joseph J. Gurney, English Quaker and philanthropist, to his wife: "I think I feel a little joyful, dearest."

Hannah Moore, English poet: "Joy!"

Alice Meynell, English poet and essayist: "This is not tragic. I am happy."

Gerard Manley Hopkins, English poet: "I am so happy, so happy."

Moritz von Schwind, Austrian painter, responding to how he felt: "Excellent."

D(avid). H(erbert). Lawrence, English novelist: "I'm better now."

Douglas Fairbanks, Sr., actor: "I've never felt better."

J(erome). I(rving). Rodale, author and health-food advocate: During a guest appearance on "The Dick Cavett Show" in 1971, Rodale, the founder of *Prevention* magazine, was boasting that thirty years earlier his doctors had given him only six months to live, but because of his diet, he would live to be a hundred. Moments later he appeared to have fallen asleep, but it was soon discovered that he had died. The taped interview was never aired.

Richard Versalle, opera singer: On Jan. 5, 1996, while performing in the Metropolitan Opera's production of Leos Janácek's *The Makropulos Affair*, the 63-year-old tenor reportedly suffered a fatal heart attack and fell from a ladder to the stage floor. "In a twist of fate worthy of an opera," wrote reporter Peter Spencer, "he had just sung the line 'Too bad you can only live so long.'"

Henry Labouchere, British statesman, noting the flare of an oil lamp at his bedside: "Flames? Not yet, I think."

Gustav Mahler, Austrian composer and conductor: "Mozart."

James Joyce, Irish novelist: "Does anybody understand?"

Georg Wilhelm Friedrich Hegel, German philosopher: "Only one man ever understood me . . . and he didn't understand me."

Pierre Auguste Renoir, French painter: "I think I am beginning to understand something of it . . . What a pity I have to go now, just when I was beginning to show promise."

Bernard de Fontenelle, French scholar: "I feel nothing except a certain difficulty in continuing to exist."

Oscar Wilde, Irish wit and playwright; penniless, sipping champagne: "I am dying as I have lived; beyond my means."

Dylan Thomas, Welsh poet, at the White Horse tavern in New York City,

1953: "I've had 18 straight whiskeys—I think that is the record."

Turlough (O')Carolan, Irish composer and harpist, requesting a cup of whiskey: "It would be hard if two such friends should part at least without kissing."

W. C. Fields (William Claude Dukenfield), American film actor, on his deathbed, allegedly said: "I've been thinking about those poor little schoolboys out here peddling their papers in cold and rain, working to support their mothers . . . On second thought, f— 'em!"

Henry David Thoreau, American writer: "Moose. Indian." Earlier, he was asked if he had made peace with God, and replied: "I was not aware that we had ever quarreled."

James Thurber, American humorist and author: "God bless . . . God damn . . ."

Buddy Rich, American drummer, reportedly said in response to a nurse, asking him if he had any allergies: "Yes—country and western music."

Robert Toombs, U.S. lawyer, states-man, and army officer: "Lend me one hundred dollars."

Henry John Temple, Lord Palmerston, British prime minister: "Die, my dear doctor? That's the last thing I shall do!"

Samuel Goldwyn, movie mogul, quoting Clifton Fadiman: "I never thought I'd live to see the day."

REVERSE PARALLELISMS

The *reverse parallelism* is a nifty literary device in which the second half of a sentence rephrases and turns around the first half. Psychologist Mardell Grothe's unpublished book "Never Let a Fool Kiss You or a Kiss Fool You" contains 2,500 examples. Here are a few from his collection.

"Ask not what your country can do for you. Ask what you can do for your country."—**former U.S. President John F. Kennedy**

66 *It's not the men in my life, it's the life in my men.* **99** —**Mae West**

"Suit the action to the word, the word to the action."—**William Shakespeare**

"I write better than those who write more quickly than I do, and quicker than those who write better than I do."—**A. J. Liebling**

Here is my best attempt at writing a reverse parallelism: "I can't get an edge in wordwise, let alone a word in edgewise." And here's a close relative of a reverse parallelism: "I fiddle with the violin, or you could say that I violate the fiddle." Some word-unit palindromic sentences in this book are similar to these. Consider: "You can cage a swallow, can't you, but you can't swallow a cage, can you?"

WORD LADDERS

By changing one letter at each step, while keeping the other letters in the same order, these words can evolve into their opposites.

PUSH	PULL
HUSH	PULE
HUSK	RULE
HULK	RUSE
HULL	RUSH
PULL	PUSH

Lewis Carroll's Head to Tail

Lewis Carroll introduced this puzzle form, which he called *doublets* (our *word ladders*, above), in *Vanity Fair*, Mar. 29, 1879. These puzzles have also been called laddergrams, word chains, word links, step words, passes, and transformations. Here's Carroll's HEAD to TAIL.

HEAD
HEAL
TEAL
TELL
TALL
TAIL

IN SHORT

Shortest English Poems

These shorts come from Martin Gardner's *Oddities & Curiosities* (1961). In Oct. 1925, the "Literary Review" column in the *New York Evening Post* featured this poem by Eli Siegel.

ONE QUESTION
I,
Why?

PALINDROME POEM
Probably the shortest poem in English, which happens to be a palindrome, was written around 1960. It is titled "Reactions to a Statement by Khrushchev That the Soviet Union Has No Desire to Meddle in the Internal Affairs of Other Nations."

O,
So?

A One-Letter American Place-Name

Y (Michigan)

Shortest Bible Verse

"Jesus wept."—**John 11:35**

A Short Correspondence

Shortly after *Les Miserables* was published in 1862, Victor Hugo, eager to know how well his book was selling, sent his publishers, Hurst and Blackett, a note which read: "?" The publishers replied: "!"

ILLOGICAL ENGLISH

The comedian Gallagher wonders why a building that is finished is not referred to as a "built," why one TV is called a "set," why one panty is considered a "pair," and why a bra is seen as a single item.

Proposition is the long term for the short term, and *propose* is the short term for the long term.—**Tim Martin, WF**

Abbreviation is a 12-letter word, *monosyllabic* has five syllables, a "near hit" is called a "near miss," and to be "out for someone" is to "have it in for someone."

TWISTED SENTENCES

Pangrams

A *pangram* is a sentence containing all the letters of the alphabet. This one by Dmitri Borgmann in Martin Gardner's *Oddities & Curiosities* (1961) uses all letters of the alphabet just once: "Cwm, fjord-bank glyphs vext quiz." A *cwm* is Welsh for "a circular valley" (*w* is a vowel in Welsh). A *glyph* is a carved figure, *vext* is a poetic spelling of vexed, and a *quiz* is an 18th century word for an eccentric. The sentence thus means "Carved figures in a valley on the bank of the fjord irritated an eccentric person."

Maxey Brook's pangrams, *WW*, May 1987, use 43 letters: "My girl wove six dozen plaid jackets before she quit." and "Her gift box of jigsaw puzzles quickly drove me nuts."

Howard W. Bergerson supplied this delightful 40-letter pangram: "Xavier picked bright yellow jonquils for Mitzi."

Here are two more: "Sympathizing would fix Quaker objectives" (36 letters); "The five boxing wizards jump quickly" (31 letters).

Tongue-Twisters

A little alliteration: "Are you copper-bottoming 'em, my man?" she asked. "No," he replied, "I'm aluminiuming 'em, mum."

Aluminium is the British spelling of what Americans know as *aluminum.*—**O'London's, Oct. 26, 1929**

"Top step's pup's pet spot."—**Leigh Mercer's tongue-twister palindrome in Martin Gardner, *Scientific American*, Sept. 1964**

"The rapid rabid rabbit ran rampant."

SEE-SAW

Mr. See and Mr. Soar were old friends. See owned a saw and Soar owned a seesaw. Now See's saw sawed Soar's seesaw before Soar saw See, which made Soar sore. Had Soar seen See's saw before See saw Soar's seesaw, then See's saw would not have sawed Soar's seesaw. But See saw Soar and Soar's seesaw before Soar saw See's saw, so See's saw sawed Soar's seesaw. It was a shame to let See soar so sore just because See's saw sawed Soar's seesaw.

ANOTHER SEA-SAW

Here is Eric Albert's offering of a false past tense: seahorse   sawhorse

IDIOTMATIC

Here are a few idioms, in the style of Bill Dana (aka José Jimenez), which never seemed to catch on.

That pancake is flatter than a . . .
Tea isn't my cup of . . .
Those flies are dropping like . . .
The rabbits are breeding like . . .
That doornail is deader than a . . .

14 ANAGRAMS IN THE MAJOR LEAGUES

◇ ◇ ◇

BY DEFINITION

Anagrams, Transposals & Mutations

An *anagram*, defined by the National Puzzlers' League, is a transposition of letters in a familiar word, name, or phrase into another, appropriate to the base. The NPL considers a *transposal* a reshuffling of letters in a name or dictionary-sanctioned word or phrase to form another, not necessarily related, word or phrase. Examples are: (1) ERIC CLAPTON—"narcoleptic" (Rik Edwards, *Longman* [1985]), (2) SENATOR—"treason" (Alfred H. Smith, *St. Nicholas*, July 1875), (3) RISE TO SPEAK—"strike a pose" (Rik Edwards, *Longman* [1985]), and (4) HERE AND NOW—"we're on hand"

(O. V. Michaelsen, *WF*, Feb. 1991).

A *mutation*, by the league's definition, is a rearrangement of a word or set of words into another, not normally used, bearing little or no relation to the base. An example is INTEGRITY—"tiny tiger." Mutations were more popular in the 19th century than today. In the NPL book *Real Puzzles* (1925), Rufus T. Strohm, aka Arty Ess, editor of *The Enigma* for 30 years, stated: "The *mutation* is the pariah of the anagram caste. It is the sort of thing one dismisses with a frown, a kick, or a curse . . . Obviously, the mental effort required to make a mutation is on a par with that required to urge a pedestrian to pick up a lost dime; which is probably the reason for the doubtful social standing of the mutation in the cosmos of puzzledom."

Incidentally, in 1886 George Haywood (Bolis) established the difference between an *anagram*, a *transposal*, and a *mutation*. William Ougheltree (Skeeziks) derived the term *mutation* from the earlier term *transmutation*. The words *mutation* and *transmutation*, as defined by Ougheltree, were never recognized by dictionary and encyclopedia authorities.

FINDING THE BEST

Basic Criteria

Several criteria can be used to judge the quality of an anagram. Experts usually agree that the ideal anagram: (1) refers clearly and specifically to the base, (2) uses standard English, (3) is transposed completely, (4) contains no extraneous or filler words, and (5) maintains parallel syntax, number, and tense with that of the familiar word, name, or phrase.

The anagram "has to pilfer," made from A SHOPLIFTER, is apt and well mixed, but does not stand on its own, parallel to the base in form, as does "a rich Tory caste," made from THE ARISTOCRACY. Since few anagrams are parallel, cohesive, apposite, and well transposed, this book includes many of the former type (A SHOPLIFTER "has to pilfer").

Some Rules of Exclusion

All in the Theme
Words which do not refer specifically to the theme detract from an anagram. The words *great* and *late great*, for instance, may be considered to detract from these anagrams about Edison and King. In THE GREAT THOMAS ALVA EDISON—"The good man, he lit vast areas." (Here the word *the* is repeated.) THE LATE, GREAT DR. MARTIN LUTHER KING—"Think tall! A dreamer greeting truth." Some puzzlers find the use of articles (*a, an, the*) acceptable in an anagram. Superfluous words often made from left-over letters are SIR(S), NOTE, and interjections such as O, OH, AH, HA, and LO.

Well-Mixed Letters
An anagram of POETRY, "Try Poe," by Hoosier (*TE*, Mar. 1934) could also be seen as flawed because only syllables are transposed. Many anagram writers feel that the number of letters repeated in sequence should not exceed three; some consider this too restricting. Most veteran puzzlers agree that an anagram should not contain any words that appear in the base.

Lengthy Anagrams
Bolis (George Haywood) pointed out that abnormally long anagram bases rarely yield good results because they tend to contain fewer words that refer directly to the subject(s). It is, however, easier to form a grammatical sentence from a long base because of the

increased number of possible letter combinations.

Just for Exercise

In this transposition exercise, I included the initials of my name to deal with the remaining letters, *O* and *M*. By adding the letters *R* and *E* to the base, I eliminated the need for initials, shown in the second example. Another criticism of the anagrams is that the bases are contrived.

I'LL SETTLE FOR WRITING ANA-GRAMS, arranging as letters will fit — O. M.

I'LL SETTLE FOR REWRITING ANA-GRAMS, arranging as *more* letters will fit.

Some of my better attempts, without the aid of a computer program, all printed in *TE*, were OSCAR WILDE—"I lace words (A WRITER *of* rare wit)" (Sept. 1990); JACKIE MASON—"a manic jokes" (Dec. 1991); PLATAN—"a plant" (June 1992); and A PSYCHI-ATRIST—"Sit, chat, pay, sir" (Dec. 1994). My ANGELIC—"nice gal" appeared in *WF*, Feb. 1995.

Avoiding Contrived Bases

The first two bases above are contrived, as is A CONE POURING RED-HOT LAVA, which when shuffled can be made into "Oh, dear! A volcano erupting."

Here is a classic with a contrived base: A FORESTER REFERS TO "a fosterer for trees" (Anglo Saxon, *Inter-Ocean*, Apr. 22, 1902).

In choosing anagrams for my top 50 list, I excluded those made from contrived bases, such as IN THE SOUTH SEA ISLANDS—"A thousand islets shine" (Ellsworth, *TE*, Jan. 1925).

Headlines & Missing Articles

Many anagrams read like newspaper headlines; they contain key words but omit the articles *a, an,* or *the*. The base and anagram STATE CRIMI-NALS—"a miscreant list" was an actual headline in a Jan. 1898 Pittsburgh newspaper. Anagrams for ISRAEL PUTNAM—"Salem Puritan" (Remardo, *TEE*, Mar. 1915), MOURN-ING—"grim noun" (Yercas, *TE*, Mar. 1933), and DORMITORY—"dirty room" (T. H., *Inter-Ocean*, May 2, 1899) relate well to the subjects.

However, I think that if the letter *A* could be used in these bases, without repeating the letter as a word, the anagrams would be enhanced. So, A DORMITORY would become "a dirty room." On the other hand, if it were possible to transpose DORMITORIES into "dirty rooms," the anagram would be parallel to the base and not require the article *a*.

CHESTER ARTHUR—"truth searcher" (Camillus, *GD*, May 5, 1883) would be improved grammatically, but not anagrammatically, by adding the initial of his middle name, forming CHESTER A. ARTHUR—"a truth searcher." Unfortunately, the word *a* in the base would also appear as a word in the anagram. In either case, "truth searcher" is too vague a description of Arthur's character and could apply to many other people. The same thing could be said about this amusing anagram, ROSS PEROT—"sore sport" (Alf, *TE*, Sept. 1992).

One highly praised example is "Bear hit den," made from HIBERNATED (Viking, *TE*, Mar. 1934). The problem with that sentence is the missing article *the*, which makes it slightly ungrammatical. (To rephrase Gertrude Stein, "There's no *the* there.") Instead, it reads like words from a script written for the Lone Ranger's friend Tonto. I prefer an anagram which reads as naturally as its base—in English as it is normally spoken or written.

Articles at Large

Many anagram bases contain what I consider forced use of the article *the* in place of *a* or *an*, as in THE NUDIST COLONY—"no untidy clothes" (Ellsworth, *TE*, Oct. 1933) and THE OVERCOAT—"cover to heat" (Kenneth, *Waverley*, Feb. 25, 1899). The article *the* seems grammatically unnecessary in these anagrams of plurals: THE CARDINALS—"in cathedrals" (Viking, *TE*, Feb. 1965), THE HURRICANES—"These churn air" (Viking, *TE*, Oct. 1931), and THE EYES—"They see." Although these break no grammatical rules, I prefer anagrams and bases in which the word *the* refers to a particular person, place, or thing, such as THE U.S. LIBRARY OF CONGRESS—"It's only for research bugs."

Interjections

In culling my top 50 list of anagrams, I also omitted anagrams containing interjections, such as THE ZOOLOGICAL GARDENS—"Oh, gaze into droll cages!" (D. C. Ver, *GD*, Oct. 15, 1898), A SEARCHLIGHT—"Ach! This glare!" (Enavlicm, *B&O*, Nov. 1931), and my favorites, GILROY, CA—"Garlic? Yo!" (Ulk, *TE*, Feb. 1993) and IT'S ALL GREEK TO ME—"Gee, talker, I'm lost." (Wabbit, *TE*, Dec. 1990).

Unmixed Letters & "I"

Not included in my list of choice anagrams are those with four or more unmixed letters, those inappropriately written in the first person, and those using the word *I*, when it refers to a nonperson. Here are some of the best "I" anagrams I've found; all work as effective declarative sentences.

THE "I's" HAVE IT

DISARMAMENT   I'm at arm's end.—Fred Domino, *TE*, June 1951

FRITO-LAY (trademark)   I fry a lot.—Tweaser, *TE*, Aug. 1988

MAINE   I am N.E.—S. L. B., *YC*, May 18, 1871

DECIMAL POINT   I'm a pencil dot.—Neophyte, *TE*, May 1977

MILITARISM   **a.** I limit arms. **b.** I limit Mars.—(a) Alec Sander, *TEE*, June 1919; (b) Barnyard, *TEE*, July 1917. Both are antonymous anagrams.

THE LIQUOR HABIT   Quit! I rob health.—Jemand, *TEE*, Dec. 1915

A POLICEMAN'S WHISTLE I am seen with all cops.—Viking, *TE*, Nov. 1933

UNITED STATES BUREAU OF FISHERIES I raise bass to feed us in the future.—Minnie Mum, *TE*, July 1925

A Matter of Choice

My main criteria for choosing the anagrams in the list of Fifty Choice Anagrams were historical content, humor, longevity of subject matter, and names, phrases, or terms that are commonly known or could be found in current reference books.

Of the thousands of anagrams I have scanned, many contain antiquated words and expressions or forgotten names and events. William Walsh, in his *Handy-Book of Literary Curiosities* (1892), stated: "After centuries of endeavor, so few really good anagrams have been rolled down to us. One may assert that all the really superb anagrams now extant might be contained in a pillbox."

Although many "choice anagrams" have been written since Walsh's time, there are fewer than one might expect, considering that over a century has passed.

But puzzlers and the public have shown renewed interest in anagrams and palindromes. Many early forms of these elegant trifles have been included in this book. Most were found in periodicals, including *The Enigma* ("in the game") and *The Eastern Enigma*.

Many come from Ross Eckler's *The New Anagrammasia* (1991).

Other word puzzlers may not share my criteria, or biases, for determining an anagram's quality. And choosing examples is necessarily subjective, no matter how strict one's criteria. Although nearly all anagrams listed here were composed as puzzles, many were judged from a grammatical point of view.

FIFTY CHOICE ANAGRAMS

Here are fifty well-composed anagrams and their authors, often bearing pseudonyms. To find full book and periodical titles, look in Key to Abbreviations, and to discover a puzzler's identity, check Puzzlers & Their Pseudonyms. Both the key and the index are in the back of this book.

AIRFIELDS aid fliers.—Ab Struse, *F-SP*, Apr. 1982

AN AISLE is a lane.—Awl Wrong, *TE*, Dec. 1939

ANIMOSITY is no amity.—Lord Baltimore, *NT*, Feb. 6, 1896

THE ARISTOCRACY, a rich Tory caste—Ess Ell, *NA*, June 2, 1906

ATHLETICS, lithe acts—Mabel P., *Pittsburgh Post*, Apr. 1, 1900

THE COMPULSORY EDUCATION LAW You must learn; police do watch.—Amaranth, *TEE*, Feb. 1916

CONSIDERATE   Care is noted.—D. C. Ver, *TEE*, June 1919

THE COUNTRYSIDE, no city dust here.—Su San, *TE*, Feb. 1948

DESPERATION
A rope ends it.
—Air Raid, *TE*, Apr. 1920

DESTINATION   It is to an end—Rizpah, *Waverley*, Nov. 19, 1898

EARNESTNESS   a stern sense—M. C. S., *Sunday Standard*, Sept. 30, 1894

EDGE TOOLS   good steel—Enavlicm, *NA*, Jan. 12, 1907

EXECUTIONS   exits on cue—Stephan R. Marlow, *F-SP*, Oct. 1981

THE EYES   They see.—Anonyme, *Puzzletown Oracle*, Jan. 15, 1896

FATHER TIME, a term thief—Damonomad, *TE*, Mar. 1934

THE HOLY GOSPEL helps theology *or* theology's help—Awl Wrong, *TE*, July 1941

INNOMINATE   no name in it—Spud, *TE*, Dec. 1922

THE LANDING OF THE PILGRIMS English, in flight, made port.—Viking, *TE*, July 1931

THE LEANING TOWER OF PISA What a foreign stone pile!—Sam Weller, *GD*, July 2, 1881

THE LOST PARADISE, Earth's ideal spot—Delian, *TS*, May 1901

MINISTERS remit sins.—O.N.E. One, *NA*, Apr. 20, 1905

NO TRESPASSING. Stop an ingress.—D. C. Ver, *GD*, Dec. 4, 1897

OLD MASTERS, art's models—Traddles, 1880s

ORCHESTRATE. Score the art.—Double H, *TE*, Nov. 1983

PASTORSHIP, parish post—Kea, *TE*, Oct. 1994

PENURIOUSNESS   no use in purses *or* no purses in use—M. C. S., *Inter-Ocean*, Oct. 8, 1901

PITTANCE, a cent tip—The Duke, *TEE*, June 1913

POSTPONED   Stopped? No.—Towhead, *TE*, Jan. 1922

PRO-LIFE   Flip Roe.—Mike Morton, 1995

RECEIVED PAYMENT; every cent paid me.—D. C. Ver, *GD*, July 14, 1897

RED TAG SALE Great deals!—Atlantic, *TE*, Apr. 1988

ROME WAS NOT BUILT IN A DAY Any labour I do wants time.—Arthur Pearson, *20th Cent. Book* (1915)

PROSPERITY is property.—Arty Fishel, *Study*, Oct. 22, 1886

SAINTLINESS, least in sins—N. Jineer, *TE*, May 1925

SALMAN RUSHDIE   Read, shun Islam! *or* Dare shun Islam!—Alf, *TE*, Apr. 1989

A SENTENCE OF DEATH faces one at the end.—Q., *TE*, Jan. 1927

A SHOPLIFTER has to pilfer.—Ess Ell, *Inter-Ocean*, Sept. 4, 1908

A SIGNAL OF DISTRESS   It's S.O.S. read in flags.—Viking, *TE*, Feb. 1932

SKIN CARE irks acne.—Howard Bergerson, *P&A* (1973)

SOUTHERN CALIFORNIA, hot sun or life in a car—Josefa Heifetz Byrne, *WW*, May 1970

A STRIP TEASER spares attire.—Awl Wrong, *TE*, July 1940

SUGGESTION   It eggs us on.—Arty Ess, *Inter-Ocean*, June 19, 1908

SURGICAL INSTRUMENTS, smart curing utensils—Francolin, *TEE*, Sept. 1915

THEOLOGICAL SEMINARIES   Sole aim: teach religions.—Atlantis, *TEE*, Feb. 1911

THREE-POINT-TWO, the "wet" portion—Sakr-el-bahr, *TE*, Apr. 1934

TRADESMEN need marts.—D. C. Ver, *NA*, Aug. 4, 1906

UPHOLSTERERS restore plush.—A. Chem, *TE*, Apr. 1930

THE U.S. LIBRARY OF CONGRESS It's only for research bugs.—Darryl Francis, *WW*, Nov. 1968

WASHINGTON CROSSING THE DELAWARE   He saw his ragged Continentals row.—Skeeziks, *Thedom*, Nov. 10, 1890

WESTERN UNION, no wire unsent—Virginia Dare, *TE*, Feb. 1922

HONORABLE-MENTION ANAGRAMS

These fifty honorable-mention anagrams seem flawed or do not appeal to my particular tastes. Many bases in these anagrams contain the grammatically unnecessary word *the*. Two of the anagrams are outdated, and a few contain alternate or nonstandard spellings (*venders*, *rime*, *learnt*, and *rassle*). Although many could be considered imperfect, all are better than most I've found.

ACETAMINOPHEN, the "no-pain" acme?—Nightowl, *TE*, May 1988

ADVERTISEMENTS   Items at venders.—Viking, *P&A* (1973)

THE ARCHEOLOGIST   He's got a hot relic.—Al Gebra, *TE*, Oct. 1963

THE ARTESIAN WELLS   Water's in all these.—Viking, *TE*, Dec. 1933

ASPERSION, no praises—Molemi, *Oracle*, Jan. 1907

THE ASSASSINATION OF PRESIDENT ABRAHAM LINCOLN   A pistol in an actor's rebel hands; a fine man is shot.—Jessie McPherrin, *TE*, Feb. 1951

THE ASTROLOGER   He got star lore.—Primrose, *Somerset Messenger*, May 18, 1898

BARGAIN HUNTERS   Run, grab in haste!—N. Jineer, *TE*, Dec. 1923

BASTARDS, sad brats—Molemi, "Anagrammasia" (1926)

THE CARICATURE, caustic art here—Awl Wrong, *TE*, July 1940

THE CARICATURISTS   Their art's caustic.—Fred Domino, *TE*, Aug. 1953

THE CHINESE RESTAURANT   Taste Hunan's rice there.—George Groth, *TE*, Aug. 1982

THE COLLEGE UNDERGRADU-ATES   Our "green" shall get educat-ed.—Molemi, *Inter-Ocean*, Jan. 19, 1912

THE COMPLETE WORKS OF WILLIAM SHAKESPEARE   Pick Marlowe; ask if *he* wrote all these poems.—Mona Lisa, *TE*, Feb. 1978

FAMILIES, life's aim—Enavlicm, *TEE*, Nov. 1917

THE DAWNING   Night waned.—Dreamer, *TE*, Feb. 1926

DESEGREGATION   Negroes get aid.—Pacifico, *TE*, July 1956

DOMESTICATED ANIMAL, docile, as man tamed it—Spica, *TEE*, 1917

DROMOMANIA   Mad, I roam on.—Awl Wrong, *TE*, Feb. 1944

THE EDUCATIONAL TELEVISION PROGRAMS   Video teaching primes us to learn a lot.—Merlin, *TE*, Dec. 1971

EQUESTRIAN, equine arts—Kenneth, *Gentleman*, May 1899

GARBAGE MAN, bag manager—Atlantic, *TE*, June 1991

"GATHER YE ROSEBUDS WHILE YE MAY." (Robert Herrick) Here's why: beauty goes dim early. —Hudu, *TE*, Jan. 1987

THE GERMAN SOLDIERS   Hitler's men are dogs!—Awl Wrong, *TE*, Dec. 1943

HUSTLERS   Let's rush!—Gemini, *TE*, July 1924

INNUMERABLE, a number line—Balmar, *AP*, May 26, 1900

INTELLIGENTSIA, an elite listing—Archimedes, *TE*, Sept. 1938

THE INTERNATIONAL MORSE CODE   Those radio men once learnt it.—Viking, *TE*, June 1972

THE LANDSCAPE GARDENER   He planted ranged acres.—Moonshine, *TE*, Apr. 1927

LIMERICKS, slick rime—Hexagony, *Inter-Ocean*, June 12, 1908

THE LORD'S DAY   Add holy rest.—Nibbs, *TEE*, Dec. 1898

THE MARIMBA Hammer a bit.—Wrong Font, *TE*, Feb. 1938

MICHELANGELO BUONARROTI'S CREATION OF ADAM A Roman ceiling, too, can house formidable art.—Talon, *TE*, Mar. 1991

THE OLD-AGE PENSION helps one in dotage.—Awl Wrong, *TE*, May 1948

AN OLD SHOE had no sole.—Neophyte, *Sunday Standard*, Apr. 1896

ONE-ARMED BANDITS, Reno's damned bait—Len Elliott, *F-SP*, Aug. 1983

THE POULTRY DEALERS They do rear pullets.—Viking, *TE*, Apr. 1937

THE PROFESSIONAL WRESTLER No sport left where I rassle.—Viking, *TE*, Sept. 1964

THE SATURDAY NIGHT SPECIAL, a gun they list as dirt cheap.—Viking, *TE*, Oct. 1972

THE SEPTUAGENARIAN, near that supine age.—Hercules, *TE*, July 1924

SNOOZE ALARMS Alas, no more Zs.—Atlantic, *TE*, Dec. 1982

"A STITCH IN TIME SAVES NINE." This is meant as incentive.—Tony Augarde, *Oxford Guide* (1984)

A SURGICAL OPERATION Pain or gore, alas, I cut.—R. Are, *AP*, Mar. 15, 1907

THE TAM-O'-SHANTER That's no mere hat!—Viking, *TE*, May 1968

TELEVISION NEWS It's now seen live.—Tut, *TE*, May 1975

"TO CAST PEARLS BEFORE SWINE" One's labor is perfect waste.—Livedevil, *TE*, ca.1938–1941

TOTAL ABSTAINERS sit not at ale bars.—Hoodwink, *TE*, Feb. 1955

THE UNITED STATES OF AMERICA So much in a tea fee started it.—Hercules, *TE*

VALENTINE POEMS, pen mates in love—Jamaica, *NA*, Aug. 19, 1905

THE VOLCANIC ERUPTIONS stir each plutonic oven.—Nypho, *TE*, June 1949

Less Perfect Anagrams

Although each of these anagrams contains four or more unshuffled letters, they are too interesting to exclude.

APPROPRIATENESS is apt, sane, proper.—R. O. Chester, *Evening Telegraph*, 1905

DISARMAMENT Amend it, Mars.—E. S. Crow, *TE*, Mar. 1927

THE INFERNAL REGIONS No final resting here!—Viking, *TE*, May 1931

IVANHOE BY SIR WALTER SCOTT, a novel by a Scottish writer—Arcanus, *NT*, Feb. 17, 1896

THE KNOW-IT-ALLS We think so tall.—Sphinx, *TE*, Nov. 1985

NOVA SCOTIA AND PRINCE EDWARD ISLAND, two Canadian provinces, lands I dread!—Dmitri Borgmann, *On Vacation* (1965)

OPERATION DESERT STORM made one terrorist stop.—Tweaser, *TE*, April 1991

THE PROFESSIONAL GAMBLER He'll bear profits on games.—Ab Struse, *TE*, July 1984

ANAGRAM VARIETIES

One-Word Anagrams

Here are apt single-word transpositions, many of which could be called *synanagrams*, a term coined by Murray Pearce in *WW*, Aug. 1971. LAUDATION—"adulation" contains five unmixed letters. "Prenatal" has been called an anagram of PATERNAL and PARENTAL, but by NPL standards, it would be considered a transposal. "Reductions" would be a more appropriate anagram of DISCOUNTS, if that were possible. Other one-word anagrams in this list which could be criticized are INAMORATA—"amatorian," IT'S—"'tis," and SABBATH—"shabbat." TAP—"pat," which are phonetic reversals, seem to be among the few nonpalindromic English words that are synonymous forward and backwards. This one-word anagram list could include the popular reversals AH!—"Ha!" and OH!—"Ho!"

IN A WORD

ADOBE abode—Ruth, *St. Nicholas*, Sept. 1876

ANGERED enraged—Kenneth, *Inter-Ocean*, Jan. 31, 1899

APT pat—King Carnival, *Evening Telegraph*, 1905

DEDUCTIONS discounted—June 1925

DETOUR routed—Cephas, *Independent*, Jan. 16, 1896

DISCOUNTER reductions

EVIL vile—T. L., *Farmer's Almanack*, 1815

FIANCÉS fancies—Ellsworth, *TE*, May 1925

HEIGHTS highest—Neophyte, *NA*, Aug. 4, 1906

INAMORATA amatorian—*Inter-Ocean*, Sept. 13, 1896

INGESTA eatings—Francolin, *TE*, Jan. 1915

IT'S 'tis

LAUDATION adulation—Arthur Pearson, *20th Cent. Standard* (1907)

LISTERIZE sterilize—Hoho, *TE*, Mar. 1943

MARS arms—Nyas, *NT*, Apr. 11, 1893

PATERNAL parental—Jason, *AP*, Sept. 15, 1902

RAISE arise—Anonyme, *TEE*, Dec. 1913

RESCUES secures—Miss T. Ree, *Central NJ Times,* May 1887

SABBATH Shabbat

SHRUB brush—Viking, *TE,* Sept. 1931

STUM must—Koe, *Harper's Young People,* July 11, 1882

TAP pat—*New Sphinx* (1806)

TONE note—R., *St. Nicholas,* May 1875

TOURING routing—Ruth, *St. Nicholas,* Sept. 1876

YEA! Aye!—Beech Nut, *Oracle,* May 1898

Anagram Shorts & Transpositions

Transposed Couplets, or Pairagrams
Here are some *transposed couplets,* or *pairagrams.* "Marine airmen" could be considered antonymous and oxymoronic. In the British magazine *Games & Puzzles,* Sept. 1975, a diversion called double anagrams was based on the same idea. Clues suggested answers that would be two-word transposals of each other. Well-mixed examples included the clue "hidden promise" with the answer "latent talent" (also used here); the clue "object in outer space" with the answer "remote meteor"; and the clue "seagoing craft" with the answer "ocean canoe." *Ocean kayak* is a valid term, but *ocean canoe* is not, to my knowledge.

Actors co-star.—Viking, *TE,* Feb. 1972

American Cinerama—Sol, Jr., *TE,* May 1954

best bets

continued unnoticed

coordinate decoration—L M. N. Terry, *AP,* Dec. 1, 1900

Elvis lives.

float aloft—Dauntless, *NA,* Jan. 27, 1906

horse/shoer (one word)—Medius, *Pittsburgh Post,* Mar. 16, 1902

latent talent—Nyas, *NT,* Nov. 29, 1894

marine airmen

married admirer—Molemi, *B&O,* Apr. 1928

Oriental relation

outer route—*O'London's,* Oct. 27, 1934

Scat, cats!—R., *St. Nicholas,* May 1875

stayed steady—Primrose, *Somerset Messenger,* Sept. 23, 1896

steno notes

streaming emigrants—Miss H. Selway, *O'London's,* Nov. 30, 1929

team mate (also written as one word)—Seer, *NA,* June 11, 1904

tramline terminal

veto vote—Swamp Angel, *Inter-Ocean,* Mar. 17, 1895

Triplet, or Trianagram

If pairagrams are admissible, then perhaps we can include a *trianagram*, which uses three terms that are anagrams of each other and reads as a sentence. You may prefer to add an article to the beginning of Eric Albert's sentence: "Discounter introduces reductions."

Antigrams—Antonymous Anagrams

Transpositions opposite in meaning to an original word or phrase are sometimes called *antigrams*, a term coined by Sans Souci in *Ardmore Puzzler*, Sept. 22, 1900. There are far fewer of these than conventional anagrams. That's probably because most appear to be discovered by the composers accidentally. One of my favorite topical examples is MONDALE—"Dole man," referring to the 1976 U.S. vice-presidential candidates Walter Mondale and Robert Dole (Larry, *TE*, Oct. 1976).

The first antigrams labeled antigrams were published in *AP*, Nov. 17, 1900. Because the coined term *antigram* could also be understood as a shortened form of the term *antigrammatic(al)*, the opposite of *grammatical*, perhaps another term would be helpful. Maybe we could call them antonymograms, antonymous anagrams, or simply opposite anagrams.

Henry E. Dudeney, editor of "Perplexities" in the *Strand*, referred in 1929 to an antigram as a word which becomes another word when reversed. A reader submitted LANIATED—"detainal" and SAMAROID—"dioramas." Lewis Carroll in the novel *Sylvie & Bruno* (1889) called this type of reversal a *semordnilap* (the term *palindromes* spelled backwards). In the *New American Encyclopedic Dictionary* (1905), the first definition of the more common term *anagram* was given as "the letters of any word read backwards." Most 20th century dictionaries, since that time, have become more sophisticated about such puzzling words.

Here are some antigrams, which can be considered antonymous anagrams.

ANTAGONIST not against—Arcanus, *TEE*, Dec. 1898

DEMONIACAL a docile man—Pygmalion, *GD*, Oct. 2, 1886

DORMITORIES tidier rooms—Sally, *TE*, Oct. 1989

DYNAMITED a tidy mend—Castet, *TE*, July 1952

EVANGELISTS evil's agents—Hi Kerr, *TE*, June 1927

HIBERNIANS banish Erin—D. C. Ver, *NA*, Sept. 8, 1906

HONOREES no heroes—Rom Dos, *TE*, July 1, 1992

INROADS no raids—Viking, *TE*, Oct. 1964

THE MORNING AFTER in great form then—Gemini, *TE*, Oct. 1925

THE OSCAR NOMINATION   It's not a cinema honor.—Atlantic, *TE*, Jan. 1993

THE PARSONAGE   so pagan there—Hoho, *TE*, Oct. 1960

PERSECUTED   due respect—*Longman* (1985)

PROTECTIONISM   nice to imports—Hercules, *TE*, Feb. 1928

REFORESTATION   no fair to trees—Te-Zir-Man, *TE*, Jan. 1990

SAINTLINESS   entails sins—Sphinx, *TE*, June 1986

A SUN WORSHIPER   I shun Ra's power.—Non Sequitur, *TE*, Nov. 1992

SWELTERING HEAT   the winter gales—A. Chem, *TE*, July 1967

UNITE(D)   untie(d)—Louisa H. Sheridan, *N&Q*, Oct. 12, 1861

THE VOLSTEAD LAW   had all "wet" votes—Larry, *TE*, Feb. 1927

WITHIN EARSHOT   "I won't hear this."—Hoodwink, *TE*, Sept. 1948

Ambigram

The term *ambigram*, an anagram ambiguously apposite or opposite in meaning from its base, was coined by Sibyl (Judith Bagai), former *TE* editor.

THE NUCLEAR REGULATORY COMMISSION   Your rules clone atomic nightmares!—Te-Zir-Man, *TE*, Feb. 1993

Transposals

The longest transposition of one scientific word into another, found so far, is HYDROXYDESOXYCORTICOSTERONE—"hydroxydeoxycorticosterones" (27 letters), which is a variant spelling of the same word; and of a nonscientific word, we have REPRESENTATIONALISM—"misrepresentational" (19 letters). The first containing 18 letters was by Mephisto in *TE*, Sept. 1980: NATURAL NECESSITIES—"inarticulatenesses," later matched by Xemu *TE*, June 1997: SECONDARY QUALITIES—"quasi-considerately." The longest well-mixed transposal is thought to be CINEMATOGRAPHER—"megachiropteran" (15 letters), found by Hercules, *TE*, Dec. 1927.

One of Albert's favorites was EARL OF COVENTRY (a card game)—"olfactory nerve." According to puzzlist and author Maxey Brooke, the earliest published transposal known was MITE—"time," by Matilda in the July 16, 1796 issue of the New York magazine *The Weekly Museum*.

COTARNINE, an organic base, is obtained by the oxidation of NARCOTINE, a crystalline alkaloid extracted from opium. ORLEANS is a city in France, and SALERNO, in Italy. The letters of the name of the independent republic in Italy, SAN MARINO, also form ROMANIANS. Film star MYRNA LOY and educator MARY LYON shared the same letters in their names, as did record producer RAY

STARK and singer KAY STARR. IRISH PECANS, shuffled, becomes SPANISH RICE; unfortunately, the former term only exists in this transposal.

In Sept. 1978 *The Wall Street Journal* reported that a motor oil manufacturer called XONEX was sued by EXXON for using the same letters in its name. Incidentally, EXON (not EXXON) was coined for the company by Dmitri Borgmann.

Triplets

Eric Albert found what is considered the longest well-mixed triple transposal: UNISON INTERVALS—NONUNIVERSALIST—INVOLUNTARINESS (15 letters). He also discovered one of the best triple transposals: CECROPIA MOTHS—PHOTOCERAMICS—COMPOSITE ARCH (13 letters).

Word Reversals

The Encyclopedia Americana (1951) stated: "The most exact anagram, sometimes termed 'palindrome,' is that formed by reading the letters backwards." This view is not shared by many, if any, modern puzzlers. A word which forms another when read backwards was originally called an "anagram," and, unofficially, a "reversion" and an "inversion." Now many puzzlers and most logologists refer to such words as a *word reversal.*

15 HISTORIC ANAGRAMS

Although many anagram collections have been available through the years, few have carefully noted the original sources of the anagrams. Here are some anagram firsts and other things to delight you about anagrams concerning historic figures and events. The first anagrams in English date from the 1500s.

◇ ◇ ◇

EARLIEST ANAGRAMS

Greeks & Egyptians

William Camden in *Remains* (1605) states that *anagrams* are thought to have been invented by the Greek philosopher and mathematician Pythagoras in the sixth century B.C. According to Eustachius, 12th century bishop of Thessalonica, the earliest-known anagrams were written by a Thracian named Lycophron, one of the Pleiades, seven honored tragic poets of Alexandria under Egyptian King Ptolemy II Philadelphus. Lycophron's obscure 260 B.C. poem

"Cassandra," about the siege of Troy in the mid-13th century B.C., contained flattering anagrams. "Made of honey" was an anagram on the name of the king, and "violet of Juno," or "Juno's violet," was an anagram of his sister, Queen Arsinoë. Another anagram by Lycophron was ATLAS— "*talas*" ("wretched").

Plato also had an interest in the art. For centuries Neoplatonists believed that anagrams revealed divinity and destiny.

According to legend, the night before the siege of Tyre, Alexander the Great dreamed that he caught a satyr leaping before him. His advisers explained that this was a good omen because the letters in the Greek word for *satyr* also formed the statement "Tyre is yours." On the following day the prediction was fulfilled.

Few humorous anagrams have been found dating before the 16th century. Rulers sometimes provided significant financial rewards to people who wrote complimentary anagrams of the ruler's name, and satirists who chose the powerful as the subject of anagram ridicule probably faced unpleasant consequences.

Of Guilds, Discoveries, Cabalists & Queens

Astronomers from the 1300s to the 1700s, such as Galileo Galilei (1564-1642), Christian Huygens (1629-1695), and Robert Hooke (1635-1703), often wrote their findings in anagrammatic codes to prevent rivals from stealing their work and church officials from interfering. Metaphors, allegories, and other symbolic codes were also used to conceal guild writings and trade secrets, most notably in alchemy.

George Puttenham (d. 1590) in *The Arte of English Poesie* (1589), arranged the letters in Queen Elizabeth's (1533-1603) Latin name, ELISSABET ANGLORUM REGINA, to form the prophetic words "*Multa regnabis sene gloria.*" ("Aged and in much glory shall ye reign.") The Queen, herself, was known to engage in anagram writing.

Thirteenth century Cabalists believed that if they arranged the letters in the Hebrew alphabet in the correct order, they could discover divine revelations and magical powers.

Anagram writing soon became a favorite pastime of scholars and the affluent throughout the world and gradually lost its mystical significance. It reached the peak of its popularity in the early 17th century when King Louis XIII (1601-1643) of France appointed Thomas Billon to be his "official anagrammatist" at a salary of 1,200 livres a year.

Eleanor Audeley, Seer Reproof

Peter Heylin records tales of 17th century anagrammatists in *Cyprianus Anglicanus, or History of the Life and Death of William Laud, Archbishop of Canterbury* (1719). In 1634 Francis Lenton, "the Queen's poet," published a book in London titled *The Inns of a Court Anagrammatist; The Masquers Masqued in Anagrams.* That same year, an incident occurred involving a self-proclaimed seer, Lady Eleanor Davies, widow of Sir John Davies, attorney-general of Ireland under King James I. Her followers believed her claims were substantiated by the fact that (by changing the *y* to an *i* and the *u* to a *v*) her maiden name, ELEANOR AUDELEY, could be rearranged to form the anagram "Reveale O Daniel." William Walsh wrote: "She pestered the world with her prophecies, gaining great repute among the unlearned by an occasional lucky guess," until she made a prophecy against Archbishop William Laud, which caused her arrest. She was tried in the Court of High Commission, where her claim was promptly invalidated by a Dean of the Arches, Dr. Lamb. Historian Peter Heylin related the event. "He shot her through and through with an arrow borrowed from her own quiver." Taking up a pen, he wrote: DAME ELEANOR DAVIES—"Never soe mad a ladie!" Despondent over the argument against her, she renounced all claims of supernatural powers.

POLITICS, LITERATURE & FATE

Protestant Reformation

During the Protestant Reformation, it was a common practice of public figures, using noms de plume, to write unfavorable anagrams of the names of their adversaries. Many writers of that period wrote under pseudonyms which were anagrams of their real names. The French humorist FRANÇOIS RABELAIS (1483-1553) published *Gargantua* (1533) and *Pantagruel* (1535) under the pen name Alcofribas Nasier. Theologian John Calvin (Jean Caulvin or Chauvin) (1509-1564), annoyed by Rabelais's decadence, rearranged the letters in *RABELAESIUS*, the Latin form of the French writer's name, into *Rabie laesus* ("afflicted with madness"). In turn, Rabelais transformed CALVIN into *jan cul* ("jackass"), substituting *j* for *i* and *u* for *v*. (The letters *v* and *j* were then new, as was *w*.) Calvin created his own pseudonyms by transposing CALVINUS into Usinulca and Alcuinus, using *v* and *u* as identical letters. He used the latter pen name in his book *Institutes of the Christian Religion* (1536).

Fate of André Pujon

For centuries, the letters *u*, *v*, and *w* were used interchangeably, as were *i*, *j*, and *y*. Other letters were *s* for *z*, *c* for *k*, and vice versa. In *Amusements Philologiques* (1808), Gabriel P. Peignot related an apocryphal French tale from the 17th century about ANDRÉ PUJON, of Rion (now Riom), France. Changing the *j* to an *i*, he transposed his name into Pendu à Rion ("hanged at Rion"). Driven to fulfill this omen, he picked a quarrel with a man, killed him, and was hanged at Rion, the center of criminal justice in the province of Auvergne (now called Clermont-Ferrand).

Casanova on Voltaire

François-Marie AROUET (1694-1778) created his pen name by adding L. J. (*Le Jeune,* "the younger") to his last name and changed the *j* to an *i* and the *u* to a *v* to form Voltaire. Giovanni Giacomo Casanova (1725-1798), the Italian *roué* ("debauchee"), surmised in his memoirs, which were written in French, collected and later published in *Histoire de ma vie* (1960), that the reason Voltaire changed his name was that he did not want to go through life being called *à rouer* ("whipping boy").

Pseudonyms

Pietro Aretino (1492-1556), a Venetian dramatist and satirist, wrote some of his works, like *La Sirena Marfisa et Angelica; Poemetti di Partenio Etiro,* under the name Partenio Etiro. Agostino Coltelini, a lesser-known Florentine poet, used the pseudonym Ostilio Contalegni.

Jonathan Swift (1667-1745) chose Cadenus, an anagram of DECANUS (the dean), as his pen name; German writer Henry OLDENBURG (1626-1678) transposed his surname into Grubendol; French jurist Charles DE MOULIN (1500-1566) formed his nom de plume, Challudie (Simon), by changing the *u* to an *i*; and Don Juan Antonio LLORENTE (1756-1823), a Spanish historian, wrote under the name Nellerto.

Before CHARLES LUTWIDGE Dodgson (1832-1898) adopted Lewis Carroll as his pseudonym, he considered, among others, Edgar Cuthwellis and Edgar U. C. Westhill.

HONORÉ de Balzac (1799-1850) was once Lord Rhoone. George BERNARD SHAW (1856-1950) rearranged the letters in his middle and last name to form his nom de plume Redbarn Wash. In Mar. 1906 and June 1907, two articles on reptiles appeared in the *National Geographic* under the alias H. A. Largelamb (A. GRAHAM BELL) (1847-1922). Dr. Seuss (THEOdor Seuss GEISEL) (1904-1991) published three books in the 1960s under the pen name Theo. Le Sieg (*Le Sieg* being Geisel spelled backwards). JIM MORRISON, of the rock band The Doors, transposed his name into "Mr. Mojo risin'" in his classic song "L.A. Woman."

Monstrous Hoax

Sir Peter Scott, a British naturalist, was reportedly so convinced of the existence of the Loch Ness Monster by photos he had seen, that he suggested it be given the technical name *Nessiteras rhombopteryx.* He had few supporters, and their number diminished even further when Nicholas Fairbairn, a Scottish member of Parliament, discovered that the proposed name was an anagram of MONSTER HOAX BY SIR PETER S., according to Willard Espy in *Another Almanac* (1980), who credits Reuters.

On the Beloved

Until the 1800s, anagrams were customarily limited to names, which were usually of the eminent and beloved. Joseph Addison (1672-1719) wrote a satirical piece in *The Spectator*, May 9, 1710, about a man who expressed his devotion to his fiancée by spending several months in isolation writing anagrams of her name; then, upon discovering that he had misspelled it, went mad and spent the rest of his life in Bedlam.

Other Masquerades

The earliest anagrams that I found not based on names appeared in the six-volume *Masquerade* (1797-1806). These included TELEGRAPH—"great help," PRESBYTERIAN—"best in prayer," and the antonymous anagrams, FUNERAL—"real fun," and ASTRONOMERS—"no more stars." All of these were referred to in the books as *transpositions*.

ON RELIGION

Biblical Verse

These Latin anagrams appeared in *N&Q*, Jan. 30, 1864. They had also been recorded in the mid- to late 1600s, with four additional lines. "*QUID EST VERITAS?*" Pilate's ques-

tion in John XV:ii, 38 to Jesus, in Latin ("What is truth?") and his reply: "*Est vir qui adest.*" ("It is the man now before you.")

Eva & Maria

Robert Southwell (1561-1595), an English Jesuit and poet, has been thought to be the first person to link the name Eva (Eve) and the Latin word *vae* in print: EVA—"*vae.*" *Vae* is Latin for "woe," and *ave* means "hail," as in "Ave Maria!"

This anagram was found in Italy in 1620. Walter Begley, an English clergyman and author of *Biblia Anagrammatica* (1904), collected nearly 1,500 Latin anagrams of this base, each said to be perfect in spelling, diction, and syntax. This is very doubtful, although Latin does lend itself well to anagrams and palindromes.

AVE MARIA GRATIA PLENA, DOMINUS TECUM!
Virgo serena, pia, munda, et immaculata.

"Hail Mary, full of grace, the Lord is with thee!

Virgin serene, pious, pure, and spotless."

Mary

George Herbert (1593-1633), 17th century clergyman and poet, created this anagram from the name Mary (Virgin Mary) in the poem "The Church," found in his collection of sacred poems and personal writings, *The Temple*, published posthumously in 1633.

MARY
Ana-{　　　}gram
ARMY

"How well her name an *army* doth present,

In whom the Lord of hosts did pitch his tent!"

Church Inscription

Also on a religious theme, here is a Latin anagram inscribed on the front of a church in Braga, Portugal.

BEATUS IOANNES MARCUS, CHRISTI DOMINI DISCIPULUS—Is in mundo pius est medicus tuis incolis Brachara.

"Blessed John Mark, disciple of Christ the Lord—He in this world is the holy healer of thy people, Braga."

Judas Iscariot

In John Taylor's poem "The Life and Death of the Virgin Mary," in *All the Workes of John Taylor* (1630), the anagram ISKARRIOTT—"traitor kis" appeared.

Pope Nono

Of Pope Pio Nono, an anonymous writer in the early 1600s exclaimed:

SUPREMUS PONTIFEX ROMANUS—"Sum Nono, super petram fixus." Translated from the Latin: SUPREME PONTIFF OF ROME—"I am Nono, founded upon the rock," or "—I am Nono, founded upon Peter." But an alternate line appeared in "The Suddaíne Turne of Fortune's Wheele," John Taylor's 1630 poem from an unpublished manuscript: *"O non sum super petram fixus."* In English: "O I am not founded upon the rock," or "O not founded upon Peter."

On Rome, Latin Word Square

Rome, the Latin *Roma*, suggests both religion and secularism. According to 17th century English poet George Herbert, these are the only legitimate Latin words possible from the city name *ROMA*: *oram* ("shore"), *ramo* ("branch"), *Maro* (Publius Vergilius Maro, better known as Virgil), *armo* ("I arm"), *amor* ("love"), and *mora* ("delay"). Three of these anagrammatic words and *Roma* easily make a reversible word square. For more word squares see chapter 21, Word Squares & Their Relatives.

ROMA WORD SQUARE

R O M A
O R A M
M A R O
A M O R

OF KINGS, CZARS & EMPERORS

James I (reign 1603-1625)

English historian and antiquarian William Camden (1551-1623) in *Remains* (1605) collected the anagram CHARLES JAMES STUART—"claimes Arthur's seat." It uses an old spelling of *claims*. This prophetic anagram of King James I by Dr. Walter Gwyn was written around 1600, before James succeeded to the English crown in 1603. King Arthur's Seat is also the name of a hill near London. Silver-tongued Joshua Sylvester, dedicating his translation of Du Barta's "La Semaine" around 1610 to King James I, created the anagram JAMES STUART—"a just master."

Carolus Rex

Consider the Latin anagram CAROLUS REX—"*Cras ero lux.*" In English: KING CHARLES—"Tomorrow I shall be light." There are two versions of this anagram's origin. Some attributed it to Charles I (1600-1649), king of England, Scotland, and Ireland. On the day before his execution, he was said to have observed a portrait on a wall with the inscription CAROLUS REX, and stated: "Those words would be more rightly read as 'Tomorrow I shall be light.'" Others credited the anagram to his son, King Charles II (1630-1685). He reportedly wrote them on a window at King Newton's Hall in Derbyshire, on the eve of his restoration to the throne in 1660.

Polish Anagram Dance

This curious anecdote of an event that took place around 1700 was found in *The Bengal Moofussul Miscellany* by George Augustus Addison, published posthumously as *Indian Reminiscences* (1837) by Edward Bull in London. Stanislaus (Leszcynski) I (1677-1766) became king of Poland and reigned intermittently between 1704 and 1735, when he became duke of Lorraine, a title he retained until his death.

"When young Stanislaus (the future king of Poland) returned from his travels, the entire Leszczynski family assembled at Lissa to celebrate his arrival with appropriate festivities. The most ingenious compliment that graced the occasion was one paid by the College of Lissa. Thirteen dancers appeared on the stage dressed as young warriors, each holding a shield on which was engraved in gold, one of the 13 letters in the name DOMUS LESCINIA. The revolutions were so arranged that at each turn the row of bucklers formed different anagrams" in this order, with seven anagrams in all: (1) *Domus Lescinia,* (2) *ades incolumis—* (3) *omnis es lucida.* (4) *Omne sis lucida—* (5) *mane sidus loci!* (6) *Sis columna dei—* (7) *I, scande solium.*

Here is a rough English translation of the Latin. (1) "(Heir to the) House of Leszczynski!" (2) "You are here, safe and sound." (3) "You are all that is wonderful." (4) "Please shine on us all." (5) "Stay with us, oh, sun of our land!" (6) "You are one of God's supporters." (7) "Come, ascend your regal throne."

Subtractive Anagram on Napoleon

In *Puzzles & Oddities* (1876) the author, M. A. A. D., gave this example of a reductive or subtractive anagram in Greek, which translates as "Napoleon, the destructive lion, goes about destroying cities." William Walsh, in his *Handy-Book* (1892), illustrated it in modern Greek script.

Napoleon	*Napoleon*
Apollyon	*apoleon*
of cities	*poleon*
the destroyer	*oleon*
a lion	*leon*
goes	*eon*
about	*on*

To Czar Nicholas

This anagram from France, addressed to Czar Nicholas I, was written in 1854, soon after the beginning of the Crimean War. The second verse is an anagram of the first. (first verse) *"A sa Majesté impériale, / le Tsar Nicolas, souverain / et autocrate de toutes les / Russies!"* (second verse) *"O ta vanité sera ta perte. / O elle isole la Russie; / tes successeurs te maudiront à / jamais!"*

It was transcribed into English by C. Lawrence Ford of Bath, England, and published in *N&Q*, Feb. 15, 1902. (first verse) "To his imperial Majesty, / Czar Nicholas, sovereign / And autocrat of all the / Russias!" (second verse) "O your vanity will be your downfall. / O it isolates Russia; / Your successors will damn you / Forever!"

ON THE FAMOUS & INFAMOUS

Here are a few anagrams on historic personages. The first two are well-known Latin anagrams on the names Napoleon Bonaparte (1769-1821), emperor of France, and Horatio Nelson (1758-1805), the British viscount and admiral known for his naval victories over Napoleon.

According to Henry Wheatley in *Of Anagrams* (1862) and the article "Anagrams & All Their Kin" in *Macmillan's*, Nov. 1862, William Holden, Rector of Chatteris, England, wrote the Horatio Nelson anagram. The earliest-known source for the anagram was Samuel Maunder's *Scientific & Literary Treasury* (1825), which had mistakenly credited it to a Dr. Burney.

In his book, Maunder included one of his own anagrams on Britain's Queen Victoria (1819-1901), shown here. In Robert Southey's *The Doctor* (1848), edited by J. W. Warter, John

Abernethy was described as an English physician, known for his eccentricity and brusqueness. The Southey book collected this anonymous anagram describing him as "Johnny the Bear." Henry Wheatley's *Of Anagrams* (1862) includes this anagram of Florence Nightingale's name, but he does not attribute it to Lewis Carroll, as many books have. The original author appears anonymous.

HORATIO NELSON *Honor est a Nilo.*
"Honor is from the Nile," referring to the naval hero's victory at the mouth of the Nile in 1798.

NAPOLEON BONAPARTE *Bona rapta, pone leno!*—George Addison, *Indian Reminiscences* (1837)
Latin for "Lay down your stolen goods, you scoundrel!"

NAPOLEON BONAPARTE No, appear not on Elba!

IRELAND Daniel R.—referring to Daniel O'Connell (1775-1847); Henry H. Breen, *N&Q*, Sept. 27, 1851

SWEDISH NIGHTINGALE Sing high, sweet Linda!—referring to Jenny Lind; *N&Q*, June 4, 1853

FLORENCE NIGHTINGALE Flit on, cheering angel.

HER MOST GRACIOUS MAJESTY ALEXANDRIA VICTORIA Ah! My extravagant joco-serious radical Minister!—Samuel Maunder, *S&L Treasury* (1825)

ENGLAND'S QUEEN VICTORIA governs a nice, quiet land—*Athenæum*, Aug. 9, 1862

THOMAS CARLYLE clearly, to sham—*Athenaeum*, Aug. 9, 1862

JOHN ABERNETHY Johnny the Bear—Robert Southey, *The Doctor* (1848)

More Historic Figures

Here are more anagrams of historic figures you will recognize—Oliver Cromwell (1599-1658), Thomas Macaulay (1800-1859), and Benjamin Disraeli (1804-1881). The first anagram refers to Cromwell's days as a farmer, and his young assistant, William. The first Baron Macaulay was an English historian, author, and statesman (1800-1859).

The anagrams on Selina Hastings (1707-1791), English jurist and author Sir Matthew Hale (1609-1676), Nicholas Cardinal Wiseman (1802-1865), French Queen Marie Antoinette (1755-1793), David Livingstone (1813-1873), and Horatio Nelson, again, are from various English publications. Many were reprinted in the book *Modern Sphinx* (1873) and later in other publications.

OLIVER CROMWELL More clover, Will.

THOMAS BABINGTON MACAULAY a big mouth's cantab anomaly—*Macmillan's*, Nov. 1862

DISRAELI   I lead, sir—*Owl*, 1867

SELINA, COUNTESS OF HUNTING-DON   See? Sound faith clings to no nun.—*Modern Sphinx* (1873)

SIR MATTHEW HALE   Law sat him there.—*Modern Sphinx* (1873)

CARDINAL WISEMAN   a calm swain in red—*Modern Sphinx* (1873)

MARIE ANTOINETTE   Tear it, men, I atone.—*Modern Sphinx* (1873)

HORATIO NELSON   as honor to Nile *or* honors at Nile—*Modern Sphinx* (1873); John B. Walsh, Evening Star, *Eurekan*, Nov. 1893

DAVID LIVINGSTONE   Go and visit Nile, D.V. (*Deo volente*, "God willing")—*Bath Gazette*, quoted in *N&Q*, Mar. 2, 1874

Of Gladstone

British politician William Gladstone (1809-1898) was a popular 19th century subject of anagrams from all political camps. On Nov. 25, 1868, Lewis Carroll recorded in his diary two anagrams: WILLIAM EWART GLADSTONE—"I, wise Mr. G., want to lead all," by an undisclosed author, and "wilt tear down *all* images," one of his own. Carroll was later credited with composing "A man will go wild at trees" and "Wild agitator means well."

A writer in *Owl*, 1867, declared: GLADSTONE—"G. leads not." On the full name WILLIAM EWART GLADSTONE, we have these anagrams, published in *Modern Sphinx* (1873), "a man to wield great wills" and "will mislead a great town." The two phrases combined make a bianagram: "A man to wield great wills will mislead a great town." Gladstone's full name also lends itself to these complete-sentence anagrams, also found in *Modern Sphinx*: "We want a mild legislator." "Wit so great will lead man." "Go, administrate law well." But here is an anagrammatic statement by a political adversary, printed in *Chambers's Journal*, Feb. 24, 1900, of the RIGHT HONOURABLE WILLIAM EWART GLADSTONE—"I'm a Whig who'll be a traitor to England's rule."

Benjamin Disraeli

On June 15, 1879 in the American puzzle journal *Modern Sphinx*, these anagrams of British politician and Prime Minister Benjamin Disraeli (1804-1881), were reprinted from an undisclosed British magazine.

THE EARL OF BEACONSFIELD   Ah! Foe (of) decent liberals!   (The) foe no liberals faced.   (of) all debaters, one chief.   Oh, Ben! Oft false, I declare.   three-faced son (of) Belial

THE EARL BEACONSFIELD   He's all force in debate.

For the Record

In *Witt's Recreations* (1807), the question was posed: PHINIAS FLETCHER—"Hath Spencer life?" Isaac Disraeli commented in *Curiosities of Literature* (1824) about the English poet Sir Thomas Wyatt (1503-1543), WIAT—"a wit."

The anagram RANDLE HOLMES—"Lo! men's herald!" comes from a Richard Blackbourne poem found in the preface of Randle Holmes's heraldic work *Academy of the Armory* (1688). The anagram ARTHUR WELLESLEY—"Truly he'll see war." appeared in George Wilkie's *Masquerade* (1797-1806).

George Addison's book *Indian Reminiscences* (1837) included a letter by Nugarum Amator containing an anagram of the first duke of Wellington, Arthur Wellesley (1769–1852), also called the Iron Duke: ARTHUR WELLESLEY—"The war yells rule!" Later this became "Ye'll rule the wars!"

These anagrams by anonymous authors were collected in Walsh's *Handy-Book* (1892). THOMAS CARLYLE—"a calm, holy rest" was written soon after his death in 1881. HORATIO NELSON—"O a nation's hero!" affirms the public's admiration.

TOPICAL ANAGRAMS

These topical enjoyments affirm puzzler D. C. Ver's words (*TE*, Nov. 1931): ANAGRAMS—"*Magna ars*" or "*Ars magna*" ("great art").

Prohibition

These appeared in the 1920s and 1930s on the subject of Prohibition and its subsequent abolition in the United States.

EIGHTEENTH AMENDMENT   End the gin, tame the men!—John James and Judith West, *Show 'em Up in Anagrams* (1929)

EIGHTEENTH AMENDMENT   Men meet gin, then death.—Astra Cielo, *Anagrams & Word Puzzles* (1930)

FRANKLIN DELANO ROOSEVELT Tons o' drink, even ale, for all!—Timothy Shy, *London News Chronicle*, 1933

On Women

Anagrams on women and women's liberation offer critiques of the female condition vis-à-vis the male establishment, whether from a male or female point of view. The MOTHER-IN-LAW anagram, the stuff of stand-up comedians, is rather extreme.

MS. STEINEM smites men.—Tut, *TE*, Dec. 1973

WOMEN'S LIBERATION   Men rib as we toil on.—Nightowl, *TE*, Oct. 1973

UNIVERSAL SUFFRAGE, guess a fearful ruin—*American Exchange & Mart*, Feb. 12, 1887

THE NEW WOMAN How we tan men.—May Le Hosmer, *GD*, Dec. 2, 1899

(A) MOTHER-IN-LAW, (a) woman Hitler—Nypho, *TE*, Apr. 1936

A Turn on Webster's

Darryl Francis in *WW*, Nov. 1968, decodes what's in a name: *WEBSTER'S THIRD NEW INTERNATIONAL DICTIONARY OF THE ENGLISH LANGUAGE*, UNABRIDGED—"When it began, this edition created one hell of a stir, 'n' *ain't* was ungrudgingly barred!"

On Reagan

No matter what these often quoted Reagan anagrams suggest, the former U.S. president was not quite the hawk many had feared.

RONALD WILSON REAGAN, insane Anglo warlord—Mike Morton, *WW*, May 1984

RONALD WILSON REAGAN, a long-insane warlord

RONALD REAGAN, a darn long era—Dr. Crypton, United Features Syndicate, Feb. 1989

RONALD REAGAN, an oral danger—Gyles Brandreth, *More Joy of Lex* (1982)

White House Speakes

A topical anagram worth mentioning is THE WHITE HOUSE SPOKESMAN—"'I mouth hot news,' he Speakes" (Hart King, *TE*, Dec. 1983), referring to White House press secretary Larry Speakes, who served during the first six years of former U.S. President Ronald Reagan's term.

Names in Trade

Dwight Gill found "tighter hams" in the trademark THIGHMASTER, and Corn Cob (*TE*, Jan. 1986) declared of ANHEUSER BUSCH—"Shun such a beer!"

Andy Aaron transposed ANDREW DICE CLAY into "Dare a lewd cynic" (*Spy*, Oct. 1990). An ambigram I composed for Clay was COMEDIAN—"O Diceman" (*TE*, Aug. 1993). The anagram GEORGE BUSH—"He bugs Gore," written in 1988, was equally apt in the 1992 U.S. presidential campaign. BEVERLY SILLS (Belle Greenough, née Silverman) was transposed into "silvery bells" by Richard Edes Harrison, collected in Willard Espy's *Another Almanac* (1980).

ON DIVERSE SUBJECTS

Historic Markers & Good Manners

These first three anagrams were found in Rev. Arthur Pearson's *Pictured Puzzles & Wordplay* (1908), probably reprinted from his column in the *London Evening Standard*. Rev. Pearson was also the author of the churchly anagram on evil, probably from his column, reprinted in his *20th Century Book of Puzzles* (1915).

LORD BEACONSFIELD'S STATUE true as Ben's stolid face

TOWER OF LONDON now one old fort

"I excel not by a pun." Turn these words into one: UNEXCEPTIONABLY

EVIL COMMUNICATIONS CORRUPT GOOD MANNERS Gossip, vice, or common cant lured man to ruin.

Popular Themes

Here are anagrams on popular themes. All except two appeared in "Transpositions" from *Masquerade* (1797-1806). The second of the two poorhouse anagrams is from Howard Bergerson's *Palindromes & Anagrams* (1973), and H. C. Laughlin's penitentiary anagram appeared in the column "Complications" in the Chicago newspaper, *Sunday Inter-Ocean*, Jan. 5, 1896. The last anagram WEALTH— "the law" accords with a comment by Ralph Waldo Emerson (1803-1882): "People say law, but they mean wealth."

DEMOCRATICAL comical trade

DETERMINATION I mean to rend it.

ENIGMATICAL in magic tale

FESTIVAL evil fast (antonymous)

PENITENTIARY Nay, I repent it! *or* Ay, repent in it!

POORHOUSE O sour hope! *or* O our hopes!

REVOLUTION to love ruin

SOVEREIGNTY 'Tis ye govern.

WEALTH the law

Human Concerns

These anagrams on human concerns varying from altered fate to tailor's alterations are from diverse 19th century publications.

CHRISTIANITY Charity's in it. *or* 'Tis in charity.—A. L. S., *AP*, Aug. 1,

1905; William Clarke, *Boy's Own Book* (1828)

PARADISE LOST   Reap sad toils.—*N&Q,* June 4, 1853

PARADISE REGAINED   Dead respire again.—*N&Q,,* June 4, 1853

FRENCH REVOLUTION   Violence run forth!—*N&Q,,* June 4, 1853

SURGEON   Go, nurse!—William Walsh, *Handy-Book* (1892)

ALTERATIONS   neat tailors— *Puzzledom* (1852)

MIDSHIPMAN   Mind his map.— John Newton, *Merry's Puzzles* (1860)

COLLECTIONS & COMPETITIONS

London Bridge Collection

For a reason unclear to me, the anagram THE TIMES—"It's theme" has been quoted for more than 130 years. It was one of many in a bundle of papers, probably dating from the mid-1800s, found in a niche of the London Bridge. On the outside of the parcel were the words: "Finder, use these well; they are all I have to leave to the world."

Unfortunately, the other anagrams included in the bundle refer to obscure subjects and forgotten names, such as RICHARD COBDEN—"Rich corn, bedad!"

Henry Wheatley's Collection

Henry Wheatley collected many commonplace and historical anagrams from the early 19th century in his book *Of Anagrams* (1862).

LAWYERS   sly ware

MISANTHROPE   Spare him not.

CRINOLINE   inner coil

PARLIAMENT   partial men

MASQUERADE   queer as mad

CHRISTIANITY   I cry that I sin.

MATRIMONY   into my arm

THE TIMES   It's theme!

Arthur Pearson's Collections

These were taken from Rev. Arthur Cyril Pearson's *20th Century Standard Puzzle Book* (1907). Most material in Rev. Pearson's book was selected from his daily puzzle column in the *London Evening Standard* between 1905 and 1907. An annual derby and other horse races are held in Epsom Downs, near London. The puzzler N. Jineer in *B&O*, Dec. 1924, later transposed the last anagram A MERRY CHRISTMAS AND A HAPPY NEW YEAR into "May many a red wreath carry happiness."

RUSSIA is ursa (a bear).

ANARCHISTS   in rash acts

EPSOM RACES   Some pacers!

PICTURESQUE   quite spruce

SLOW READING   a single word

THE OXFORD AND CAMBRIDGE ANNUAL BOAT RACE   Much extra load on board can bring a defeat.

VICTORIA THE FIRST, QUEEN OF GREAT BRITAIN AND IRELAND, AND EMPRESS OF INDIA   Fit for a bard, I claim inspired strain, /The sad and even tenor of a quiet reign.

THE ANGLO-JAPANESE TREATY OF ALLIANCE   Hail, gallant East! Fear not, enjoy peace.

DENMARK   dark men (antonymous)

A MERRY CHRISTMAS AND A HAPPY NEW YEAR   Many a sad heart can whisper my prayer. *or* My prayer and wishes reach many a part.

Amaranth, "Anagrammasia" (1926)

A Pittsburgh attorney, Newton Lovejoy (1874-1932), known to puzzlers as Amaranth, was a versatile and prolific pioneer in American puzzledom. In 1926 he completed his unpublished book "Anagrammasia," which contains about 5,000 collected anagrams, a brief puzzle history, commentary, and a review of his own work. He sent seven copies (one in Braille) to other NPL members. Only the master and fewer than five of the original mimeographed copies of his book have survived. NPL members continued to add to Lovejoy's collection.

Ross Eckler, New Anagrammasia (1991)

Ross Eckler released Lovejoy's collection, with NPL additions, and those from other sources in *The New Anagrammasia* (1991), part of a *Word Ways* monograph series. The monograph contains nearly 9,000 anagrams and antigrams from more than 90 sources. Eckler's version differs from Amaranth's in that it contains very few anagrams of personal names and no anagrams of more than 24 letters.

Verdant Green, 1878-1898 Collection

Verdant Green (H. C. Vansant) in an article titled "Anagrammasia" in *TEE*, Dec. 1898, provided a useful list of anagrams published from 1878 to 1898. The article was updated by Majolica in *TEE*, Dec. 1903, as "Anagrammasia Continued." This should not be confused with the above two collections with a similar title.

Ecclesiastical Gazette Competition

On Sept. 15, 1886, the editor of the *Ecclesiastical Gazette*, a British journal, published the results of a competition for the best anagrams on the names of seven bishops, TURNER, SANCROFT, LLOYD, KEN, LAKE, WHITE, and TRELAWNEY, sent to the Tower for libel in 1688. Two hundred twelve anagrams were submitted to the editor; the first two here were prizewinners.

O let the well-known rank defy a cruel tyrant's ire.

Keenly ye work and wrestle all for ancient truth.

Nay, stern ruler, we will not kneel to thy dark face.

What can royal wrath do to conscience and labour?

The faithful fathers will not read a royal act.

Notes & Queries Contest

These anagrams appeared in *Notes & Queries* in 1851 and 1903 issues as anagrams on the full magazine name *NOTES AND QUERIES*, with the word *and* spelled out.

O send in a request!—Hermes, Oct. 25, 1851

No end as I request.—Daniel Stone, Nov. 1, 1851

a question sender—Daniel Stone, Nov. 1, 1851

reasoned inquest—C. P. Phin, Jan. 3, 1903

enquires on dates—C. P. Phin, Jan. 3, 1903

Baltimore & Ohio Magazine

The two anagrams on the Baltimore & Ohio were taken from the puzzle column "In the Realm of the Riddle" from *Baltimore & Ohio Magazine.*

BALTIMORE AND OHIO RAILROAD   Load him aboard, oriole train!—Atlas, Aug. 1922

THE BALTIMORE AND OHIO   I behold a train to home.—N. Jineer, Jan. 1923

chapter 16

SENSE & NONSENSE ANAGRAMS

Anagrams, after all, invite a sense of play, but they are also governed by the law of letters, each letter being carefully appointed to its place. Here are some anagrams on familiar themes and some to amuse you.

◇ ◇ ◇

ANAGRAM MUSINGS

Consider. Through the magic of letter-shuffling, a BENGALI can be transformed into a BELGIAN, WILD BOARS into RABID OWLS, the game of POLO into POOL, and a MELON into a LEMON. The word SANITARY can be transposed into the opposite anagram NASTY AIR. But by adding the prefix IN- to the base, an apposite anagram can be made: INSANITARY then would become IN NASTY AIR. Puzzlers responsible for these transformations are Rik Edwards, *Longman* (1985), for Bengali; Arthur Pearson, *Pictured Puzzles & Wordplay* (1908), for wild boars and (in)sanitary; and Chin-Chin, *Washington Post*, Dec. 9, 1883, for melon.

CHRONOLOGICAL LIAR

One may admit to dyslexia at age 32, but a person spelling out FORTY-FIVE would naturally make an anagramatist suspicious. Rik Edwards's *Longman Anagram Dictionary* (1985) shows that these letters conceal the words and age OVER FIFTY.

"RELATED"

The solution to these clues in verse from Malcolm Tent, *TE*, Apr. 1995, is an anagram containing four unmixed letters: "We're a family for peace, yet there's always a war on. / We could say the word is an oxymoron."

DAMN KIN!

MANKIND

CHEATERS' ANAGRAMS

IDEALISTIC   italicised (British spelling)—Rik Edwards, *Longman* (1985)

"QUESTION?"   in quotes—Rik Edwards, *Longman* (1985)

MISSPELLINGS   simpl, singels—Deacon, *TE*, Nov. 1990

ROAST TURKEY?   Try our steak.—Arthur Pearson, *20th Cent. Standard* (1907)

ANAGRAMMATIC CALCULATIONS

To satisfy the curious, Nugarum Amator calculated the possible combinations of letters up to twelve. These sums were collected in George Addison's *Indian Reminiscences* (1837).

Two letters produce 2 changes.

Three letters produce 6 changes.

Four letters produce 24 changes.

Five letters produce 120 changes.

Six letters produce 720 changes.

Seven letters produce 5,040 changes.

Eight letters produce 40,320 changes.

Nine letters produce 362,880 changes.

Ten letters produce 3,628,800 changes.

. . . and twelve letters produce 479,001,600 changes.

Sums: Allowing that 20 words of 12 letters each can be written in one minute, then, according to this accounting, writing out the full number of possible combinations that a 12-letter word could produce would require 45 years and 207 days.

ANAGRAMMATIC CROSS-REFERENCES

SEPARATE (see "apart")—Arty Fishel, *GD*, Mar. 5, 1887

INFIDEL (find "lie")—*American Agriculturist*, May 1861

OPERAS (re: soap)—David Morice, *WW*, Feb. 1995

TELEVISION SET
(see "it's not live")
—David Morice, WW, Feb. 1995

HURRY TO THE REAR

Eric Albert called my attention to this anagram which shifts the first letter, *c*, to the last position in the new word.

CABARET   a bar, etc.—Hoho, *TE,* Dec. 1941

DIABOLICAL TRANSFORMATIONS

An article, "On Anagrams," published in *Belgravia* magazine, Sept. 1896, declared that Great Britain's promising offspring, Tasmania, is much to be commiserated. She is said to have forsaken her old name of Van Diemen's Land, since it sounded somewhat diabolical in origin. It is clear, however, that His Infernal Majesty will not lightly yield his dominion, for in TASMANIA we find the startling announcement: "I am Satan."

Saint, Santa, Satan

SANTA   Satan—Madda Boutem, *TE,* Jan. 1940

A SAINT   I, Satan—Sphinx, *TE,* Feb. 1985

ANAGRAM PUZZLES

The number of letters for each word of the solution to the anagram puzzle is shown in parentheses after the puzzle, except when all letters of the clue

are used to form a single-word answer. Asterisks indicate capitalized words. No clues are given to the single-word bases. The answers are on p. 115.

1. I'm any martial. (1 8 3)

2. minus lace

3. I tap, I slug. (1 8)

4. flour and oats (7 5)

5. Name this famous path. (3 7 2 *6)

6. All right, a hint: a demented TV wit. (*TV show title.* 4 5 4 5 9)

7. trees, for a hint (3 4 6)

8. hint: hotel (3 *6)

9. hint: Leo (3 4)

10. She isn't Leo. (3 7)

11. cat; no Leo. (2 6)

12. often a fun dream (4 3 7)

13. a very hidden author (*5 *5 *7)

14. Swen or Inga (*)

15. AAU term

16. Spend it.

17. Idle? Sure!

18. time taxers

19. on any screen (*4 *7)

20. Topic: cone, lava, ruin (1 8 8)

A FEW BY THE NUMBERS

At least three *apposite numerical transpositons* have been found, using contrived bases. The first, by Emmo W. (*TE,* Apr. 1948), is in English, and the last two, by Lee Sallows (*WW*, Feb. 1992), are in Spanish.

ELEVEN + TWO = twelve + one

CATORCE + UNO (14 + 1) = once + cuatro (11 + 4)

DOCE + TRES (12 + 3) = trece + dos (13 + 2)

A YEAR IN RHYME

Here are three poems containing all the letters in the names of the twelve months; Rev. Arthur Pearson may have written all three. The first includes the poem title in the anagram. It is from his *20th Century Standard Puzzle Book* (1907) and probably appeared in his *London Evening Standard* column a year or two earlier.

The second poem was in Rev. Pearson's article "Anagrams and All Their Kin," *Chambers's Journal*, Feb. 24, 1900. We've titled it "Merry." These two poems inspired the optimistic third verse we've titled "Inspiration," found in Rev. Pearson's *20th Century Book of Puzzles* (1915).

A POEM
Just a jury by number
Each scrap of year—
A number recording
Every jumble, tumble, tear.

MERRY
Merry, durable, just grace
My every future month embrace;
No jars remain, joy bubble up apace.

INSPIRATION
Burst, joybud, happy let me be,
Come turn, brave year!
A grumbler's murmur I can face,
Enjoy a jeer.

UNITE-UNTIE IN VERSE

A *telestich poem* is one in which the final letters of the lines form a word. In this poem, a *double acrostic*, the letters at both the beginning and the end of the lines form a word. The two words here—*unite* and *untie*—make an opposite anagram. This poem, published in *N&Q*, Oct. 12, 1861, was written by Louisa H. Sheridan, who has been referred to as "the rival of Tom Hood in talent and wit." The French term *goût* means "taste, style, or preference."

Unite and *untie* are the same, so say yoU;
Not in wedlock, I we'en, has this unity beeN;
In the drama of marriage, each wandering *goûT*
To a new face would fly, all except you and I,
Each seeking to alter the 'spell' in their scenE.

THE LONG & SHORT OF IT

The shortest anagrams in English, OH!—"Ho!" and AH!—"Ha!," are also reversals and palindromes when read as couplets. The latter anagram, written by Palea, was quoted in *GD*, June 4, 1898.

The base of the next anagram, about the Declaration of Independence, is somewhat contrived, but it is one of the best of the long examples. The author is Ann S. Thetics; it was printed in *TE*, Jan. 1924.

SIGNING OUR DECLARATION OF INDEPENDENCE OF THE UNITED STATES OF AMERICA   Thirteen Colonies post defiance dead against future foreign dominance.

In the book *Of Anagrams* (1862), Henry Wheatley stated that the longest specimen he had found was in Spanish, on the Marques de Astorga and all his titles, from Francisco de la Torre y Sebil's *Luces de la aurora días sol* ("Lights of Daybreak"), containing eight lines of about 140 letters.

ON HEARST

John Winkler's biography of William Randolph Hearst tells how the *New York World* once copied from Hearst's *New York Journal* an obituary on one "Reflipe W. Thanuz." THANUZ was the phonetic spelling of "the news" and REFLIPE W. was "we pilfer" spelled backwards. A reviewer of Winkler's book recalled that the *New York World* retaliated by inserting the name "Lister A. Raah" into a story. After the *New York Journal* had printed the story, it was pointed out that the name was an anagram of HEARST A LIAR. Martin Gardner describes these events in *Oddities & Curiosities* (1961).

SOLUTIONS TO "ANAGRAM PUZZLES"

1. a military man—Arcanus, *TE*, Sept. 1935

2. masculine—Hoho, *TE*, Aug. 1946

3. a pugilist—Molemi, *TE*, Nov. 1945

4. natural foods—Ai, *TE*, Feb. 1994

5. the Isthmus of Panama—Amaranth, *Inter-Ocean*, Jan. 13, 1911

6. "Late Night with David Letterman"—O. V. Michaelsen, *TE*, Sept. 1990

7. the rain forest—Te-Zir-Man, *TE*, Oct. 1989

8. the Hilton—Atlantic, *TE*, May 1982

9. the lion—Francolin, *TE*, May 1915

10. the lioness—Te-Zir-Man, *TE*, May 1987

11. an ocelot—Ulk, *TE*, Apr. 1986

12. fame and fortune—Ruthless, *TE*, Apr. 1989

13. Henry David Thoreau—Ab Struse, *TE*, Mar. 1988

14. Norwegians—Kamel, *TE*, Jan. 1982

15. amateur—Atlantic, *TE*, Jan. 1982

16. stipend—Barnyard, *TE*, Oct. 1917

17. leisured—Stocles, *TE*, Mar. 1920

18. taximeters—Merlin, *TE*, Oct. 1971

19. Sean Connery—Rom Dos, *TE*, Nov. 1990

20. a volcanic eruption—Ab Struse, *TE*, Mar. 1980

17 ANAGRAMS FOR THE WELL-READ

◇ ◇ ◇

LITERARY ANAGRAMS
from John O'London's Weekly

These anagrams on famous lines from poems, plays, and other works by literary lions were found in the column "Literary Competitions" in *John O'London's Weekly* from 1929 to 1942. The original quote appears in capital letters.

"DEAR IS THE MEMORY OF OUR WEDDED LIVES."—Alfred, Lord Tennyson's "The Lotus-Eaters" (1832; 1842)   "Love's treasured word edified my home."—H. H. Gyde, Dec. 2, 1933

"MAN WANTS BUT LITTLE, NOR THAT LITTLE LONG."—Edward Young's *The Complaint, or Night Thoughts on Life, Death, & Immortality* (1742-1745)   "Truth? Not! All betting men still want a lot."—Miss R. E. Speight, Jan. 25, 1930

"THERE IS DELIGHT IN SINGING, THOUGH NONE HEAR."—Walter Savage Landor's "To Robert Browning" (1845)   "I raise the tune high, no dog then lingers nigh."—Mrs. M. A. M. Macalister, Oct. 6, 1934

"EARTH HAS NOT ANYTHING TO SHOW MORE FAIR."—William Wordsworth's "Composed upon Westminster Bridge, September 3, 1802"   "A white hoarfrost neath night's moon-ray."—May 1930

"LIVES OF GREAT MEN ALL REMIND US."—Henry Wadsworth Longfellow's "A Psalm of Life" (1838)   "Small toil never framed genius."—Mrs. B. Woodward, Jan. 16, 1929

"HAPLY SOME HOARY-HEADED

SWAIN MAY SAY:"—Thomas Gray's "An Elegy Written in a Country Churchyard" (1751; 1768) "Away, sad shame! A hair-dye's my only hope."—Rev. Fred James, Sept. 17, 1937

"OUR LITTLE SYSTEMS HAVE THEIR DAY."—Alfred, Lord Tennyson's *Idylls of the King* (1885) "Ah, yes! Mortals die, yet truth lives."—S. W. Parker, Jan. 6, 1939

"ONE GOOD TURN DESERVES ANOTHER."—variation of John Heywood's "One good turn asketh another." *Proverbes, Part 1* (1546) "Do rogues endorse that? No, never!"—J. Yeoman, Jan. 26, 1929

"'WHERE CAN IT BE—THIS LAND OF ELDORADO?'"—Edgar Allan Poe's "Eldorado" (1849) "Here, if we toil hard and do noble acts."—J. F. Shine, May 4, 1929

"HOW HAPPY COULD I BE WITH EITHER."—John Gay's *The Beggar's Opera* (1728) "But pray, which do I elope with, eh?"—E. Pinnock, Aug. 10, 1929

TURNS ON SHAKESPEARE

"BUT O HOW VILE AN IDOL PROVES THIS GOD."—William Shakespeare's *Twelfth Night* (1599) "Have no doubt; to worship gold is evil."—Mrs. Dean, July 28, 1934

"ANGELS AND MINISTERS OF GRACE DEFEND US!"—William Shakespeare's *Hamlet* (1600) "from Satan's seeds' degrading influence."—Mrs. V. M. Reynolds, Feb. 13, 1942

"FRAILTY, THY NAME IS WOMAN!"—William Shakespeare's *Hamlet* (1600) "It's a whim of male tyranny."—J. G. Hassocks, Feb. 9, 1935

COMMENT ON CORREGGIO

"SOME MEN PRETEND THEY THINK IT BLISS."— reference to (Antonio Allegri da) Correggio's painting "Jupiter and Io" (1532) "The interested nimble nymph to kiss."—Mrs. E. H. Fatkin, Jan. 11, 1930

LITERARY FELLOWS

The Charles Dickens (1812-1870) anagram appeared Feb. 12, 1887, in an article from Leonard Dacre's four-part series "Anagrams & Chronograms" in *American Exchange & Mart*. Anagrams on Henry Wadsworth Longfellow (1807-1882); Alfred, Lord Tennyson (1809-1892); Thomas Moore (1779-1852); Edgar Allan Poe (1809-1849); Benjamin Disraeli (1804-1881); and William Shakespeare appeared in *American N&Q*, Nov. 10, 1888.

The puzzler Bolis wrote the famous Dante Gabriel Rossetti (1828-1882) anagram when he was 19 years old. Rossetti was the same age when he wrote his idealistic poem "The Blessed Damozel" in 1847. Although this anagram is one of the best known, I do not consider it among the best. The anagrams on Voltaire are from the sources noted.

CHARLES DICKENS   Cheer sick lands.—*American Exchange & Mart,* Feb. 12, 1887

HENRY WADSWORTH LONGFEL-LOW   won half the New World's glory

ALFRED TENNYSON   fans one tenderly

ALFRED TENNYSON, POET LAURE-ATE   neat sonnet, or deep tearful lay

THOMAS MOORE   *Homo amor est.* ("Man is love.")

EDGAR ALLAN POE   a long peal; read *or* a long, pale read

DISRAELI   idle airs

WILLIAM SHAKESPEARE   He's like a lamp, I swear!

WILLIAM SHAKSPEARE (alternate spelling)   We praise him, ask all.

DANTE GABRIEL ROSSETTI   greatest idealist born—Bolis, *GD,* Nov. 8, 1884

VOLTAIRE   *O alte vir!* ("Oh, noble man!")—*Belgravia,* Sept. 1896

FRANÇOIS DE VOLTAIRE   I said, "O France, revolt!"—L. Z. H., *TE,* Sept. 1924

GILBERT & SULLIVAN

This anagram by Mangie, *TE,* Sept. 1975, is popularly quoted: H.M.S. PINAFORE—"name for ship."

ANAGRAM TALES & HISTORIC FEATS

Writing a poem or tale using anagrams is certainly a feat. When the subject is history, events mingle with imagination even more than usual. Anagrammatic oarsmen may row unsteadily and slightly off-course, and, despite all their exertion, the whole may not be as satisfying as an isolated line or two. But the tales here of "Washington Crossing the Delaware" and of "The Lent Oars" from the master word *monastery* are heroic efforts.

Shulman's "Washington Crossing the Delaware"

Every line in David Shulman's sonnet "Washington Crossing the Delaware" is an anagram of its title. The sonnet was first published in *TE,* June 1936. Despite its grammatical flaws (strained anagrams), it remains an impressive achievement.

Line Notes on Shulman's Sonnet
Here are some glosses and historical notes about anagrams contained in selected lines. About the eighth line, "He saw his ragged Continentals row," and the first, "A hard, howling, tossing, water scene," it's more likely that Washington "saw nothing," one critic complained. Edwin Drood transposed the first line into "Watch a soldier hang on, steering S.W." Drood suggests, as a joke, a different route,

WASHINGTON CROSSING THE DELAWARE

David Shulman (1936)

A hard, howling, tossing, water scene;
Strong tide was washing hero clean.
"How cold!" Weather stings as in anger.
O silent night shows war ace danger!

The cold waters swashing on in rage.
Redcoats warn slow his hint engage.
When general's star action wish'd "Go!"
He saw his ragged Continentals row.

Ah, he stands—sailor crew went going,
And so this general watches rowing.
He hastens—Winter again grows cold;
A wet crew gain Hessian stronghold.
George can't lose war with 's hands in;
He's astern—so, go alight, crew, and win!

perhaps through the more scenic state of Delaware rather than the historic crossing from Pennsylvania to New Jersey.

Shulman's first anagram line "A hard, howling, tossing, water scene," by puzzler Jim Jam, appeared in the column "Knit Knots," in the *Norristown* (Pennsylvania) *Herald & Free Press*, Sept. 9, 1879. "Knit Knots" also printed the first published anagram on the base WASHINGTON CROSSING THE DELAWARE, submitted by Graham (Levi G. DeLee), July 8, 1879.

The fifth line was the solution to a clue by Percy Vere, "Read this event on history's page." The puzzle was first published in the column "Modern Anagrams" in *Harper's Young People*, July 11, 1882.

Hercules had composed the 12th line, "A wet crew gain Hessian stronghold," first published in *TE*, May 1932. Skeeziks first used the eighth line "He saw his ragged Continentals row" in a rhymed verse on the theme of Washington's crossing in *Thedom*, Nov. 10, 1890.

Skeeziks was the first to incorporate multiple anagrams of WASHINGTON CROSS-ING THE DELAWARE into rhymed verse. Here is his version from the 1890 puzzle broadside, *Thedom*, published in Newburgh, New York.

GEO. W.'S CLANS, IN NIGHT DASH O'ER WATER
Skeeziks (1890)

Proemial

AS G. WAS HERE, ON A COLD WINTER'S NIGHT,
He spoke of *whole*, as a General might.

"Yes!" shouted his officers, "*Whole* must be allowed"—
GO, GENERAL W! TAN THIS HESSIAN CROWD!

"What strategy in *whole*! can we ever forget,
GO, W! GET RAHL'S HESSIAN CROWD IN A NET!"

IN COLD WEATHER, HESSIANS WANT GROG—
"The dream not of *whole*, bent on slaughter."

Three cheers for *whole*! amid the ice and snow.
HE SAW HIS RAGGED CONTINENTALS ROW.

Awaken! Rah! Assuredly, *complete* will trouble you!
A HERO'S CREW IS HASTENING, TO LAND G. W.

All patriots will adhere *whole*, marshalling his band—
G. W. IS ASHORE, CREW HASTENING TO LAND.

Sequent

Vain resist *total*, to take possession—
W.'S CROWD GETTING ONE RAHL, A HESSIAN.

To the enemy, *complete* proved quite a surprise—
AS G. W. GETS O'ER WITH CANNON, RAHL DIES.

OH! TRENTON IS REGAINED! G. W. HAS CLAWS!
For *total* won the fight, and helped a noble cause.

G. W., WISE SCHOLAR HAS GAINED TRENTON.
To gain it, was what *total* was so bent on.

This piece found in an Edinburgh, Scotland, newspaper in the mid-1800s contains fifty mutations of the word *monastery*. It was later collected in William Dobson's *Literary Frivolities, Fancies, Follies & Frolics* (1880).

The Lent Oars

I am a boatman on the Lago Maggiore, but, fool that I am, I lent my oars to the monks of St. Thomas's, who used to cross the lake in their own boat, and who, on my inquiring about them, vowed they never had got them. I spoke to the mayor of the canton, who transmitted a letter my dear Mary had written, and promised he would send for an answer himself.

Having waited for some time rather impatiently, I set off to the monastery to inquire if the *mayor sent* or not for the answer to *Mary's note* about *my ten oars*. The abbot had gone on a visit to the adjoining convent, and I was informed that the letter was sent there, and they thought it likely my oars were there too. I went thither, and on gaining admission, I inquired if the answer had been sent for. "*Ay, monster*," said she, "though *ten mayors* had sent they would not have got one." "Come, come, *no mastery* over me; *may no rest* be mine here or hereafter if I do not have my oars! *Yes, matron*, there is *one St. Mary* to whom I shall pray for interference." "See your *stone Mary* there," said she, pointing to an image of the blessed Virgin set in the wall. I prostrated myself before it, saying, "O *my one star*, my Mary! Look down *on my tears*, and *O try means* to get me back my oars. May my soul, which has *met no rays* of thine for long, *store many* favors now. Oh! Mary, do *so try, amen*." On rising I was astounded on hearing the matron exclaim, "*My! Treason!*" Woman though she was, I could have smitten her to the ground, for here came the abbot angrily and anxiously inquiring, "What treason?" Taking me for a French spy, he approached cautiously, but seeing as *yet no arms* about me, he grew bolder, and caused me to be searched for *army notes* or papers.

Though he found nothing, I could scarce prevail upon him to grant a truce *or amnesty* till I could explain my errand. "*Ay, no terms* with the villain," said he, threatening to *tan my sore* hide for me. I remonstrated, "Stay, Ermon, be not hasty; I trump you no *mean story* in showing you this," and here I showed him my *torn, seamy* coat, as evidence that no government had favored me with a degree in *money arts*. "*Yet Romans*," said he, "call *Rome nasty*, and I suspected that you were one of that kind." "No, *my senator*, I am nothing great, but I am not so bad as that." I was glad to get off without further mentioning my oars, and left the place.

I was terribly vexed, however, at the way affairs had turned out, so that I could not help telling my care to an old woman I met not far off, and whom I knew. "Do you see *yon stream* on this side of the lake?" Said I: "*O m'ny tears* have I shed there; I never refused to lend an oar when asked, but no one *sent my oar* back, till now I have lost them all." "Dear me, that's scandalous; take *a rest on my* bundle for a short time; I am sure I saw *Tom N. Sayer* with some of them, and I'll just run over and see." I did as she said, and had not long to wait for her return. "*Ye ran most* nimbly, but how sped you?" At no great *rate, my son*; he has some, but he ran away." "Ran away!" I exclaimed. "*Yes, Tom ran*, though I told him you meant to *say no term* of payment for the bother you had been put to." "May he rot—*yes, man, rot*—for his roguery; by all the bloody heroes, from *Mars to Ney*, were I a tailor I would *try to seam* till I found him; and then—. But I am no tailor, I am but a boatman; so I see no way to make up my loss but by laying a little *on my rates* of passage or smuggling a trifle of *Morny's tea*."

"If a *tear, my son*, would avail thee anything, I would shed plenty; but you *may rest on* my doing what I can for you, so neither hinder *nor stay me* just now, as I must away." "Good-bye," said I; "but may Old Davy *tar my nose* for me if I don't watch that chap. Fine way for a poor *tar's money* to go, always buying oars. Yes, Tom, I'll be down *smart on ye* some of these days."

Thoroughly disgusted, I turned *my toes, ran* swiftly home, and vowed myself a *snore at my* ease, unless my *mentor say* me nay.

MONASTERY Afterwords
Other transpositions of MONASTERY are *myronates, So try "amen," Tory means, oysterman, Romany set, stray omen, story name, Tom yearns, yon stream, store many, one smarty*, and "*Yes, matron*." Anglo Saxon in "Puzzledom" in *GD*, Sept. 9, 1902, found *O many rest*. Opposite anagrams of the word are *more nasty* and *or mean sty*. MONASTERIES was transposed into *Amen stories* by Lord Baltimore, *GD*, Apr. 4, 1896, and *No mates, sire*, by Su San, *TE*, Dec. 1932.

18 PALINDROMES

RUNNING BACK WORDS

A *palindrome* is a word, phrase, or number that reads the same backwards as forward; the word comes from the Greek *palindromos*, which means "running back again." The first palindromic sentences in English were printed in 1614.

Sotades & Muses

The palindrome, sometimes considered a form of anagram, has also been called an *inversion, cancrine, reciprocal,* or *Sotadic* or *Sotadean phrase* or *verse,* after the third century B.C. Greek poet Sotades. The poet was said to have degraded his muse by devoting his verse to harsh and vulgar satire. Legend has it that he wrote a poem lampooning his ruler, King Ptolemy II Philadelphus, who, in retribution, had him sealed in a box and dumped into the sea.

Sotadea carmina became the term for derisive verses, which probably were complimentary when read in the opposite direction. These verses were in the form of *word-unit palindromes*; in these each word is taken as a unit, rather than each letter. Although Sotades has long been associated with the palindrome, no palindromes were found in the few surviving fragments of his poems.

Accolades to the Palindrome

A coherent palindromic sentence is more difficult to compose than an anagram (an apposite transposition). Robert Thomsen in *Games, Anyone?* (1965) even went so far as to say: "If you are able to create one simple sentence that is a perfect palindrome, yours is a life well spent." In 1929, a competitor in the column "Prose & Verse Competitions" of the London weekly *Everyman* wrote: "A palindrome may seem a simple problem on the surface, but as a matter of fact it is difficult enough to tax to the utmost the sharpest of wits."

Some of the best-known palindromes are these: "Able was I ere I saw Elba" in Charles Bombaugh's *Gleanings* (1867). "Madam, I'm Adam" from Henry Wheatley's *Of Anagrams* (1862); and "a man, a plan, a canal, Panama!" by Leigh Mercer, *N&Q*, Nov. 13, 1948, as a tribute to George Washington Goethals, Panama Canal builder.

Palindromes also would seem to generate palindromes, just as literary quotes generate other quotes through decades and even through centuries. A palindrome echoing Mercer's original, "a mar on a panorama," written by T. H., appeared in *Ardmore Puzzler*, July 1899. Thirty years later, a palindromist named Lubin came up with "a dog, a panic in a pagoda" in *Everyman*, Nov. 28, 1929. Around 1970, J(ames). A. Lindon penned "a dog, a pant, a panic in a patna pagoda." Closer to Mercer's theme was Edward Wolpow's "A man appals—I slap Panama." On former U.S. President George Bush's invasion of that country in 1989 came the palindrome "a man, a pain, a mania, Panama." Jon Agee in *Go Hang a Salami—I'm a Lasagna Hog* (1991) rephrased the familiar formula, "a car, a man, a maraca."

A PALINDROME COLLECTION

Letter-Unit Palindromes

Many palindromes collected here were found in rare magazines, books, and newspapers. Several are from G. R. Clarke's *Palindromes* (1887), which contains thirty-three examples, each illustrated by the author. Some come from *Ardmore Puzzler*, a privately issued magazine published from 1899 to 1909; the newspaper column "Complications" from the *Inter-Ocean*, both the Chicago daily and Sunday editions, in the late 1890s and 1906; and "Enigmatic Oddities" in the *Pittsburgh Post* in 1900. *The Enigma*, a popular source for palindromes, was called *The Eastern Enigma* before 1920.

Many palindromes are from Dmitri Borgmann's *Language on Vacation* (1965) and *Beyond Language* (1967), and Howard Bergerson's *Palindromes & Anagrams* (1973). J(ames). A. Lindon and Leigh Mercer were major contributors to Borgmann's and Bergerson's books. Mercer (1893?-1978) joined the NPL in 1952 under the palindromic pseudonym of Roger G. M'Gregor.

Other sources include Martin Gardner's *Oddities & Curiosities* (1961), Charles Bombaugh's *Gleanings from the Harvest Fields of Literature, Science & Art* (1867-1890 editions), John Pool's *Lid off a Daffodil* (1982), Stephen Chism's *From A to Zotamorf*

(1992), Jon Agee's *Go Hang a Salami* (1991), Jon Agee's *So Many Dynamos (& Other Palindromes)* (1994), Joaquin and Maura Kuhn's *Rats Live on No Evil Star* (1981), Arthur Pearson's *Pictured Puzzles & Wordplay* (1908), and Jeff Grant's *The Palindromicon* (1992).

Michael Donner's "Six I's" is a particularly interesting example because it also works as "IIIIII," from his 1996 book *I Love Me, vol. I*, which is itself a palindrome, with the subtitle *S. Wordrow's Palindrome Encyclopedia.* Many of the palindromes by John Connett have not been previously published.

Because palindromes, like folklore, have many versions and variations, often anonymously composed, it may be nearly impossible to find the original authors. Many palindromes collected here come from the earliest-known sources. Unattributed palindromes are anonymous. Sometimes palindromes seem to write themselves, often with unfortunate results for the subject. Others, when collected, create witty dialogue or the stuff of radio drama.

The Key to Abbreviations at the back of the book will help you decipher shortened book titles, abbreviations for periodicals, and popular puzzle columns found in attributions. The Puzzlers & Their Pseudonyms index will help you discover the identity of puzzlers.

FIRST WORDS

1. a. Adam: "Name me man." **b.** The Creator: "Name Me, man."
—(a, b) Michael Donner, *I Love Me, vol. I* (1996)

2. a. "Madam, (it is [in Eden] I sit.) I'm Adam." **b.** Eve: "Eve."
—(a) without parentheses, Henry Wheatley, *Of Anagrams* (1862); brackets, Leigh Mercer, *N&Q*, Jan. 10, 1948; parentheses, John Connett, *WW*, May 1996; (b) Henry Wheatley, *Of Anagrams* (1862)

3. "Now Eve, we're here, we've won."
—Howard Bergerson, *P&A* (1973)

4. Mad, a detail of Eden: one defoliated Adam.
—Tut, *TE*, Mar. 1974

5. Cain, a (mono)maniac.
—Atlantis, *AP*, Dec. 1, 1907

6. a. Eve damned Eden, mad Eve! **b.** Mad (at) Adam!
—(a, b) Arthur Pearson, *20th Cent. Standard* (1907)

7. a. Eve is a sieve! **b.** Even Eve?
—(a) Joaquin and Maura Kuhn, *Rats Live* (1981); (b) Ruthven, *Ballou's Monthly*, May 1873

ALL AT SEA

8. a. "Pull up, Eva, we're here. Wave, pull up!" **b.** "Pull up if I pull up."
—(a) Leigh Mercer, *N&Q*, Feb. 1953; (b) Howard Bergerson, *P&A* (1973)

9. a. Delia sailed, Eva waved, Elias ailed. **b.** Delia sailed as a sad Elias ailed. **c.** "Sail, Elias."

—(a, b) Dmitri Borgmann in Martin Gardner, *O&C* (1961); (c) Joaquin and Maura Kuhn, *Rats Live* (1981)

10. a. "No word," I say, as I'd row on. **b.** No word, no bond, row on.
—(a) M. C. S., *Inter-Ocean*, July 26, 1896; (b) Leigh Mercer, *N&Q*, Feb. 1952

11. a. "Nora, a raft! Is it far, Aaron?" **b.** "Raft far."
—Jon Agee, *Go Hang* (1991); Joaquin and Maura Kuhn, *Rats Live* (1981)

12. "You bet! I sure can omit Tim on a cerusite buoy!"
—J. A. Lindon in Howard Bergerson, *P&A* (1973)

RIGHT, BUT NO CIGAR

13. a. "Cigar? Toss it in a can, it is so tragic." / But sad Eva saved a stub. **b.** Cigar Tom made ting in a can ignited ammo. Tragic. **c.** Cigar tosser: I fret, fall ill, after fires so tragic.
—(a) J. A. Lindon in Howard Bergerson, *P&A* (1973); (b) Smith, Tim S., *TE*, Aug. 1975; (c) Smith, Tim S., Oct. 1967

DRINKS ALL AROUND

14. "Here so long? No loser, eh?" [Still on that barstool?]
—Leigh Mercer, *N&Q*, Nov. 2, 1946

15. Wasted, Ted was.
—O. V. Michaelsen

16. Put (it) up.
—*Atlantis*, AP, Dec. 1, 1907

17. Tip it.

18. a. "Yo! Bottoms up! U.S. motto, boy!" **b.** Campus motto: "Bottoms up, Mac!" **c.** Ban campus motto: "Bottoms up, MacNab."
—(a) Howard Bergerson, *P&A* (1973); (b) anonymous; (c) Leigh Mercer, *N&Q*, Nov. 2, 1946

19. "Ron, I'm a minor."
—Jon Agee, *Dynamos* (1994)

20. "No sot, nor Ottawa (legal age) law at Toronto, son."
—Henry Campkin, *N&Q*, Mar. 8, 1873

21.
"Lager, sir, is regal!"
—J. A. Lindon in Howard Bergerson, *P&A* (1973)

22. "Regal was I ere I saw lager."
—*O'London's*, Aug. 31, 1929

23. a. Drawn I ginward. **b.** "O gin, on (, on) I go!"
—(a) Tut, *TE*, Sept. 1974; (b) Graham Reynolds in Howard Bergerson, *P&A* (1973)

24. Stewed, a jade wets.
—J. A. Lindon in Howard Bergerson, *P&A* (1973)

25. a. Not sober (re: Boston). **b.** "Pure" Boston did not sober up.
—(a) Michael Taub, *Atlantic Unbound*,

Aug. 30, 1996; (b) Dmitri Borgmann, *On Vacation* (1965)

26. Nog eroded Oregon.
—Joaquin and Maura Kuhn, *Rats Live* (1981)

SPORTING CHANCES

27. "Yes, a call, a bat, a ball, a Casey!"
—J. A. Lindon in Howard Bergerson, *P&A* (1973)

28. "SNAFU? Oy, Boston! O do not sob, you fans!"
—Erich W. R., *Atlantic Unbound*, Aug. 30, 1996

29. a. "Boston, O do not sob." **b.** Boston did *not* sob. **c.** "I did not sob, Boston, did I?"
—(a) Joaquin and Maura Kuhn, *Rats Live* (1981); (b) Howard Richler, *WW*, Nov. 1991; (c) L. P. Flash, *Atlantic Unbound*, Aug. 30, 1996

30. So many dynamos!
—Atlantis, *GD*, June 7, 1905

31. a. "Now (I see, referees), I won." **b.** "Now I nod; egged on, I won." **c.** "No, *we* won."
—(a) Atlantis, *AP*, Dec. 1, 1907; (b) Cornel G. Ormsby; (c) Atlantis, *AP*, Dec. 1, 1907

LITTLE WARS

32. a. "Now, sir, a war is won!" **b.** A war at Tarawa.
—(a) Howard Bergerson, *P&A* (1973); (b) Martin Gardner, *O&C* (1961)

33. "Nam? Raw war man."
—Jouko I. Valta, "International Palindromes" page, *WWW*, Dec. 1995

34. "Hanoi, dare we use radio? Nah."
—Ron Howes, *Atlantic Unbound*, Aug. 30, 1996

35. Live wartime did emit raw evil.
—Howard Richler, *WW*, Feb. 1991

36. Erin (is) in ire.
—Joaquin and Maura Kuhn, *Rats Live* (1981)

37. Able foe of Elba?
—George Chaiyar, *NY World*, Dec. 11, 1921

38. "Able was I ere I saw Elba."
—Charles Bombaugh, *Gleanings* (1867)

39. Elba, Rome, memorable.
—Evergreen, *TE*, June 1956

40. Poor troop! A side divided is a poor troop.
—Tut, *TE*, June 1977

41. Ed is on *no* side.
—Jon Agee, *Go Hang* (1991)

42. Dumb mobs bomb mud.
—Neil (Fred) Picciotto's "Gigantic List of Palindromes," *WWW*, Dec. 1, 1995

43. a. "Draw, O Caesar! Erase a coward!" **b.** "Draw, O Howard!" **c.** (drawn inward) **d.** "Draw, O coward!"
—(a) Leigh Mercer, *N&Q*, Nov. 13, 1948; (b) J. A. Lindon's poem title in Howard Bergerson, *P&A* (1973); (c) Arthur Pearson, *PP&W* (1908); (d) G. R. Clarke, *Palindromes* (1887)

44. "Sir, I soon saw I was no Osiris."
—Dmitri Borgmann, *On Vacation* (1965)

FOOD, GLORIOUS FOOD

45. **a.** Stressed? ([or] Stress, Ed?) Not on desserts. **b.** No lemon(s), no melon. **c.** "I saw desserts, I'd no lemons, alas, no melon; distressed was I." **d.** "Stressed was I, sad, alas, to order a redroot salad as I saw desserts." **e.** "Salad, alas." **f.** "Boredom à la mode, Rob?" **g.** Desserts I desire not, so, lost one, rise distressed. **h.** "Norah's dessert, Sid, distressed Sharon." **i.** "Desserts, sis?" Sensuousness is stressed. (a mutual passion for sweets) **j.** "Stressed, Flo? Wolf desserts!"
—(a) Howard Richler, *WW*, May 1991; (b) Enavlicm, *TEE*, June 1912; (c) Leigh Mercer, *N&Q*, Nov. 2, 1946; (d) T. P. O'Brien, *London Times*, July 18, 1973; (e) anonymous; (f) Jon Agee, *Dynamos* (1994); (g) *TE*, 1942; Henry Campkin, *N&Q*, Mar. 8, 1873; (h) John Connett, Feb. 1996; (i) O. V. Michaelsen; (j) Howard Richler, *WW*, Nov. 1995

46. **a.** Stir grits. **b.** Ma handed Edna ham. **c.** O slaw, also! **d.** "Doc, note, I dissent. A fast never prevents a fatness. I diet on cod." **e.** "Dish Sid a radish. Sid?" "Mash Sid a radish, Sam." **f.** (No!) Not a ton (on)! / Note! Not one ton. **g.** "Spoon it in. Oops!" **h.** "Won ton? (No, Don.) Not now." **i.** "May we nab a new yam?" **j.** "Ana, nab a banana." **k.** "Ana nabs Bob's banana." **l.** "Yo, banana boy."
—(a) Joaquin and Maura Kuhn, *Rats Live* (1981); (b) J. A. Lindon in Howard Bergerson, *P&A* (1973); (c) Joaquin and Maura Kuhn, *Rats Live* (1981); (d) probably Peter Hilton, 1943; (e) John Connett, May 1996; (f) Coxy, *NA*, Aug. 13, 1904; R. C. O'Brien, *New York World*, Nov. 20, 1921; "not a ton" in G. R. Clarke, *Palindromes* (1887); (g) Jon Agee, *Dynamos* (1994); (h) R, *St. Nicholas*, May 1875; parentheses anonymous; (i) Mabel P., *Pittsburgh Post*, Aug. 5, 1900; (j) John Pool, *Daffodil* (1982); (k) David Woodside, *WW*, Aug. 1996; (l) anonymous

WINE, WOMEN & SONG

47. "Deny me not; atone, my Ned."
—Howard Bergerson, *P&A* (1973)

48. **a.** "Ned, I am now a won maiden." **b.** "Now, Ned, I am a maiden won." **c.** "Now, Ned, I am a maiden nun. Ned, I am a maiden won."
—(a) *American N&Q*, Jan. 5, 1889; (b) Gertrude Rowe, *Everyman*, Nov. 28, 1929; (c) Leigh Mercer, *N&Q*, Nov. 2, 1946

49. "Ma is a nun, as I am."
—Dmitri Borgmann, *On Vacation* (1965)

50. **a.** "Norma is as selfless as I am, Ron." **b.** *Shortened versions*: "Norma, I am Ron." "Ma is as selfless as I am."
—(a) J. A. Lindon in Martin Gardner, *Scientific American*, Sept. 1964; (b) anonymous

51. Harass (selfless) Sarah?
—Dmitri Borgmann, *On Vacation*
(1965)

52. "Madame, not one man is selfless;
I name not one, madam."
—Howard Bergerson, *P&A* (1973)

53. a. Rail (at a) liar! **b.** "Rail on, O
liar!" **c.** Liars (, alas,) rail.
—(a) R. G., *St. Nicholas*, Feb. 1875;
(b) parentheses in G. R. Clarke,
Palindromes (1887); (c) Leigh Mercer
in Howard Bergerson, *P&A* (1973)

54. a. "Can I attain a C?" **b.** Egad! A
base tone denotes a bad age! **c.**
"Treble, Delbert!" **d.** "Mother at song,
no star, eh, Tom?" **e.** "If I had a hi-fi!"
f. La, not atonal! **g.** "Eton, for one
tenor of 'note.'" **h.** "Ron, Eton mis-
tress asserts I'm no tenor." **i.** Gnostic,
a tacit song.
—(a) Howard Richler, *WW*, May 1992;
(b) Arthur Pearson, *20th Cent.*
Standard (1907); (c) anonymous; (d)
L. C., *O'London's*, Aug. 31, 1929; (e)
Jon Agee, *Go Hang* (1991); (f) J. A.
Lindon in Howard Bergerson, *P&A*
(1973); (g) Ron Howes, *Atlantic*
Unbound, Aug. 30, 1996; (h) Howard
Bergerson, *P&A* (1973); (i) Howard
Richler, *WW*, Nov. 1991; derived from
Howard Bergerson in Dmitri
Borgmann, *Beyond Language* (1967)

55. "Sex, Rex? A trap, Artaxerxes."
—Tut, *TE*, Apr. 1972

56. Party (booby) trap!
—Joaquin and Maura Kuhn, *Rats Live*
(1981)

57. Sex? Even a Dane vexes!
—Howard Richler, *WW*, May 1993

58. Sol led Rob to hot bordellos.
—Tom Nobel, *WW*, May 1995

59. I saw Ed under Deb's bed; red,
nude was I.
—John Connett, Mar. 1996

60. "Revolt, love!" raved Eva. "Revolt,
lover!"
—Howard Bergerson, *P&A* (1973)

61. Won't lovers revolt now?
—Leigh Mercer, *N&Q*, Oct. 16, 1948

62. "Deb, smash Sam's bed!"
—Stephen Chism, *From A to Zotamorf*
(1992)

63.
"Did Eve peep?"
"Eve did."
—W. Williams, *Everyman*,
Nov. 28, 1929

64. Anna: "Did Bob peep?" Bob: "Did
Anna?"
—Dmitri Borgmann, *On Vacation*
(1965)

65. "Did I disrobe Jeb or Sid?"—"I
did?"
—John Connett, July 1996

66. "O, desire! Rise, do!"
—John Pool, *Daffodil* (1982)

67. "Rise, lame male! Sir?"
—J. A. Lindon, *WW*, Nov. 1971

68. **a.** "Sex at my gym taxes!" **b.** ("Naomi), sex at noon taxes!" (I moan).
—(a) Howard Richler, *WW*, Nov. 1991; (b) Michael Gartner, *St. Louis Post-Dispatch*, 1972, in Willard Espy, *An Almanac* (1975); parentheses by anonymous

69. "I moan, ('Live on, O evil,') Naomi!"
—Charles Bombaugh, *Gleanings* (1890); also Dmitri Borgmann in Martin Gardner, *O&C* (1961); parentheses by anonymous

70.

Revere her ever!

—Graham, *Washington Post*, Sept. 21, 1884

71. **a.** "Ned, go gag Ogden." **b.** "Lace me, Portia! Wait! Rope me, Cal!" **c.** Egad! No bondage! **d.** "Wo, Nemo! Toss a lasso to me, *now!*" **e.** "Tie it." **f.** "Noose?" "Soon." **g.** "Lash Sal!" **h.** "Nail Ian!" **i.** "Nail, Lillian!" **j.** Knock! Conk! **k.** Reliant nailer! **l.** "Slap my gym pals." **m.** "Eh? Cane my men, odd one? My men ache!" **n.** No's in unison. **o.** "Want serene rest?" "Naw."
—(a) J. A. Lindon, *P&A* (1973); (b)

John Connett, Feb. 1996; (c, f–k) Joaquin and Maura Kuhn, *Rats Live* (1981); (d) Dona Smith, *Wo, Nemo! Toss a Lasso to Me, NOW!* (1993); (e) anonymous; (l, m) John Connett, Dec. 1995; (n) Joaquin and Maura Kuhn, *Rats Live* (1981); (o) Jon Agee, *Dynamos* (1994)

72. **a.** Sores? Alas, Eros. **b.** Eros saw I was sore. **c.** "Eros! Sidney! My end is sore." **d.** "Sore dermis! I'm red, Eros." **e.** Red? No wonder! **f.** So renowned, I, a maiden, won Eros.
—(a) anonymous; (b) Atlantis, *AP*, Dec. 7, 1901; (c) Willard Espy, *Another Anmanac* (1980); (d) O. V. Michaelsen; (e) anonymous; (f) Frans Folks, *GD*, Nov. 28, 1903

ECOLOGY

73. To Lake Erie rim, all a mire; I reek a lot!
—Smith, Tim S., *TE*, Oct. 1973

74. We passed Odessa. Pew!
—John Connett, Nov. 1995

75. A mar on a panorama.
—T. H., *AP*, July 1889

76. **a.** Niagara, O roar again! **b.** Niagara, eh? I hear again!
—(a, b) Atlantis, *TEE*, Apr. 1914

77. **a.** "Eva, can I stab bats in a cave?" **b.** "Eva, can I evade Dave in a cave?" **c.** "Eva, can I put a Manet (torn, rotten, a mat) up in a cave?"
—(a) El Uqsor, *TE*, Oct. 1956; (b) John Connett, *WWW*, 1995; (c) John Connett, Jan. 1996 in *Palindromist*, Winter 1996

DRAWING IT ALL OUT

78. a. Trades opposed art. **b.** No, it is (opposed. Art sees trade's) opposition. **c.** Trade ye no (mere) moneyed art!
—(a) anonymous; (b) Henry Campkin, *N&Q*, Mar. 8, 1873; (c) Leigh Mercer, *N&Q*, Nov. 2, 1946

79. "Degas, are we not drawn onward, we freer few, drawn onward to new eras aged?"
—Dmitri Borgmann, *On Vacation* (1965)

80. An era came: Macarena.
—Fred Klein, *Palindromist*, winter 1996

81. "Did Dean aid Diana?" "Ed did."
—Dmitri Borgmann, *On Vacation* (1965)

82. "Did I draw Della too tall, Edward?" "I did?"
—Dmitri Borgmann in Martin Gardner, *O&C* (1961)

WHO'S THERE?

83. Ed is busy. Subside!
—Jon Agee, *Dynamos* (1994)

84. "Al, let's go hog Stella."
—John Pool, *Daffodil* (1982)

85. a. Al lets Della call Ed "Stella." **b.** A "Lola?"
—(a) Dmitri Borgmann, *On Vacation* (1965); (b) J. A. Lindon in Howard Bergerson, *P&A* (1973)

86. a. "I did, did I?" **b.** "He did, eh?"
—(a) Enavlicm, *TEE*, June 1912; (b) anonymous

WHODUNIT?

87. a. Stella won(dered:) no wallets(?). **b.** Stella won(dered: "Roy ordered) no wallets?"
—(a, b) Leigh Mercer, *N&Q*, Feb. 1953; (a, b) parentheses Dmitri Borgmann, *On Vacation* (1965)

88. Rev.: "Ned, Nina made Ed a 'man' in Denver."
—John Connett, Dec. 1995

89. a. "Did Hannah say as Hannah did?" **b.** "No, son."
—(a) Leigh Mercer, *N&Q*, Feb. 1953; (b) Joaquin and Maura Kuhn, *Rats Live* (1981)

90. "Did Ione take Kate?" "No, I did."
—Dmitri Borgmann in Martin Gardner, *O&C* (1961)

91. "Did I, ameliorating Nita, roil Ema?" "I did?"
—Howard Bergerson, *P&A* (1973)

92. "Did I fish? Tim's rod or Smith's, if I did."
—J. A. Lindon in Howard Bergerson, *P&A* (1973)

93. "Did I do, O God! Did I as I said I'd do? Good, I did!"
—Dmitri Borgmann in Martin Gardner, *O&C* (1961)

94. Marge lets Norah see Sharon's telegram.
—Dmitri Borgmann in Martin Gardner, *O&C* (1961)

95. Norah's moods (, alas,) doom Sharon.
—Dmitri Borgmann in Martin Gardner, *O&C* (1961)

96. Della called.
—Stephen Chism, *From A to Zotmorf* (1992)

SNOOPS

97. a. "Oh, who was it I saw, oh who?" **b.** "Oh, who was in a VW van I saw? Oh, who?"
—(a) Atlantis, *AP*, Dec. 1, 1907; Enavlicm, *TEE*, June 1912; (b) Ulk, *TE*, May 1994. Both are based on "Was it a rat I saw?" from G. R. Clarke's *Palindromes* (1887).

98. Nosy son!
—Joaquin and Maura Kuhn, *Rats Live* (1981)

99. Was it a (bar or a) bat I saw?
—anonymous; parentheses, Martin Gardner, *O&C* (1961)

100. a. "A rod. Not a bar, a baton, Dora." **b.** "Not a bastion? No, it's a baton." **c.** "No, it's a bastion." **d.** Dora sees a rod. **e.** No, it's a bar of gold—a bad log for a bastion.
—(a) Howard Bergerson, *P&A* (1973); (b) anonymous and O. V. Michaelsen; (c) anonymous; (d) G. R. Clarke, *Palindromes* (1887); (e) Henry Campkin, *N&Q*, Mar. 8, 1873

UNDONE

101. Not *seven* on a mere man, *one* vest on!
—J. A. Lindon in Howard Bergerson, *P&A* (1973)

102. Stiff fits?
—Jon Agee, *Dynamos* (1994)

103. No dresser, Don!
—Jon Agee, *Dynamos* (1994)

104. a. "Got a tog?" **b.** "Anita got a toga, Tina."
— (a) Carter Bennett, (b) John Connett, *WW*, May 1995

105. "Massive Levi's, Sam!"
—Jon Agee, *Dynamos* (1994)

106. Tug at a gut.
—John Pool, *Daffodil* (1982)

INVASION & EVASION

107. "Sue," Tom (smiles, "Selim) smote us."
—Leigh Mercer, *N&Q*, Aug. 30, 1952; "Selim smiles" in G. R. Clarke, *Palindromes* (1887)

108.
"Dammit, I'm mad!"
—Enavlicm, *TEE*, June 1912

109. "Max, I stay *away* at six a.m.!"
—Howard Bergerson, *P&A* (1973)

110. "Evade (*me,*) Dave?"/ "Evade (no one,) Dave."
—Howard Richler, *WW*, Nov. 1995

111. "He won't, ah, *wander*, Edna. What now, eh?"
—John Jensen, "Official Palindrome List," *WWW*, April 1995

112. "Marc, scram!" *or* Marc: "Scram!"

113. "No, sir, away! A papaya war is on!"
—Jon Agee, *Dynamos* (1994)

YOUR MONEY OR YOUR LIFE

114. *A lawyer named* Otto made Ned a motto: (read with #115)

115. *Si nummi immunis.* ("Give me my fee and I warrant you free.")
—William Camden, *Remains* (1605)

116. See? Few owe fees.
—Leigh Mercer, *N&Q*, Oct. 16, 1948

117. Pay on time, emit no yap.
—Benjamin C. Pearson, *Everyman*, Nov. 28, 1929

118. Borrow or rob.
—G. R. Clarke, *Palindromes* (1887)

119. Too long no loot.
—Joaquin and Maura Kuhn, *Rats Live* (1981)

120. Stole lots.
—Joaquin and Maura Kuhn, *Rats Live* (1981)

121. Sue us!
—Joaquin and Maura Kuhn, *Rats Live* (1981); #107, shortened version

122. Must sell at tallest sum.
—Howard Bergerson, *P&A* (1973)

123. a. "Sums are deified, Erasmus."
b. Sums are not set as a test on Erasmus.
—(a) Howard Richler, *WW*, May 1993; (b) Leigh Mercer, *N&Q*, July 8, 1950; Mabel P., "Sums are not on Erasmus," *Pittsburgh Post*, July 8, 1900

124. Sad? I'm Midas!
—Tony Augarde, *Oxford Guide* (1984)

FLEEING MADNESS

125. a. "Mad? Am I, madam?" **b.** "No, old loon!"
—(a) anonymous; (b) Joaquin and Maura Kuhn, *Rats Live* (1981)

126. "Nurse, I spy Gypsies! Run!" **b.** Nurses run.
—(a) Leigh Mercer, *N&Q*, Aug. 30, 1952; (a, b) G. R. Clarke, *Palindromes* (1887)

127. a. I roam as a Maori. **b.** I roamed under it as a tired, nude Maori.
—(a) M. C. S., *Inter-Ocean*, Jan. 31, 1897; (b) Blackstone, *TE*, Oct. 1936

128. a. Too far (, Edna, we wander) afoot. **b.** Too flat! A fatal foot. **c.** Too fat a foot!
—(a) Molemi, *Inter-Ocean*, Mar. 1, 1906; (b) John Connett, May 1996; (c) G. R. Clarke, *Palindromes* (1887)

129. Selim's tired. No wonder, it's miles.
—Leigh Mercer, *N&Q*, July 8, 1950

130. "I did not limp, Milton, did I?"
—John Connett, July 1996

131. I run in Uri.
—Hal Ober, *Atlantic Unbound*, Aug. 30, 1996

132. "I'm runnin'!"—Nurmi
—Jane Prins, *Games*, Apr. 1992

133. Yale ran (in) a relay.
—*TE*, June 1956

AUTOSHOP

134. a. Race pony? Nope, car. **b.** One car race, no?
—(a) Tom Deneau; (b) anonymous

135. a. A Toyota (race car)? A Toyota? **b.** A Toyota's a Toyota.

136. Race fast, safe car!
—J. A. Lindon, *WW*, Nov. 1971

137. 'Tis in a DeSoto sedan I sit.
—John Connett in John Jensen, "Official Palindrome List," *WWW*, 1995

138. Gateman sees name, garage man sees name tag.
—Leigh Mercer, *N&Q*, Feb. 1953

BIG MAN ON CAMPUS

139. a. Was raw tap ale not a gag at one lap at Warsaw? **b.** Was a raw tap ale not a reviver at one lap at Warsaw?
—(a) *O'London's*, Aug. 31, 1929; (b) anonymous

140. "Hey, no mere ceremony, eh?"
—John Connett, *WWW*, 1995

141. In a regal age ran I.
—Leigh Mercer, *N&Q*, Sept. 7, 1946

DIAMONDS & JADES, JACKS & MAIDS

142. Diamond light, Odo, doth gild no maid.
—M. C. S., *Inter-Ocean*, Jan. 10, 1899

143. Eve saw diamond, erred; no maid was Eve.
—J. A. Lindon in Howard Bergerson, *P&A* (1973)

144. Deb, Boris eyed a jade. Yes, I too, Otis, eyed a jade. Yes, I robbed.
—John Connett, Jan. 1996

NET RESULTS

145. a. Ten animals I slam in a net. **b.** Net torn, even rotten. **c.** Net safe—rotten net to refasten.
—(a) Atlantis, *TEE*, Apr. 1914; (b) Howard Richler, *WW*, May 1992; (c) J. A. Lindon in Howard Bergerson, *P&A* (1973)

PEELINGS

146. Emil asleep, Hannah peels a lime.
—Dmitri Borgmann, *On Vacation* (1965)

147. a. "Emil, a sleepy baby peels a lime?" **b.** "No, Mel, a sleepy baby peels a lemon."
—(a) anonymous; (b) Jouko I. Valta, "International Palindromes" page, *WWW*, Dec. 1995

148.

Sleepy Liza lazily peels.

—Smith, Tim S., *TE*, Apr. 1976

149. R. E. Lee, potato peeler.
—Crossman, Jr., in Dr. Crypton, *Science Digest*, Feb. 1983

YOU DO IT

150. "We'll let Dad tell Lew." *or* "Si, we'll let Dad tell Lewis."
—El Uqsor, *TE*, 1958

151. "Lew, Otto has a hot towel."
—Atlantis, *TEE*, Apr. 1914

152. Dump mud.
—Jon Agee, *Go Hang* (1991)

153. Draw no dray a yard onward.
—Arthur Pearson, *PP&W* (1908)

154. Draw putrid dirt upward.
—Dmitri Borgmann, *On Vacation* (1965)

155. Till it, O Toro. Rototill it!
—John Connett, June 1996

156. a. Bog dirt up a sidetrack carted is a putrid gob. **b.** Live dirt up a sidetrack carted is a putrid evil.
—(a) anonymous; (b) Dmitri Borgmann in Martin Gardner, *O&C* (1961)

POLITICS AS USUAL

157. Won't S.A.L.T. last now?
—J. A. Lindon, *WW*, Nov. 1971

158. Wonder if Sununu's fired now.
—David J. Ray, *San Francisco Chronicle*, 1991

159. a. Retract (it), Carter! **b.** Won't Carter retract now? **c.** Do-gooder, retract! Carter, redo! O God! **d.** Retracting, I sign it "Carter." **e.** To last, Carter retracts a lot.
—(a, b) Howard Richler, *WW*, Nov. 1991; (c) Mark Saltveit, *Palindromist*, winter 1996; (d) anonymous in Howard Bergerson, *P&A* (1973); (e) Edward Scher in Willard Espy, *Another Almanac* (1980)

160. a. O Democrat(s) star, come, do! **b.** Star comedy (by) Democrats!
—Enavlicm, *NA*, Sept. 8, 1906; (b) Atlantis, *Inter-Ocean*, 1906: "Star comedy as I say 'Democrats.'"

161. a. Rise to vote, sir. **b.** Name now one man. **c.** Now Lon Nol won. **d.** Now rely, Tyler won.
—(a) Leigh Mercer, *N&Q*, Sept. 7, 1946; "Rise, Sir," Atlantis, *AP*, Dec. 1, 1907; (b) "Name no one(,) man" in Charles Bombaugh, *Gleanings* (1860); (c) Fred J. Abrahams in William Safire, "On Language," *NY Times Magazine*, 1989; (d) Dave Morice, *Alphabet Avenue* (1997)

162. a. Taft: fat. **b.** Want fat Taft? Naw.
—(a) Dmitri Borgmann, *On Vacation* (1965); (b) Enavlicm, *TEE*, June 1912

163. Bob's a snake; Kansas Bob.
—Pikmee and Ellen Auriti, *Atlantic Unbound*, Aug. 30, 1996. Political comment about former Republican senator from Kansas Bob Dole.

164. Sparta's one rule: lure no satraps!
—Ron Howes, *Atlantic Unbound*, Aug. 30, 1996

165. A rah, a shah, Sahara.
—Marg B., *Atlantic Unbound*, Aug. 30, 1996

WATERGATE

166. Pure vocal lips spill a cover-up.
—Smith, Tim S., *TE*, July 1973

167. Hoopla cover-ups must suborn, in robust sums, pure vocal "pooh."
—Tut, *TE*, Sept. 1973

IRAN-CONTRA

168. North gift? Casey era? C.I.A.'s or Bush's law? Walsh sub rosa? I care, yes! Act! Fight Ron!
—Matthew K. Franklin, *WW*, May 1988. William Casey was C.I.A. director; Lawrence Walsh served as independent counsel in the Iran-Contra investigation, begun in 1986.

PANAMA, 1989

169. A man, a pain, a mania, Panama.
—Brian Hall "Public Domain Palindrome Page," *WWW*, 1995

170. a. Noriega casts a cage: Iron. **b.** Noriega can idle, held in a cage— iron.
—(a) David Morice, *WW*, Nov. 1991; (b) *Games*, Apr. 1992

171. A foray far from home—/ This is how George will now / rewrite a palindrome: "A man appals. I slap Panama."
—Newrow, *TE*, Mar. 1990

PERSIAN GULF WAR

172. a. Drat Saddam, a mad dastard! **b.** Mad dastard, a sad rat—Saddam. **c.** A red rat, Saddam! A mad dastard era! **d.** Mad dash, eh, Saddam?
—(a) Howard Richler, *WW*, Nov. 1990; "Drat Sadat, a dastard," Michael Miller in Willard Espy, *Another Almanac* (1980); (b) Brian Hall, "Public Domain Palindrome Page," *WWW*, 1995; (c) David Morice, *WW*, May 1992; (d) Howard Richler, *WW*, Nov. 1992

BOSNIA

173. a. Bosnia: Pain. Sob. **b.** Bosnia gasps again! (sob).
—(a) Winfred S. Emmons, *WW*, Feb. 1994; (b) Tom Deneau, *Atlantic Unbound*, Aug. 30, 1996

GOING PLACES

174. An ole crab was I ere I saw Barcelona.

175. a. "Not Cohocton!" **b.** "Not New York!" Roy went on.
—(a) Michael Donner, *I Love Me, vol. I* (1996). Cohocton is a river and town in New York State. (b) Leigh Mercer, *N&Q*, Oct. 16, 1948

176. Ned, go to hot Ogden!
—Emily P. Arulpragasm, *Atlantic Unbound*, Aug. 30, 1996

177. O go to Togo!
—Michael Donner, *I Love Me, vol. I* (1996)

178. Oh . . . to go to Togo, tho?
—Emily P. Arulpragasam, *Atlantic Unbound*, Aug. 30, 1996

179. O go t' Boston, not (sob) Togo!
—Peter N. Horne, *Atlantic Unbound*, Aug. 30, 1996

180.
Haiti? Ah!
—Joaquin and Maura Kuhn,
Rats Live (1981)

181. a. "No, sir, (prefer) prison." **b.** "Golf? No, sir, prefer prison flog."
—(a) without parentheses, Svensk Grandy-bo, *Farmer's Wife*, Aug. 1908; (b) Howard Bergerson, *P&A* (1973)

182. a. Viva! Let no evil revel, ever. Live on, Tel Aviv! **b.** Viva, le Tel Aviv!
—(a) El Uqsor, *TE*, June 1957; (b) Dmitri Borgmann, *On Vacation* (1965)

183. One (resort rose): Reno!
—Tom Deneau, *Atlantic Unbound*, Aug. 30, 1996

MARTHA, AMY & MA

184. "Here, help Martha. Ah! Trample her, eh?"
—Atlantis, *TEE*, Apr. 1914

185. "Amy, must I jujitsu my ma?"
—Jon Agee, *Go Hang* (1991)

186. "Ample help, Ma?"
—William Irvine, *If I Had a Hi-Fi* (1992)

ABOUT ROSES

187. "Lapses? Order red roses, pal."
—Jim Beloff, *Palindromist*, spring 1997

188. "Red roses run no risk, sir, on nurse's order."
—Howard Bergerson, *P&A* (1973)

189. Red Rose; madame's order.
—C. B. Humphrey, *Everyman*, Nov. 28, 1929

190. a. "No misses ordered roses, Simon." **b.** "(E)no misses ordered roses, Simon(e)."
—(a) Enavlicm, *TEE*, June 1912; (b) parentheses later

TAN OR HIDE

191. a. Sun at noon, tan us. **b.** "Wanna tan?" "Naw."
—(a) Smith, Tim S., *TE*, June 1973; (b) Jon Agee, *Go Hang* (1991)

OUTERSPACE

192. Tons of UFOs? Not.
—Jouko I. Valta, "International Palindromes" page, *WWW*, Dec. 1995

193.

Hell, a spacecraft farce caps all, eh?

—Howard Bergerson, *P&A* (1973)

194. SPACESUIT! (I use caps.)
—John Connett, *Palindromist*, Winter 1996

TAKING STEPS

195. Poor Dan is in a droop.
—Leigh Mercer, *N&Q*, Oct. 16, 1948

196. Now I draw an award I won!
—George M. Woodcock, *NY Recorder*, Feb. 1893; Woodcock won an award for this contest entry.

197. a. Step on no pets. **b.** Step not on pets.
—(a) C. A. H. Greene, *Farmer's Wife*, Aug. 1910; (b) G. R. Clarke, *Palindromes* (1887)

SOMETHING FOOLISH

198. 'Tis Ivan, on a visit.
—Leigh Mercer, *N&Q*, Oct. 16, 1948

199. I'm a fool—aloof am I.
—Su San, *TE*, Oct. 1926

200. Drab as a (fool, as aloof as a) bard.
—*O'London's*, Aug. 31, 1929; parentheses, Leigh Mercer, *N&Q*, Aug. 30, 1952

201. Is it I? It is I.

202. Diana saw Dr. Awkward was an aid.
—Atlantis, *TEE*, Apr. 1914

203. Avid (as a) diva.
—Howard Bergerson, *P&A* (1973)

OOPS!

204. a. Pupils slip up. **b.** "Pupils!" I say, as I slip up. **c.** An error, Rena.
—(a) anonymous; (b) J. A. Lindon in Howard Bergerson, *P&A* (1973); (c) Jon Agee, *Dynamos* (1994)

205.

Pa's a sap.

—Martin Gardner, *O&C* (1961)

206. A new order began; a more Roman age bred Rowena.
—El Uqsor, *TE*, Sept. 1958

207. a. Egad, Loretta has Adams as mad as a hatter! Old age? **b.** Old? Lo!
—(a) Hercules, *TE*, early 1930s; (b) anonymous

GOOD & EVIL

208. Deny a God, O gay Ned?
—John Connett, Dec. 1995

209. Allah, lave Valhalla!
—Howard Bergerson, *P&A* (1973)

210. St. Simon sees no mists.
—Dmitri Borgmann, *On Vacation* (1965)

211. a. No evils live on. **b.** No evil's deeds live on. **c.** No evil sagas live on.
—(a) anonymous; (b) Philip Morse, *Pittsburgh Post*, Mar. 1900; (c) Mrs. M. K. Barnes, *O'London's*, Dec. 1, 1939

212. No devil's deeds lived on.
—*Everyman*, Nov. 28, 1929

213.
Lived on decaf, faced no devil.

—Brian Hall, "Public Domain Palindrome Page," *WWW*, 1995

214. a. Dog-deifiers reified God. **b.** Dog as a devil deified, lived as a god.
—(a) anonymous; (b) Arthur Pearson, *PP&W* (1908)

215. "God as all!" I saw it, felt it, left; I was ill as a dog.
—Cornel G. Ormsby

216. Ah, Satan, no smug smirk rims gums on Natasha.
—Howard Bergerson, *P&A* (1973). *Natasha* is a diminutive of *Natalie*, "Christmas child."

217. "Satan, oscillate my metallic sonatas!"
—Tony Augarde, *Oxford Guide* (1984)

218. Revered now, I live on. O did I do no evil, I wonder? Ever?
—Howard Bergerson, *P&A* (1973)

219. Did Bob live evil? Bob did.
—G. R. Clarke, *Palindromes* (1887)

220. Live on, O do! to do no evil.

221. a. Live on (tenet:) no evil. **b.** Live not on evil. **c.** Live not on evil, madame; live not on evil.
—(a) *Everyman*, Nov. 28, 1929; (b) *American N&Q*, Jan. 5, 1889; (c) Dmitri Borgmann in Martin Gardner, *O&C* (1961)

222. "Reviled did I live," (said I, as) evil I did deliver.
—Leigh Mercer, *N&Q*, Nov. 2, 1946

223. Do Good's deeds live on? No, Evil's deeds do, O God!
—Howard Bergerson, *P&A* (1973); "Do good's deeds live never even? Evil's deeds do, O God!" in Arthur Pearson, *20th Cent. Standard* (1907)

PARTING WORDS

224. To the Devil: "Live, O Devil, revel ever; live, do evil!"
—J. A. Lindon in Martin Gardner, *O&C* (1961)

225. To the Deity: "Do, O God, no evil deed; live on, do good!"
—J. A. Lindon in Martin Gardner, *O&C* (1961)

CREATING PALS

Earliest Palindrome

John Taylor, author of the earliest-known palindromic sentence in English, wrote: "This line is the same backwards as it is forward, and I will give any man five shillings apiece for as many as they can make in English: 'Lewd did I live & evil I did dwel.'"

Taylor's palindrome was found in Nathaniel Butler's *The Nipping or Snipping of Abuses* (1614). The ampersand (*&*) used to be a letter of the English alphabet, and from the 1300s to the 1600s, *dwel* was an acceptable spelling of our modern *dwell.* An updated version of his palindrome would read: "Evil I did dwell; lewd did I live."

Longest Palindromic Words

According to the *Guinness Book of World Records* (1993), the longest palindromic word is the coined term *saippuak(ivi)kauppias* (19 letters), which means "a dealer in lye" (caustic soda). The word, said to be Finnish, was derived from the German word *seife* ("soap") and *kauppias*, from *kaufer* ("buyer or dealer") or *kaufen* ("to buy"). Apparently, the longest American English palindromic word is *releveler* (spelled *releveller* in Britain). The longest found in the *OED* is *tattarrattat* (12 letters), and the longest palindromic place-name in America seems to be Wassamassaw, a swamp north of Charleston, South Carolina. It is an American Indian word meaning "the worst place ever seen."

Transformations

In "Triplets—An Added Dimension," *Word Ways*, Nov. 1991, Peter Newby demonstrated how one well-known palindrome can be transformed into another.

LIVE	NOT	ON	EVIL
LIE	NO	ONE	VIL
LE	O	DONE	VI
E	AO	DOE	I
EN	A	OE	IN
ENS	HA	E	INN
DENS	HAD	EA	INNE
DENIS	AD	ENA	INNED
DENNIS	AND	EDNA	SINNED

David Morice holds the record for the longest English word used in a palindrome: *antiparasympathomimetically* (27 letters).

FOREIGN-LANGUAGE PALINDROMES

Dutch *"Moooie zeden in Ede,' zeei oom."* ("'Nice customs in Ede,' said Uncle.")

Finnish *"Nisumaa oli isasi ilo aamusin."* ("The field of wheat was your father's joy in the morning.") *"Isa, ala myy myymalaasi."* ("Father, don't sell your shop.") *"Nalli laukee taas; saat eekua lillan!"* ("The detonator is exploding again; your butt will be toasted!")

French *"Etna, lave devalante."* ("Etna, spreading lava.") *"A l'autel elle alla. Elle le tua la."* ("To the altar she went. She killed him there.")

German *"Bei leid lieh stets heil die lieb."* ("In sorrow, love always lent security," or, "In trouble, comfort is lent by love.") This appears in Charles Bombaugh's *Gleanings* (1875).

Greek *"Niyon anomhmata, mh monan oyin."* ("Wash your sins, not only your face." *or* "Purify the mind as well as the body.") Compare this to the second verse in Psalms 51: "Wash me throughly from mine iniquity, and cleanse me from my sin." It is believed that the Greek inscription dates back to the sixth century. It was found on a baptismal font in Hagia Sophia in Istanbul, Turkey.

Icelandic *"Allar munum ralla."* ("We shall all have a wild time.")

Italian *"Ove regnai piangere vo."* ("I go to weep where I once ruled.")

Latin *"Acide me malo, sed non desola me, medica."* ("Disgustingly I prefer myself, but do not leave me, healing woman.") *"Si nummi immunis."* ("Give me my fee and I warrant you free.") The translation is by William Camden in *Remains* (1605).

Portuguese *"Atai a gaiola, saloia gaiata!"* ("Tie the cage, naughty rustic girl!")

Spanish *"Sobornos son robos."* ("Bribes are robberies.") *"Sacara maracas."* ("He will take out the maracas.") *"Osos, somos soso."* ("Bears, we lack flavor!") *"Anita lava la tina."* ("Anita [little Anne] washes the bathtub.") *"Yo de todo te doy."* ("I give you a bit of everything.") The first three—about bribes, maracas, and bears—are by Mark Saltveit.

Swedish *"Ni talar bra Latin."* ("You speak good Latin.")

Welsh *"Lladd dafad ddall."* ("Kill a blind sheep.") This palindrome in *N&Q,* July 7, 1853, was written a year earlier.

Japanese Palindromes

Ernest W. Clement of Tokyo, Japan, provided the Japanese palindromes and description of their various forms here in a letter to the editor of *The Dial*, a Chicago magazine, May 25, 1916.

"The subject of palindromes happened to come up in my class the other day. After I had given the most common English example, I asked for some examples of Japanese palindromes. This brought out specimens of three or four kinds: those which appear when written in the Japanese syllabary (*kana*); those in Chinese ideographs; those in Roman letters; and those in two of these kinds at one and the same time. A few of these examples may be cited here.

"*Sa-to To-sa* (also read *To-sake*) is a personal name that makes a palindrome in both the Japanese syllabary and the Chinese ideographs. *Mi-wa-ta Rin-zo, Ku-bo-deva Yassu-hisa,* and *Wata-nabe Watara* are personal names that form palindromes only with Chinese ideographs (indicated with syllables), although in the last case there is a hint of the palindrome in the Roman letters. *A-ka-sa-ka,* the name of a Tokyo suburb, is a palindrome only in Japanese. *Kitsu-tsu-ki* ('woodpecker') is another example. *Ta-ke-ya ga ya-ke-ta* ('The bamboo shop has burned.') forms a palindrome in Japanese kana only.

There are two Japanese poems (of 31 syllables) that make good palindromes; but, being artificial, they do not make good sense, so I shall not attempt any translation thereof. The first one is called '*Hatsu-yume*,' or 'First Dream' (of the New Year). It is written on a sheet of paper, folded in the shape of a ship, and laid under the pillow, as a charm to ensure a good dream. It reads:"

Na-ka (ga)-ki yo no
To-o no ne-mu-ri no

Mi-na me-za-me
Na-mi no-ri mu-ne no
O-to no yo-ki ka na.

Here is an English translation from Dmitri Borgmann's *Language on Vacation* (1965). "Everybody wakes up from the sound sleep of a long night—winter. How delightful the sound of the oars of a fishing boat on the sea."

"It should be explained," Clement continues, "that *ka* and *ga* are written with the same character, with diacritical marks (in prose) to indicate the 'muddy' sound of *ga*; and that *mu* and *fu* are interchangeable. So the poem is a better palindrome in Japanese kana than when it is transliterated into Roman letters."

The next poem is "a first-class palindrome in the Japanese syllabary."

To-ku ta-ta-shi
Sa-to no ta-ka-mu-ra
Yu-ki shi-ro-shi
Ki-yu-ra-mu ka-ta no
To-sa-shi ta-ta-ku to.

Here is Clement's translation: "I wished to depart swiftly, for the bamboo grove of the village was white with snow. I intended to knock at the door of the house on the side where the snow would probably have melted."

"Note how the verbal palindrome, '*shi-ro-shi*,'" Clement says, "forms the pivot, exactly in the center. This poem was written by a famous scholar, Dr. Haga. The Japanese syllabary lends itself admirably to the forming of palindromes."

Roma–Amor

The poem "Roma–Amor," said to be based on a verse written by Sotades around 250 B.C., is one of many suppressed by the papacy during the Protestant Reformation. Many writings from that period contained palindromic lines or verses using the words *Roma* ("Rome" or "Roman") and *amor* ("love" or "love affairs"). The translation of the poem was given by A. B. R. in *N&Q*, Feb. 2, 1856.

> *Roma, ibi tibi sedes—ibi tibi Amor;*
> *Rom, etsi te terret et iste Amor,*
> *Ibi etsi vis te non esse—sed es ibi,*
> *Roma te tenet et Amor.*

> "At Rome you live—at Rome you love;
> From Rome that love may you affright,
> Although you'd leave—you never move,
> For love and Rome both bar your flight."

Rude Latin

William Camden in *Remains* (1605) provided a Latin palindrome and this explanation: "A scholar and a gentleman, living in a rude country town where he received little respect, wrote this with a coal in the town hall: *'Subi dura a rudibus.'* ('Endure rough treatment from uncultured brutes.')"

Bilingual Palindrome

In March 1866 *Our Young Folks* magazine featured this remarkable English and Latin palindrome, contributed by James C. P., which has the same meaning in both directions: "Anger? 'Tis safe never. Bar it! Use love! *Evoles ut ira breve nefas sit; regna!*" ("Rise up, in order that your anger may be but a brief madness; control it!") The palindrome is not in classic Latin.

Latin Defense

"On Palindromes," *New Monthly Magazine*, 1821: "For the most beautiful example, we must turn to the annals of our own country (England), and to a woman. In the reign of Queen Elizabeth, when the education of women rendered them frequently superior to the other sex, a lady (of nobility) being banished from the Court on suspicion of her being too familiar with a great lord in favor, gave this device: The moon covered by a cloud, and the following palindrome for a motto: '*ablata at alba*'—'obscured, but pure.'" The magazine continues, "This kind of composition was never in any example of which we know so heightened by appropriateness and delicacy of sentiment."

William Camden in *Remains* (1605) gave the palindrome as "*ablata & alba.*" Other translations of the palindrome were "banished but blameless" and "out of sight, but still white."

19 PLAYFUL & BEWITCHING PALS

PALS IN RIDDLE & RHYME

John Taylor's Palindromes

New Monthly Magazine in 1821 stated that, despite the fact that there were so many palindromic English words, the only known palindromic letter-unit sentence in English was "Lewd did I live & evil I did dwel," by John Taylor, the water poet, in 1614. However, he had written at least two others, as shown in one of his poems, published that same year. This Taylor poem is found in Nathaniel Butler's *Nipping or Snipping of Abuses,* or *Woolgathering of Witte* (1614).

> To Anna, Queen of Great Britaine—
>
> These backward and these forward lines I send
> To you right Royall high majesticke hand;
> And like the guilty prisoner I attend
> Your censure wherein bliss or bale doth stand.
>
> If I condemned be, I cannot grudge,
> For never Poet had a juster judge.
>
> *Deer Maddam Reed:*
> *Deem if I meed.*

Edgar Allan Poe (1809-1849) has been credited as the author of this acrostic puzzle when he was 18 in *The Saturday Evening Post*, 1827. The solution is composed of palindromic words.

> First find out a word that doth silence proclaim,
> An backwards and forwards is always the same;
> Then next you must find a feminine name
> That backwards and forwards is always the same;
> An act or a writing or parchment whose name
> Both backwards and forwards is always the same;
> A fruit that is rare whose botanical name
> Read backwards and forwards is always the same;
> A note used in music which time doth proclaim,
> And backwards and forwards is always the same;
> Their initials connected a title will frame
> That is justly the due of the fair married dame,
> Which backwards and forwards is always the same.

Here's the solution.

```
M   U     M
A   N   N A
D   E   E D
A   N A N A
M   I N I M
```

Swift on Carrots

Edgar Allan Poe's acrostic is reminiscent of a poem written by Jonathan Swift (1667-1745) in 1711, referring to Queen Anna (Anne), "Carrot," the redheaded Duchess of Somerset, and her bedchamber lady, Lady Masham, who was a friend of Swift's. This acrostic appears in Tony Augarde's *Oxford Guide* (1984); the solution is of course the queen's name, Anna.

> Root out these carrots, O thou, whose name
> Is backwards and forwards always the same;
> And keep close to thee always that name,
> Which backwards and forwards is almost the same.

MORE PALINDROME AMUSEMENTS

Cats & Dogs

About cats and dogs, in anagrams we have SCAT—CATS! (R., *St. Nicholas*, May 1875); GREYHOUND—"Hey, dog, run!" (King Carnival, *GD*, Oct. 1, 1898); and STAGHOUND—"A dog hunts." (Atlantis, *AP*, Aug. 1, 1905).

Palindromists offer us "Revolt a cat lover" by Dale Reed in *Science Digest*, Feb. 1983; "Stack cats" in Jon Agee's *Go Hang* (1997); "Stacy's super-aware pussy cats!" poem by James A. Lindon in Howard Bergerson's *Palindromes & Anagrams* (1973); and by anonymous writers, "Senile felines?" and "We mew." About dogs we have "Go, dog!" "Dog, as a devil deified, lived as a god," from Arthur Pearson's *Pictured Puzzles & Wordplay* (1908); and "God save Eva's dog!" by Neil "Fred" Picciotto.

Musical Palindromes

Many musical palindromes have been composed, but I am aware of only one song in which the melody and lyric are palindromic. It is the Spanish: "*Somos o no somos.*" ("Are we, or are we not?") According to *Palindromist*, spring 1997, the song was performed at a New York party thrown by Jon Agee to celebrate his book *So Many Dynamos!* (1994).

Mickey Mackenzie, a Michigan musician, composed an instrumental jazz piece, "Gnostic Illicit Song," that must be played with the chord progression "A-B-C-B-A."

Addition

Peter Newby, *WW*, Nov. 1993, provides this palindromic response to the anagram "ELEVEN + TWO = twelve + one."

One + nine = nine? No.

A Hoot

Molemi wrote the palindrome "too hot to hoot," printed in the column "In Mystic Mood," *Farmer's Wife*, May 1911. Fill in the missing letters indicated by asterisks for the palindrome.

In 1995, the NPL changed the way clues were given to this type of puzzle. Now, only the verse(s) and number of letters in each word of the palindrome are provided, and each capitalized word is indicated by an asterisk.

'Twas a night succeeding days
Of Midsummer's fiercest blaze,
Silent as a graveyard ghost
Sat an owl upon a post.
"Come," said I, "O strigine fowl!
Why so silent? Speak, O owl!"
The owl gave just one glance at me:
"*oo *o* *o *oo*, to whoo!" said he.

Another Owl

Jon Agee in *Go Hang* (1991) gave us the palindrome "Mr. Owl ate my metal worm."

Versifying the Palindrome

These three verses, written by Tut (James I. Rambo) in the 1970s and published in *TE*, conclude with palindromes (italicized). The custard palindrome (without the verse) first appeared in G. R. Clarke's *Palindromes* (1887).

> Quiche Lorraine?
> Oh, not again!
> *Drat such custard!*
>
> Make it more simple!
> No puzzler's atrocity
> Stays afloat long on a flood
> Of verbosity.
> *Edit, damn it! Solemn word ties lessen;*
> *I drown wordiness, else it drown me;*
> *lost in mad tide.*
>
> From moral heights unscaled by ardent beaux,
> Our miss still contemplates her blameless bed;
> Though supplicants abhor these pesky woes,
> The florist suffers most—when all is said!
> *Sir! I rose. No men, as late pained rage lapses.*
> *Order red roses, pale gardenia petals, anemones, or iris!*

PALINDROMIC NAMES

Adaven, Nevada a community in Nye County, Nevada

Anuta Catuna winner of the New York Marathon and Olympics contender

Aoxomoxoa title of a 1969 album by the Grateful Dead

Apollo, PA Pennsylvania town cited by Enavlicm, *TEE,* June 1912

Dr. Awkward Dr. Michael Awkward, University of Pennsylvania English professor, found by Jon Agee

Emily's Sassy Lime teenage southern California punk trio

Kavon Novak a suggested, but discarded pseudonym for film star Kim Novak (b. Marilyn Novak)

Leon Noel French ambassador to Poland before World War II

Live Evil a 1983 record album by the rock band Black Sabath

Lon Nol president of Cambodia from 1970 to 1975 (d. 1985)

Ogopogo alleged sea creature of Lake Okanogan, British Columbia, referred to as the (North) American Loch Ness monster. The first documented sighting of the creature was in 1852. The creature's name does not come, as many had supposed, from any language of Pacific Coast tribes found in the province. It may have been derived from a 1920s British music hall song.

Olé ELO! record album title by the Electric Light Orchestra

Omaha, MO town in Missouri

Revilo P. Oliver (III) professor emeritus, University of Illinois at Urbana

Robert Trebor Two actors were born with this name. One, better known as Bob Trebor, was also a radio talk show host on San Francisco's KGO in the 1970s.

S. Addidas French branch of the Addidas corporation

"SOS" (by **Abba**) a 1976 hit song and the Swedish group who recorded it

Sydney Yendys the pen name of English poet Sydney Dobell (1824-1874)

UFO Tofu record album title by Béla Fleck & the Flecktones

U Nu prime minister of Burma from the late 1950s to the early 1960s

Wolf Flow a 1992 horror novel by K. W. Jeter

No Place

Michael Donner in *I Love Me, Vol. I* (1996), mentions the place-name **Point No Point**. There are at least two; one in Stratford, Connecticut, and another near Port Townsend, Washington.

Businesses

Yreka Bakery, which has a palindromic name, baked bread in Yreka, California, for over a century. According to *American N&Q,* Jan. 5, 1889, it was owned by a certain S. Gilligs (palindromic name). This establishment's name, mentioned in *Our Young Folks,* Mar. 1866, dates back more than 130 years. The editor of "Our Letter Box" column in *Our Young Folks* called such palindromes *inversions.*

West Miner Street, in Yreka, had two businesses with palindromic names. Next to the bakery was the **Yrella Gallery**. At last report, the gallery was still in operation.

Elite Tile is the name of a business in Walnut Creek, California.

Games' Famous Names

In Apr. 1992, *Games* magazine ran a contest for palindromes containing famous names. The results were given in the June 1992 issue, with the grand prize awarded to Douglas Fink for "Lisa Bonet ate no basil." Runners-up included, from A Palindrome Collection on p. 124, #170 on Noriega and #132 that refers to Finland's Paavo Nurmi, 1920s Olympic track and field medalist. Here are a few more from *Games,* June 1992.

Vanna, wanna *V?*—Mike Griffin

(. . . Yawn.) Madonna fan? No damn way!—Susan Leslie and Robert Siegel

Plan no damn Madonna LP!

O, Geronimo: No minor ego!—David Morice

Oh, no! Don Ho!—several submitted

"Is Don Adams mad?" (a nod.) "Sí."—Susan C. Ridgeway

"Damn! I, Agassi, miss again! Mad!"—John Leavy

Harpo & Oprah

Here's one by an anonymous writer about the casualties of fame not found in *Games* magazine: "Ed, I saw Harpo Marx ram Oprah W. aside."

HOOPLA

Irish Gathering

English is a difficult language for the palindromist; long palindrome sentences tend to abandon grammar and sense. This palindrome by Enavlicm, *TE*, Nov. 1934, is a good example. It inspired Dmitri Borgmann's palindromic collection of English proper names "Dennis . . . sinned" (see Persons Unknown) and is based on Enavlicm's "(Oh,) sir, I'm Iris(h, O!)," printed in *TEE*, June 1912. I have omitted 18 letters from this palindrome since the words could offend.

"Hah, sir, I'm Irish, Ah! Now sit! . . . Go! Droop! Stop! Onward! Don't nod, put it up! Too hot to hoot? Ha, ha, hah! Tag Agatha, ha, hah! Oh, who sinned? Noel, Carol, 'Mad Alice,' Caleb, Mike, 'Bab,' Leo, Jane, Lysle, Nesbit, Ann, Adolf, Leah, Parker, Ruby, Enoc, Selim, Syd, Algy, Emmit, Alec, Irene, Eli, Edna, Ned, 'Lo,' Gregory, 'Snap,' Amaryllis, Leroy, Darby, 'Cul,' Tod, Nell, Aaron, 'Live Hannah,' 'Evil Nora,' Allen, Dot, Lucy, Brady, Orel, Silly, Rama, Pansy, Roger, Golden and Eileen, Eric, Ela, Timmy, Gladys, Miles, Coney, Burr, 'Ek,' Raphael, Flo, Dan, Nat, Ibsen, Elsy, Lena, Joel, Babe, Kim, Bela, Cecil, Adam, Lora, Cleon, Dennis! Oh, who? Ha, ha, hah! Tag Agatha, ha, hah! Too hot to hoot? Put it up! Don't nod! Draw no pots (poor dog) . . . 'Tis won! Hah, sir, I'm Irish, ah!"

An earlier version was "Oh, sir, Irish, O!" by Willy Wisp (possibly W. G. Scribner) in *Our Young Folks*, Mar. 1867. "Draw pupil's lip upward," appeared in the Aug. 1866 issue, perhaps also by Willy Wisp. "Don't nod" and "put (it) up" were credited to Atlantis in the *Ardmore Puzzler*, Dec. 1, 1907.

In the Apr. 1866 *Our Young Folks*, W. G. S. (possibly W. G. Scribner) contributed the palindrome "Snug & raw was I ere I saw war & guns." An alternative to this palindrome could be "Snug, raw was I ere I saw war guns." Other classics include Charles T.'s "red root put to order" in *Our Young Folks*, Apr. 1866; Robert G. Evans's "never odd or even" in *B&O*, June 1930; and J. H. Armington's "live on, time; emit no evil" in *GD*, Mar. 28, 1891.

Persons Unknown

This palindrome is composed entirely of proper names listed in "A Pronouncing Vocabulary of Common English Given Names" from *Webster's Seventh New Collegiate Dictionary*

(1963). It is based on Enavlicm's "Ha, sir, I'm Irish, ah!" and on "Dennis (Krats) and Edna (Stark) sinned," by Evergreen, *TE*, June 1956. The palindrome appears in Dmitri Borgmann's *On Vacation* (1965).

"Dennis, Nell, Edna, Leon, Nedra, Anita, Rolf, Nora, Alice, Carol, Leo, Jane, Reed, Dena, Dale, Basil, Rae, Penny, Lana, Dave, Denny, Lena, Ida, Bernadette, Ben, Ray, Lila, Nina, Jo, Ira, Mara, Sara, Mario, Jan, Ina, Lily, Arne, Bette, Dan, Reba, Diane, Lynn, Ed, Eva, Dana, Lynne, Pearl, Isabel, Ada, Ned, Dee, Rena, Joel, Lora, Cecil, Aaron, Flora, Tina, Arden, Noel, and Ellen sinned."

Orgy

Clement Wood's "The Orgy" appears in Willard Espy's *The Word's Gotten Out* (1989).

"Di, Al, Togo, Böll, Edna, Todd, Adolf, Sir Obadiah Turner, Ollie, Nora, El, silly Rama, Yma Sumac, St. Toby, Cal, Mike, Graf Alfie, Leila, Roz, Owen, Gallos, Reg, Nina Noyes, Mary, Lionel, Lana, Essex, Rex, Dr. Olim, Sal, Isobel, Ed, Axel, Ann, Odile, Leon, Bill (a Pole), Ginger, gay Ogden MacColl, Ewen Enid, Ansel, Gore, Lady Block, Cindy, Sam, Ronny, Llewellyn, Norma, Syd, Nick Colby, Dale, Rog, Les, Nadine Newell, Occam, Ned, Goya, Greg, Nigel, Opal, Lib, Noel, Eli, Donna, Lex, Adele, Bo, Silas, Milord Xerxes, Sean Allen, Oily Ramsey, Onan, Ingersoll, Agnew, Oz, Oralie, Leif LaFarge, Kim, Lacy, Botts, Camus, Amy, Amaryllis, Lear, O'Neill, Oren, Ruth, Aida, Boris, Flo, Dad, Dot, and El Lobo got laid."

WORD-UNIT PALINDROMES

A Palindromic Epitaph

A Lyon verse, or Sidonius verse, as it was sometimes called, is a word-unit palindrome, like "The Witch's Prayer," which when read backwards often answers or gives the verse an opposite meaning. Caius Sollius Sidonius Apollinaris, a Gallo-Roman writer from Lyon, France, has been credited with its invention in the fifth century. This example, a sort of epitaph by an unknown author, was probably written in the 1700s or earlier. It was found in St. Winwalloe's churchyard, five miles south of Helston in Cornwall, England. Its words can be read in four directions.

Shall	we	all	die?
We	shall	die	all!
All	die	shall	we?
Die	all	we	shall!

Aphoristic Palindromes

Here is a proverbial word-unit palindrome: "Eat to live; never live to eat." Here are more contemporary examples of word-unit palindromes that make ready aphorisms.

God knows man. What is doubtful is what man knows God?—G. J. Blundell, *New Statesman*, ca. 1970

Do geese see God? See! Geese do! (The first sentence is a letter-unit palindrome. Combined, the sentences form a word-unit palindrome.)

All for one and one for all.—Alexandre Dumas, *The Three Musketeers* (1844)

Women understand men; few men understand women.—Naomi Marks, *New Statesman*, ca. 1970

Case development: Arrested suspect calls Doctor Brothers. Doctor calls suspect "arrested development case."—*WW*, Nov. 1987, NPL contest

James A. Lindon's Collection

Here are five palindromes written by James A. Lindon, published in various sources. The first is from *WW*, ca. 1970; the next two were published in Martin Gardner's "Mathematical Games" in *Scientific American* (second, Aug. 1970; third, Sept. 1964); and the last two were in Martin Gardner's *Oddities & Curiosities* (1961).

So patient a doctor to doctor a patient so.

You can cage a swallow, can't you, but you can't swallow a cage, can you?

Amusing is that company of fond people bores people fond of company that is amusing.

King, are you glad you are king?

What! So he is hanged, is he? So what?

Will Shortz & NPR Competition

These winning palindromes come from a competition run by Will Shortz on National Public Radio's "Weekend Edition," Sunday. They were first published in *WW*, Feb. 1997; Shortz wrote: "The quality of the results greatly exceeded my expectations. In fact, some of the submissions might well become new classics." First, the runners-up.

RUNNERS-UP

Fall leaves after leaves fall.—Betsy Mirarchi

Will my love love my will?—John Hesemann

Please me by standing by me, please!—Peter Stein

Escher, drawing hands, drew hands drawing Escher.—John Meade

Blessed are they that believe that they are blessed.—Hugh Hazelrigg

Says Mom, "What do you do?" You do what Mom says.—Natalie Heiman

You know, I did little for you, for little did I know you.—Patrick Robbins

"Did I say you never say, 'Never say never?' You say I did."—Bill O'Malley

GRAND PRIZE

The grand prize went to Peter Stein of San Francisco (another of his is quoted above), for his future headline out of Washington, D.C.: "First Ladies Rule the State and State the Rule—'Ladies First!'"

This legendary Latin word-unit palindrome, supposedly mentioned in Joseph Addison's writings, was printed in Dmitri Borgmann's *Beyond Language* (1967). Borgmann, in his little joke, claimed he found the Witch's Prayer in the 14th century tome *The Complete Manual of Witchcraft*, published in Belfast, Ireland. Read forward, it offers encouraging religious advice, but when read in reverse, it endorses sin.

"PRAYER"

Delicias fuge ne frangaris crimine, verum
Coelica tu quaeras, ne male dispereas;
Respicias tua, non cujusvis quaerito gesta
Carpere, sed laudes, nec preme veridicos;
Judicio fore te praesentem conspice toto
Tempore: nec Christum, te rogo, despicias;
Salvificum pete, nec secteris daemona, Christum
Dilige, nequaquam tu mala concupito.

Here is an English translation. "Shun pleasures of the flesh, lest you be broken by crime; seek the things of Heaven, lest your end be an evil one; consider your own deeds, and do not seek to slander someone else's, but praise them, and do not suppress those who speak the truth; always realize that you must stand before a judgment; I beg you, do not despise Christ, seek him who gives salvation, and do not follow the Devil; love Christ, and do not lust at all after evil."

PRAYER REVERSED

Concupito mala, tu nequaquam dilige Christum;
Daemona secteris, nec pete salvificum;
Despicias, rogo te, Christum: nec tempore toto
Conspice praesentem to fore judicio;
Veridicos preme, nec laudes, sed carpere gesta
Quaerito cujusvis, non tua respicias.
Dispereas male, ne quaeras tu coelica, verum
Crimine frangaris, ne fuge delicias.

This prayer in reverse translates into English: "Lust after evil, and do not at all love Christ; you follow the Devil, do not seek Him who gives you salvation; despise Christ, I beg you, and realize that never will you stand before a judgment; suppress those who speak the truth, and do not praise the deeds of anyone, but seek to slander them; do not consider your own; let your end be an evil one, do not seek the things of Heaven; let yourself be broken by crime, do not shun pleasures of the flesh."

LINE-UNIT PALINDROMES

James A. Lindon invented the line-unit palindrome. The original version of Lindon's poem "Doppelgänger" was printed Dmitri Borgmann's *Beyond Language* (1967). Howard Bergerson in *Palindromes & Anagrams* (1973) presented this revision. The poem reads the same from the first to the last line as it does from the last line to the first.

DOPPELGÄNGER

Entering the lonely house with my wife
I saw him for the first time
Peering furtively from behind a bush—
Blackness that moved,
A shape amid the shadows,
A momentary glimpse of gleaming eyes
Revealed in the ragged moon.
A closer look (he seemed to turn) might have
Put him to flight forever—
I dared not
(For reasons that I failed to understand),
Though I knew I should act at once.

I puzzled over it, hiding alone,
Watching the woman as she neared the gate.
He came, and I saw him crouching
Night after night.
Night after night
He came, and I saw him crouching,
Watching the woman as she neared the gate.

I puzzled over it, hiding alone—
Though I knew I should act at once,
For reasons that I failed to understand
I dared not
Put him to flight forever.

A closer look (he seemed to turn) might have
Revealed in the ragged moon
A momentary glimpse of gleaming eyes,
A shape amid the shadows,
Blackness that moved.

Peering furtively from behind a bush,
I saw him, for the first time,
Entering the lonely house with my wife.

20 WORD REVERSALS & THEIR PALS

COMPOSED IN REVERSE

This short dictionary of words and couplets will be helpful to those interested in composing palindromes. Archaic and obsolete words are excluded, as are many alternative spellings, foreign and obscure words and names, and localized trade names. I compiled this list with puzzle colleague Kent Aldershof.

Dmitri Borgmann's *On Vacation* (1965) and Jeff Grant's *Palindromicon* (1992) are also good sources of palindromic words and word reversals.

You could, of course, cull palindrome collections, like that beginning on p. 124, for appropriate palindromic words. But we've made it easier for you. Here is A Dictionary of Reversals, and A Dictionary of One-Word Palindromes appears on p.160.

A Dictionary of Reversals

able   Elba
ABM   MBA
abut   tuba
a cap   paca (rodent)
a dad   dada
Adaven (Nevada)   Nevada
ados   soda
a gar   Raga (Sudan)
a garb   Braga (Portugal)
a gem   mega
ages   Sega (trade name)
a goy   yoga
Ah!   Ha!
Ah, Satan!   Natasha
ailed   Delia
ail Amos   Somalia
aim   MIA, Mia
ajar   Raja, raja
a knot   Tonka (trademark)

Al, al   L.A., la
Allah   halla
alley   yella
am   ma
a mal-   lama
a Mede   edema
amiced   decima
am Ron   Norma
an   Na, na
an ad   Dana
an aid   Diana
and   DNA
a Ned, an Ed   Dena
a need   Deena
an era   arena
an id   Dina
animal   lamina
a nit   Tina
a nob   bona
an ole crab   Barcelona
an Omar   Ramona
anon   Nona
ante   (Mt.) Etna
a nut   tuna
a pan   Napa (California)
a pap   Papa
a pat   tapa
ape   EPA
a pup   pupa
a rap   para-
are   ERA, era
a repo   opera
ares   sera (plural of *serum*)
a rev   Vera
Ari   IRA, Ira
a roc   Cora
a rod   Dora
a Ron   Nora
array   Yarra (river, Australia)
arret   terra

Aryan   nay, Ra
a sip   Pisa
a slab   balsa
a tad   data
a tram   Marta
a tsar (czar)   Rasta
(Albert) Camus   sumac
Avalon   no lava
ave   Eva
avid   diva
Avis   Siva (Shiva)
Avon   Nova, nova
ay   ya
a war at   Tarawa
a yam   Maya
(Francis) Bacon, bacon   no cab
bad   dab
bag   gab
bal   lab
Balder   red Lab (Labrador retreiver)
bals   slab
ban   nab
banyan   nay, nab
bar a   Arab
bard   drab
bat   tab
baton   no tab
bats   stab
bed   Deb, deb (Debbie, debutante)
(Brian) Benben (actor)   neb-neb
bid   dib
bin   nib
binder   red nib
bog   gob
bon   nob
bonder   red nob
brag   garb
bro   orb
bros.   sorb
bud   dub

bun nub
buns snub
bur rub
burg grub
bus sub
but tub
buts stub
cam mac
cap pac
cares serac
caw WAC
cit. (citizen, cited) tic
cod doc
cork (Ray) Kroc
cram marc
crap parc (park)
dahs shad
dam mad
Damon nomad
dat tad
daw wad
de Ed
decaf faced
decal laced
decap paced
decider rediced
dedal laded
deem meed
deer reed
defer refed
deifier reified
Deiter retied
Delbert trebled
delf fled
deli I led
delit tiled
deliver reviled
demit timed
den Ned
Dennis sinned

Denton (town) not Ned
depot toped
depots stoped
dessert tressed
desserts stressed
detar rated
devas saved
devil lived
dew wed
dial laid
dialer relaid
diaper repaid
dig gid
dig rut turgid
dim mid
dimit timid
dine Enid
dioramas samaroid
do od
dog god
don nod
doom mood
door rood
DOS, dos sod
draw ward
drawer reward
Draw? No. onward
drawn us sunward
Draw, oh. Howard
draws sward
Draw? Yah. Hayward
dray yard
ear Rae
Edam (city) made
Edison no side
edit tide
eel Lee, lee
e'en née
eh? he
el le

Elaps	spale	gums	smug
Elbert	treble	guns	snug
Ellen	Nelle	gut	tug
Eliot	toile	hahs	shah
em	me	haiku	Ukiah, California
Emil	lime	hales	selah
emir	rime (alternate spelling)	har har	rah, rah
emit	time	Harpo	Oprah
ergo	ogre	harpoon	No, Oprah.
Eris	rise	Harrison	No sir, rah!
Eros	sore	haw	wah (panda)
Eton	note	hay	yah
Evian (trademark)	naïve	ho	oh
Evan	nave	hoop	pooh
evil	live	I'm, alas	salami
fir	rif	idol	Lodi (town)
fires	serif	I'm	mi
flow	wolf	I maim	Miami
gal	lag	I moan	Naomi
gals	slag	Ira's	sari
gar	rag	IRS	sri
gas	sag	is	si
gat	tag	it	Ti, ti
gateman	name tag	jar	raj
gats	stag	Kay	yak
gel	leg	keel	leek
gem	Meg	keels	sleek
Gibbons	snob, big	keep	peek
(Bill) Giles	(Bud) Selig	knaps	spank
gin	nig (to nidge)	knar	rank
girder	red rig	knits	stink
girt	trig	K.O.	O.K.
gnat	tang	Kool (trade name)	look
gnats	stang (British dialect)	lap	pal
gnaw	Wang	lair	rial
gnus	sung	lager	regal
golf	flog	leer	reel
got	tog	Leon	Noël, noel
gulp	plug	liar	rail
gum	mug	lien	Neil

leper   repel

lever   revel

lit   'til

loop   pool

loops   spool

loot   tool

looter   retool

loots   stool

mal-   lam

map   Pam

maps   spam, Spam (trade name)

mar   RAM, ram

marcs   scram

mart   tram

Mason, mason   No, Sam.

mat   tam (tam-o'-shanter)

may   yam

meet   teem

Megan   nag 'em

megaton   not a gem

Mets   stem

mho   (Georg Simon) Ohm, ohm

moor   room

mot   Tom, tom

motmot   tom-tom

murmur   Rum! Rum!

Mustafa (Kemal)   a fat sum

namer   reman

nap   pan

naps   span

nature's   Serutan (trade name)

Nemo   omen

net   ten

nip   pin

nips   spin

nit   tin

no   on

Nola's   salon

no mar   Ramon

no net   tenon

nor   Ron

Norton   not Ron

Norris   sir, Ron

no scut   Tucson (Arizona)

not   ton

no tar   rat on, Raton (New Mexico)

notes   Seton

no tip   piton

not narcs   Scranton (city)

not now   wonton

not sip   piston

now   won

nut   tun

nuts   stun

oat   Tao

os   so

Oy!   Yo!

pacer   recap

pals   slap

pans   snap

par   rap

parcs   scrap

part   trap

parts   strap

pa's   sap

pat   tap

pay   yap

peels   sleep

per   rep

(Ross) Perot   to rep

pets   step

pilot   to lip

pins   snip

pit   tip

piton   no tip

(Henri) Pitot, pitot (tube)   to tip

pools   sloop

ports   strop

pot   top

pots   stop

rat tar

rats star

raw war

rebut tuber

recaps spacer

red net tender

red now wonder

redraw; red, raw warder

reknit tinker

reknits stinker

relit tiler

remit timer

repot toper

rewets stewer

rot tor

saps spas

satraps Sparta's

saved Vedas

saw was

scares seracs

sew Wes (Wesley)

Sex? Aw! waxes

sex is sixes

shay yahs (yesses)

sit 'tis

sleets steels

sloops spools

smart trams

smut Tums (trade name)

snaps spans

snips spins

snoops spoons

snoot toons

spans snaps

spat taps

spay yaps

spaz zaps

spit tips

sports strops

spot tops

spots stops

sprat tarps

stat tats

stew wets

straw warts

Suez Zeus

sway yaws

T. Eliot toilet

tort trot

way yaw

DROP-LETTER REVERSALS

In order to make palindromic phrases, first make reversals of the words in this list by dropping the first or last letter. Dmitri Borgmann calls these *drop-letter reversals*, and wordsmith Chris McManus calls them *embedded reversals*. Borgmann's *Language on Vacation* (1965) supplied these examples. *Pollage* is a rare word for "poll tax," "capitation," or "extortion."

*a*ssuaged degauss

*a*rab-yaws sway bar

*o*ne myriad dairymen

*r*egallop pollage

*r*euniter retinue

*s*ibilate et alibi

animativ*e* vitamin A

dairyma*n* a myriad

relativ*e* vitaler

rotativel*y* levitator

ANCHORED REVERSALS

In these *anchored reversals* created by Dmitri Borgmann in *Language on Vacation* (1965) the first letter in each word or name is dropped.

*C*atalpa   *L*a Plata (Argentina)
*N*airobi (Kenya)   *c*iboria

IN A WORD, SINGULAR PALINDROMES

These single-word palindromes will help you think in reverse and compose pals of your own.

A Dictionary of One-Word Palindromes

ABA / Aba (city) /aba
Abba (music group)
Ada (Ohio and trade name)
aga (agha)
aha
ah-ha
aiaia (aiaiai)
aka / a.k.a.
ala / à la
alla
alula
AMA
amma
ana
anna
anona
Asosa (Ethiopia)
bib
bob
boob

bub
Cabac (Michigan)
civic
dad
deed
degaged
degged (British dialect)
deified
deled
denned
detannated
dewed
did
dud
ecce
eke
Eleele (Hawaii)
ere
esse
Eve/eve
ewe
Gagag (India)
gag
gig
Glenelg (Maryland, Scotland, Nova Scotia)
hah
hah-hah
huh
Idi (Sumatra, Indonesia)
Ii (river and town, Finland)
Ili (river and district, Russia)
Iliili (American Samoa)
Iki (Island, Japan)
Imi (Ethiopia)
Inini (French Guiana)
Iri (South Korea)
Iriri (river, Brazil)
kaiak (kayak)
Kanak

Kanakanak (Arkansas)	pep
Kavak (town in Turkey)	pip
kayak (kaiak)	pip-pip
kayakayak (Arkansas)	poop
Kazak	pop
Keek	pull(-)up
Kinik (Turkey)	pup
kook	put(-)up
krk (island and town, Yugoslavia)	radar
Kuk (river, Arkansas)	redder
La Sal (Utah)	refer
Laval (France and Quebec province)	Reger (Missouri)
lavalaval	reifier
ma'am	Remer (Minnesota)
madam	repaper
Malayalam	retter
marram	reviver
Matam (Senegal)	rotator
minim	rotavator
Mirrim (lake, Uruguay)	rotor
mom	sagas
mum	sanas
Navan (Ireland)	sayas
Neuquen (river and town, Argentina)	Sebes (Romania)
non	sees
noon	seesees
Noyon (France)	seities
nun	sememes
oho	semès
Ohopoho (Zaminia, Africa)	sesses
Okonoko (West Virginia)	sexes
omo- (shoulder)	shas
Oruro (Bolivia)	siris
Oso (Washington, and river, Zaire)	sis
Otto	sisis
Owo (Nigeria)	Socos (trade name)
Oyo (Nigeria)	solos
Oxo (trade name)	SOS
pap	stats
peep	stets

Tahat (mountain, Algeria)

tat

tebet

tenet

terret

Tip-it / Tippit (game)

tit

TNT

Tommot (Russia)

toot

tot

Towot (Sudan)

Tumut (New South Wales, Australia)

Turut (Iran and Turkey)

(King) Tut / tut

tut-tut

Wakaw (Saskatchewan)

Wassamassaw (South Carolina)

Wassaw (sound, Georgia)

Waw-waw (pedal)

wow

Xanax (trade name)

Yessey (Siberia, Russia)

Ziz (Morocco)

zzzz (buzzing or snoring sound)

CALL BACK

These people's forenames and surnames come in part from collections by Dmitri Borgmann's *Language on Vacation* (1965) and Jeff Grant's *Palindromicon* (1992).

Abba

Ada

Anissina   (M., French Olympic ice dancer)

Anna

Asa

Ava

Bab   "the Bab," Ali Muhammad of Shiraz (1819-1850), Persian religious leader; founder of Bab, also called Babi

Bob

Drakard   John, English newspaper proprietor (1775-1854)

Eve

Hannah   forename and surname

Harrah   Bill, casino founder; Toby, infielder

Kazak   Eddie, infielder

Kerek   Angela, German tennis star

Lil   short for Lilian and Lillian

Llull   Ramon, Catalan mystic and poet (ca. 1235-1316)

Nan   short for Anne and Anna

Nen   Robb, pitcher; Dick, first baseman

Odo   Eudes, French king, 888-898

Ono   Yoko

Otto

Redder   Johnny, infielder

Reyer   Louis, French composer

Sabas   Sylvia, French tennis star

Salas   Mark, catcher; a town in Peru

Seles   Monica, U.S. tennis star

Soros   George, financier

Viv *or* Vyv   Vivian

Yy   pen name of Robert Lynd, meaning "too wise"

VERTICAL PALINDROMES

Identify the palindromic word this verse, found in Arthur Pearson's *20th Century Standard Puzzle Book* (1907), suggests.

A turning point in every day,
Reversed I do not alter.
One half of me says haste away!
The other bids me falter.

The solution is *noon*. Other vertical palindromes are the word *dollop*, the trade name *OXO*, and the auto-antonymous phrase "NO *X* IN NIXON." John M. Culkin calls these invertograms and others have called them vertizontals.

Vertical Reversal

up   dn

PHONETIC PALS & REVERSALS

Here are some phonetic palindromes and reversals. I could add many other examples to both lists. Phonetically palindromic dialogue could be written if enough of these words were found. The phonetic palindrome "top spot" is also a literal or graphic palindrome.

Phonetic Palindromes

crew-work / work-crew
dry yard
easy
Funny enough.
Let Bob tell.
new moon
selfless
Sorry, Ross.

Talk, Scott.
to boot
top spot
We revere you.
We taught you.
Y'all lie.
You're caught! Talk; Roy.
You're damn mad, Roy!

Phonetic Reversals

Bach / bock   cob
back(s)   (s)cab
bar   rob
boar / bore   robe
buck   cub
butt(s)   (s)tub
cap   pack
(s)coops   spook(s)
crawl   lark
cup   Puck / puck
ether   earthy (antonymous)
feel   life
fleshpot   top shelf
fox   scoff
play   yelp
pore   rope
(s)crew   work(s)
tart   trot
we   you

IN REVERSE

BOSS in reverse reads SSOB (double S.O.B.). STROHS ON TAP, reading backwards, spells "Pat no shorts." EMBARGO—"O grab me!" (which reads palindromically "Embargo, go grab me!") was the nickname given to

Thomas Jefferson's Embargo Act of 1808, because of the many who flagrantly violated it. EVIAN, the name of a bottled water, is a reversal of "naïve." In 1968, STEVIE WONDER recorded under the anonym of Eivets Rednow, presumably to avoid a breech of contract suit by Motown Records. Fashion designer Arnold ISAACS found that his last name in reverse, Scaasi, spells success.

Sumarongi, a reversal of IGNORA-MUS, was the name of a tribe in Samuel Butler's (1835–1902) novel *Erewhon* (1872), a near-reversal of NOWHERE.

The surname MAHARG is Graham spelled backwards (probably "gray home" in Old English). One story has it that during a British dispute the name was reversed to protect those named Graham from persecution. The name Yokum is a phonetic reversal of MCCOY. Acting baseball commissioner Bud SELIG's name is a reversal of Bill GILES, president of the Philadelphia Phillies.

WORDS RECONSIDERED

LIVE ON REVILED reads backwards as "Deliver no evil." By inserting "sides reversed is" between the two phrases (a trick devised by Leigh Mercer in 1946), it forms the palindrome "'Deliver no evil,' sides reversed, is 'Live on reviled.'"

Another type of reversal is a sentence that can be read in both directions word by word, but which is not palindromic. Consider these century-old examples: "Scandalous society and life make gossips frantic." Or, "Frantic gossips make life and society scandalous."

21 WORD SQUARES & THEIR RELATIVES

HISTORIC WORD SQUARES

Mining Early Word Squares

The first palindromic sentences in English were printed in 1614, and the first English anagrams date from the 1500s. Word squares, in Latin and Greek, date back more than 2,000 years. Aristotle and Plato referred to them, and ancient Romans also enjoyed them.

The Latin word square "Sator-Rotas" was found during excavations at Pompeii, Italy, which had been buried with Herculaneum by an eruption of Mount Vesuvius in 79 A.D. The same word square was also found at archaeological sites in England and Mesopotamia. It is a combination of an acrostic and a palindrome, and its words can be read in four directions.

This Latin word square can be read, "*Sator arepo tenet opera rotas.*" Here are three possible English translations: (1) "Plant a piece of land with true seed, and the result will be as harmonious as the motion of the wheel." (2) "The reaper shall cease from his toil as the mower works his wheel." (3) Assuming Arepo is a proper name, "Arepo, the sower, guides the wheels with care." Or, "Arepo, the sower, works with the help of a wheel."

SATOR-ROTAS WORD SQUARE

```
S A T O R
A R E P O
T E N E T
O P E R A
R O T A S
```

Letters from the "Sator-Rotas" word square may be rearranged to compose a prayer: *"Oro Te, Pater; oro Te, Pater; sanas."* ("I pray to Thee, Father; I pray to thee, Father; Thou healest.") The letters also form a cross of the Latin word(s) for "Our Father," *Pater Noster* or *Paternoster,* which begin "The Lord's Prayer," found in Matthew 6:9-13 and Luke 11:2-4 in the Latin, or Vulgate, version of the Bible. Tony Augarde in *Oxford Guide* (1984) explains that the central word *tenet* (which is itself a palindrome) forms a cross in the original word square, while the remaining letters (two *A*'s and two *O*'s) can be placed at the ends of the cross to represent alpha and omega—the beginning and the end, according to Revelations, 21:6. Here is the "Paternoster Cross."

PATERNOSTER CROSS

```
                A

                P
                A
                T
                E
                R
A  P A T E R N O S T E R   O
                O
                S
                T
                E
                R

                O
```

Related Magic Squares

Tantalus in *John O'London's Weekly,* Sept 7, 1929, wrote about the magic square, long admired by mathematicians. He observed that Albert Dürer's engraving "Melencolia I" (melancholy) may be the first example in art of a *magic square,* or *Nasik square,* borrowing the name of the town in India where the first investigator of these figures lived.

In a *fourth-order magic square,* like that used by Dürer, there are 16 cells, with four rows and four columns. The numbers 1 to 16 are placed so that they total 34 in any direction. The four corners of

DÜRER'S MAGIC SQUARE (1514)

16	3	2	13
5	10	11	8
9	6	7	12
4	15	14	1

the square also add up to 34. There are other combinations of the numbers 1 to 16 which will give a total of 34 for any set of four figures forming a square. Tantalus observed that the two numbers in the middle cells of the bottom row of this magic square give the date of the painting, 1514.

Construction of magic squares was a very old pastime in the East, which continues today. Mathematicians enjoy them, and their mystical properties appeal to the superstitious. They were often engraved in metal or stone and worn as charms against plague and other evils.

WORD SQUARES & CROSSWORDS

These word squares by H. E. P. (probably Harriet Eleanor Phillimon) appeared in the London journal *N&Q*, July 16, 1859.

WORD SQUARES
H. E. P. (1859)

```
S C A R        A I S L E
C U B E        I D I O M
A B L E        S I E V E
R E E L        L O V E R
               E M E R Y

               C R E S T
C R E W        R E A C H
R A V E        E A G E R
E V E R        S C E N E
W E R E        T H R E E

               M I G H T
J U S T        I D L E R
U G L Y        G L I D E
S L I P        H E D G E
T Y P E        T R E E S
```

Form Puzzles & Early Crosswords

Form puzzles, such as word diamonds and squares, were predecessors of the *crossword*. More closely related to the crossword are the difficult and rare double forms, in which vertical and horizontal words differ. In an ordinary word square, each word runs in both directions, like the word *scar* in the first row and first column of H. E. P.'s word square above. Because a form puzzle contains no black squares, it requires more skill to construct than a crossword. Forms and crosswords are certainly more difficult to build than to solve.

Arthur Wynne originated the first crossword as we know it, then called a *word-cross*, published in the *New York World* Sunday supplement, Dec. 21, 1913. The first book of crosswords published in America appeared Apr. 10, 1924. In 1925, British newspapers adopted the American crossword, which developed a more difficult style of its own, and *les mots croisés* began appearing in France.

Constructing Word Squares

In making a word square or form puzzle, words with alternating vowels and consonants are the easiest to build on. The more consonants in the words, especially in the bottom row, the more difficult it is to create. The letters Q, J, X, V, and Z are especially challenging to the form-builder. When composing or solving a large form puzzle, at least a large dictionary and a gazetteer or atlas are essential.

Although there are no established rules in form-building, many puzzlers advise against using proper names and abbreviations not listed in standard references. A perfect form puzzle, in my view, contains no slang words, phrases, or terms that are hyphenated, rare, archaic, obsolete, regional, or strictly foreign.

Although phrases and nondictionary words are acceptable to many formists, very few are shown in the forms in this book. Many examples included here are composed of current common words.

According to puzzle historian Theodore G. Meyer, the earliest-known word square in English uses just three words "cat ate tea." It appeared in the early 1850s in "a little volume published for the curious."

```
C A T
A T E
T E A
```

Palindromic Four-Word Squares

In 1860 the *American Almanac* featured a palindromic four-word square containing three English words, *time, item,* and *emit.* According Dr. Joseph Emerson Worcester in *The Geographical Dictionary* (1817), *Meti,* the fourth word, was the name of a town in Abyssinia (now Ethiopia).

The earliest-known palindromic word square published in America which contained no foreign words was by Nellie Jay (Nellie Jones) found in "Round the Evening Lamp," in the Boston magazine *Our Young Folks,* May 1871.

PALINDROMIC FOUR-WORD SQUARES
(1860)

```
T I M E
I T E M
M E T I
E M I T
```

Nellie Jay (1871)

```
S T E W
T I D E
E D I T
W E T S
```

FIVE-WORD SQUARES

An anonymous contributor to *N&Q,* Sept. 3, 1859, provided a word square we've titled "Warning," which reads across and down: "Leave Ellen alone, venom enemy!" Compare this with the word square on p. 167 that could be read as a complete sentence: "Might idler glide hedge trees?" The puzzler states: "The conclusion to be drawn from exercises of this kind is that four letters are nothing at all; that five letters are so easy that nothing is worth notice unless the combination has meaning. Six letters, done in any way, are respectable, and seven letters would be a triumph. I have seen only one combination of five letters with meaning, as follows, given me by the friend who made it."

WARNING
(1859)

```
L E A V E
E L L E N
A L O N E
V E N O M
E N E M Y
```

Charlie B. composed the first American-made five-word square ("Light-Trent") published. It appeared in the "Headwork" column of *Our Boys & Girls*, also called *Oliver Optic's Magazine*, Feb. 1, 1868. It is similar to the five-word square "Might idler glide hedge trees?" on p. 167. Oliver Optic was the pseudonym of the magazine's editor, William Taylor Adams (1822-1897), father of puzzledom and noted story writer for young readers. Imperial made the first double word square, printed in the Toledo, Ohio, magazine, *Our Boys*, Feb. 1, 1871.

What we call word squares today were called both "word squares" and "square words" until the term *word square* was officially defined in the 1879 *Supplement to Webster's Unabridged Dictionary*: "a series of words so arranged that they can be read vertically and horizontally with the like result" resembling that shown below.

EARLIEST AMERICAN
FIVE-WORD SQUARE
Charlie B. (1868)

```
L I G H T
I D L E R
G L A R E
H E R O N
T R E N T
```

WEBSTER'S 1879 EXAMPLE

```
H E A R T
E M B E R
A B U S E
R E S I N
T R E N T
```

FIRST DOUBLE WORD SQUARE
Imperial (1871)

```
T E R M
A L O E
P L A T
S A M E
```

Double Five-Word Square

Niagara made the first double five-word square found in *Our Boys & Girls*, Feb. 1875.

DOUBLE FIVE-WORD SQUARE
Niagara (1875)

```
S T A M P
M A L A R
A P O D E
R I N G S
T R E E S
```

Palindromes & Cryptograms

This palindromic cryptogrammatic five-word square by Skeeziks was found in the column "Puzzledom" in *Golden Days*, Dec. 3, 1884.

PALINDROMIC CRYPTOGRAM
Skeeziks (1884)

```
3 2  1 2 3      L A S A L
2 5  4 5 2      A N O N A
1 4  3 4 1      S O L O S
2 5  4 5 2      A N O N A
3 2  1 2 3      L A S A L
```

The crypt solution is the word *salon*.

Polyglot Word Squares

Here are some polyglot word squares. The first one, "Polyglot" by D. C. Ver, appeared in *Ardmore Puzzler*, Jan. 15, 1907, and the second one, a ten-language double word square, was created by Chris Long on a computer in 1992.

In the five-word square titled "Polyglot," the word *damen* is German; *amico*, Italian; *mitos*, Greek; *école*, French; and *noses*, English.

POLYGLOT
D. C. Ver (1907)

```
D A M E N
A M I C O
M I T O S
E C O L E
N O S E S
```

The computer-made double word square boasts these words and ten languages: (across) *aagje*, Dutch; *falot*, French; *flirt*, English; *yttra*, Swedish; *rotol*, Italian; (down) *affyr*, Danish; *aalto*, Finnish; *glitt*, German; *jorro*, Spanish; and *ettal*, Norwegian.

POLYGLOT DOUBLE
Chris Long & Computer (1992)

```
A A G J E
F A L O T
F L I R T
Y T T R A
R O T O L
```

Connected Squares

To complicate puzzle construction still more, here are three five-word squares neatly connected to create a single form puzzle. "Connected Squares" was created by the puzzler Pedestrian for the *Danbury News* column "Witch Knots," May 13, 1876.

CONNECTED SQUARES
Pedestrian (1876)

```
                J U D E A
                U S I N G
                D I V A N
                E N A T E
C H A M P A G N E S U P P E R
H O N O R           P O L K A
A N I M A           P L A I N
M O M U S           E K I N G
P R A S E           R A N G E
```

SIX-WORD SQUARES

Circle & Square Squared

The first six-word square here, "Circle Squared," that begins with the word *circle* and ends with the word *esteem*, was first published in *N&Q*, July 2, 1859 and later in *Wilkes' Spirit of the Times*, Sept. 2, 1859. The second "improved" version omits the proper name Icarus and substitutes four new words (*inures, rudest, crease,* and *lessee*) for the former four middle words (*Icarus, rarest, create, lustre*). The second version appeared in Dmitri Borgmann's *Language on Vacation* (1965). And then we have Dmitri Borgmann's "Square Squared," published in *Newsweek*, Nov. 2, 1964.

CIRCLE SQUARED (1859)

```
C I R C L E
I C A R U S
R A R E S T
C R E A T E
L U S T R E
E S T E E M
```

"IMPROVED" CIRCLE SQUARED
(1965)

```
C I R C L E
I N U R E S
R U D E S T
C R E A S E
L E S S E E
E S T E E M
```

SQUARE SQUARED
Dmitri Borgmann (1964)

```
S Q U A R E
Q I N T A R
U N L A C E
A T A V I C
R A C I S T
E R E C T S
```

Our Young Folks Challenge

A. Langdon Root composed the first American-made six-word square, published in *Our Young Folks* magazine, Mar. 1871. The readers were given the first two words, *scions* and *catnip*, and offered the challenge of finding the other four. Of the 28 puzzlers who responded, 11 completed it. Here is the solution.

SIX-WORD CHALLENGE
(1871)

```
S C I O N S
C A T N I P
I T H A C A
O N A G E R
N I C E S T
S P A R T A
```

Several contributors formed another word square in which NICENE replaced NICEST, and SPARED, SPARES, and SPARER replaced SPARTA. Hitty Maginn stated in the Feb. 1871 issue that he made more than 100 attempts at a six-word square. In the four months following the published solution, the magazine received over two dozen six-word squares from readers. In the June issue, the editors challenged readers with a seven-word square, but results were disappointing.

WORD CUBES

Still Six Abreast

Jeff Grant in *WW*, Aug. 1978, presented these six interrelated six-word cubes. All words are from the *OED*. Each boldface letter in the upper left corner of each word cube, taken together, spells the word REMADE. Also, each of the original words from the first cube becomes the first row and first column of the succeeding cube. So, the word *enamel* heads the second cube, *macula* the third, *amulet* the fourth, *delete* the fifth, and *elater* the sixth. Also note the diagonal repetition of the word *ere* in the sixth cube.

You can also read across all six cubes. Start, for instance, with the second row of each, and read across "enamel, narine, arenas, minime, enamor, and lesere." If you read down the second cube, you will find the same words repeated. This works for all six rows, the third row matching the third cube, etc., just as all words (save the first word) from the first cube head succeeding cubes.

```
R EMADE      E NAMEL      M ACULA
E NAMEL      N ARINE      A RENAS
M ACULA      A RENAS      C ERITE
A MULET      M INIME      U NITER
D ELETE      E NAMOR      L ATERE
E LATER      L ESERE      A SERED


A MULET      D ELETE      E LATER
M INIME      E NAMOR      L ESERE
U NITER      L ATERE      A SERED
L ITOTE      E METIN      T ERENE
E METIN      T ORIED      E RENDE
T ERENE      E RENDE      R EDEEM
```

Windmill

Walter Shedlofsky in *WW*, Aug. 1973, provided this windmill of a six-word square.

```
E S C A R P
S I E V E R
C E R I S E
A V I S O S
R E S O R T
P R E S T I S S I M O
            S O O N E R
            S O R T E D
            I N T A K E
            M E E K E R
            O R D E R S
```

Word Square with Rhymed Verse Clues

The first word square printed with clues in rhymed verse was this six-word square by puzzler S. E. G. in *Our Young Folks*, May 1871.

WORD-SQUARE PUZZLE
S. E. G. (1871)

Without my first, naught can be made.	M A T T E R
My second, we wish our friends to do.	A R R I V E
To sit on my third, I am afraid.	T R I P O D
Some love my fourth, alas! 'Tis true.	T I P P L E
To see my fifth, we watch the flowers,	E V O L V E
And for my last, ask heavenly powers.	R E D E E M

Double Six-Word Squares

The puzzler Rose Budd is credited with making the first double six-word square, printed in *Danbury News*, summer 1876. But Gil Blas created the first widely-recognized example in *Wild Oats*, Aug. 22, 1878.

DOUBLE SIX-WORD SQUARE
Gil Blas (1878)

```
P A N A D A
O B E L U S
M A C L E S
A T T U N E
D E O D A R
E R N E S T
```

The words used in these double six-word squares can be found in most unabridged dictionaries. The first two squares contain most common words. The first is by Eric, published in *TE*, Dec. 1990, and the second by M. D(ouglas). McIlroy, published in *WW*, 1976, was computer-made. The third and fourth double word-squares were also computer-made by Chris Long in 1992. The words in these last two double word-squares can be found in the unabridged second edition of *Webster's New International Dictionary* (1960). The letters *X* and *J* in the top and bottom words of the fourth word-square are difficult to use in form-building.

DOUBLE SIX-WORD SQUARES

Eric (1990)	M. D. McIlroy & Computer (1976)	Chris Long & Computer (1992)	Chris Long & Computer (1992)
A S S E T S	S C H I S T	S Q U A R E	S C O L E X
S C H L E P	P R I N C E	T U N N E R	W I R I L Y
T H R A L L	R A T T O N	R O S O L I	A N A N A S
H O O P L A	I N T E N D	Y T T R I C	R E C E N T
M O U S E Y	T I E R C E	C H O A N A	A N L A C E
A L D E R S	E A R N E R	H A W K E D	J E E R E R

Progressive Word Squares

The puzzler Sphinx made the first progressive word square, published in *Wild Oats*, Oct. 8, 1876. In the progressive word square, the second letter of each word begins the word in the succeeding line. The earliest progressive six-word square was by puzzlers Ben J. Min and Comet. The two puzzle-makers independently submitted the same word combination to Hal Hazard, editor of "Marginalia" in the newspaper *Baltimore Item*. The progressive six-word square was published Mar. 19, 1881.

PROGRESSIVE SIX-WORD SQUARE
Ben J. Min and Comet (1881)

R E L A T E
E L A T E S
L A T E S T
A T E S T E
T E S T E R
E S T E R S

SEVEN-WORD SQUARES

First Seven

The first seven-word square appeared by Skeeziks in *Wild Oats*, June 27, 1877. Here are glosses on some of the words in the seven-word square: *Camargo* is a town in Bolivia, and the word *osselet* means "a small bone, such as one of the three in the ear's tympanic cavity."

SEVEN-WORD SQUARE
Skeeziks (1877)

```
C A M A R G O
A T O N E R S
M O T I V E S
A N I L I N E
R E V I V A L
G R E N A D E
O S S E L E T
```

OBSOLETE WORDS—
O So Old, Webster!

Magnificent Sevens

These seven-word squares (1 to 8) contain no phrases, no proper names, and no obsolete, rare, archaic, or hyphenated words. (1) The first seven-word square in our collection is by puzzler Hal Hazard; it appeared in "Puzzle Calls" in the *Newark Sunday Call*, May 6, 1888. (2) The second is a later version of a word square composed by William Fenwick, of the British Puzzlers' League, found in "Our Puzzle Column," the *Henry Republican* of Aug. 17, 1882. The first and second words in the original were *targets* and *avernat* (*avernal* is more familiar), and the sixth word was *stayers*. (3) A. F. Holt created this seven-word square, published in the *Henry Republican*, May 1, 1884. It uses the British spelling *sceptre*. (4, 5) These two seven-word squares are from a set of 15 by puzzler Simon Ease from the July 3, 1884 *Henry Republican*. (6, 7) These two seven-word squares were made by Chris Long on a computer in 1992. (8) Dmitri Borgmann said this seven-word square was the best square he had seen of this size. It was computer-generated by M. D. McIlroy, *WW*, Nov. 1975.

O. N. E. One composed the OBSOLETE WORDS anagram, used in our heading. It was found in "The Newark Puzzler," *NA*, Oct. 28, 1905.

1. Hal Hazard (1888)

```
P R E P A R E
R E M O D E L
E M U L A T E
P O L E M I C
A D A M A N T
R E T I N U E
E L E C T E D
```

2. William Fenwick (1882)

```
M E R G E R S
E T E R N A L
R E G A T T A
G R A V I T Y
E N T I T L E
R A T T L E R
S L A Y E R S
```

3. A. F. Holt (1884)

```
R O A S T E R
O B S C E N E
A S S E R T S
S C E P T R E
T E R T I A N
E N T R A N T
R E S E N T S
```

4. Simon Ease (1884)

```
I M P A S T O
M O U N T E D
P U R G E R Y
A N G L E R S
S T E E V E S
T E R R E N E
O D Y S S E Y
```

5. Simon Ease (1884)

```
N E S T L E S
E N T R A N T
S T R A N G E
T R A I T O R
L A N T E R N
E N G O R G E
S T E R N E R
```

6. Chris Long & Computer (1992)

```
V I S C E R A
I M P A N E L
S P I T T L E
C A T E R E R
E N T R E A T
R E L E A S E
A L E R T E D
```

7. Chris Long & Computer (1992)

```
M A C A B R E
A M A T E U R
C A N T A T A
A T T E S T S
B E A S T I E
R U T T I E R
E R A S E R S
```

8. M. D. McIlroy (1975)

```
W A S S A I L
A N T E N N A
S T R I N G Y
S E I Z U R E
A N N U L A R
I N G R A T E
L A Y E R E D
```

Seven Up

According to Sherlock Holmes, master word-square and form builder, it is ten times more difficult to build an eight-word square than a seven-word square, and ten times as hard to compose a nine-word square than an eight-word square. A double eight-word square has been thought to be as difficult to compose as the nine-word square.

The first double seven-word and eight-word squares contained very obscure words, as did the first regular nine-word square, shown here.

Chris Long's computer-made double seven-word square from 1992 is the best "double seven" I've seen. It contains no proper nouns and all words are in Webster's second unabridged dictionary.

Sherlock Holmes, at age 70, produced, without computer assistance, what I consider the second best double seven-word square, published in *TE*, Aug. 1972, and shown here. His word square contains no proper nouns, 11 words are found in Webster's second unabridged dictionary, including *vincent* (rare), meaning "victorious."

Mattie Jay published the first double seven-word square in the "Salmagundi" column of the *Baltimore Sunday News*, Oct. 19, 1882.

FIRST DOUBLE SEVEN-WORD SQUARE
Mattie Jay (1882)

```
C A R A M A N
A L A M O D E
R A V E L E D
A T E L E N E
B E N I S O N
A R E N O S E
S E R E N E S
```

"BEST" DOUBLE SEVEN-WORD SQUARE
Chris Long & Computer (1992)

```
S M A S H E S
P O N T I N E
I N G R A T E
R E L A T E R
A S I N I N E
L I N G O T S
S A G E N E S
```

DOUBLE SEVEN-WORD SQUARE
Sherlock Holmes (1972)

```
M A R A R I E
I D O L I N G
S E M E N C E
A L A R G E S
V I N C E N T
E N C E N S E
R E E S T E D
```

EIGHT-WORD SQUARES
Eights First

Dona Telore, who edited the monthly journal *Fairmount Puzzler*, built the first eight-word square on June 18, 1884 and published it July 31, 1884. He composed it nearly a month and a half before an identical square was published under the pseudonyms C. U. Rious and Will Dexter. Use of the same combination of words was coincidental. Dona Telore explained that he had not printed his word square sooner because he wanted to sell it, but had not received a suitable offer.

About two weeks before he claimed to have composed his eight-word square, *Newark Puzzler* editor Adonis showed at least three of his own to other formists. Each of his word squares was missing one letter. C. U. Rious, after reading Dona Telore's claim that he made an eight-word square, but not seeing Telore's word square or that by Adonis (below), submitted his nearly finished square to Will Dexter. Dexter finished it with four letters, by using a larger dictionary.

FIRST EIGHT-WORD SQUARE
Dona Telore (1884)

```
G A D A W A R A
A N E L A C E S
D E T A S T E S
A L A N T I N E
W A S T I N G S
A C T I N I A S
R E E N G A G E
A S S E S S E D
```

EIGHT-WORD SQUARE
Adonis (1884)

```
_ R A G T A R A
R E T R A C E S
A T L A N T E S
G R A P L I N E
T A N L I N G S
A C T I N I A S
R E E N G A G E
A S S E S S E D
```

EIGHT-WORD SQUARE
Simon Ease (1884)

```
B A P T I S T A
A T L A N T E S
P L U N D E R S
T A N N I N G E
I N D I C T E R
S T E N T E S T
T E R G E S T E
A S S E R T E D
```

EIGHT-WORD SQUARE
C. U. Rious (1884)

```
P A R A P A R A
A N E L A C E S
R E   A S T E S
L A N T I N E A
P A S T I N G S
A C T I N I A S
R E E N G A G E
A S S E S S E D
```

REVISED EIGHT-WORD SQUARE
Jarep & Bolis (1884)

```
B A P T I S T A
A I L A N T U S
P L U N D E R S
T A N N I N G E
I N D I C T E R
S T E N T E S T
T U R G E S C E
A S S E R T E D
```

Simon Ease made the second eight-word square to be published; it appeared Sept. 13, 1884 in "Our Puzzle Column," *Henry Republican*. Jarep, the first puzzler to compile a word list for building forms, showed Bolis how, by altering two words, the geographical name *Tergeste* could be eliminated in the word square. *Tergeste* is replaced with *turgesce* and the second word *Atlantes* with *ailantus*. That left only two objectionable words, *Baptista*, a character from Shakespeare's *Taming of the Shrew* (1593), and *Tanninge*, another geographical name. Jarep and Bolis's revised eight-word square appeared in *Newark Puzzler*, Oct. 1884.

Eric Albert composed the "Best Eight-Word Square" on a computer. (See p.179.) All of its words are in Webster's second unabridged dictionary, except *pimenton*, which appears in *Webster's New World Dictionary*, third college edition. Margaretta Strohm built the "'Second Best' Eight-Word Square," without computer aid. The original word in the sixth position was *cantoral*, according to *TE*, Nov. 1926.

BEST EIGHT-WORD SQUARE
Eric Albert & Computer (1989)

```
O P A L E S C E
P I M E N T O N
A M E N D I N G
L E N T A N D O
E N D A N G E R
S T I N G I N G
C O N D E N S E
E N G O R G E D
```

FIRST DOUBLE EIGHT-WORD SQUARE
Tunste (1901)

```
F A T A L I S M
A M A R A N T A
T A L E N G E S
A R E S T E R S
L A N T E N N E
I N T E R N A T
S T E N N E T T
T E S S E R A E
```

"SECOND BEST" EIGHT-WORD SQUARE
Margaretta Strohm (1926)

```
A G A R I C U S
G E N E R A N T
A N A C O N D A
R E C A N T E R
I R O N W O R T
C A N T O N A L
U N D E R A G E
S T A R T L E D
```

"Q" EIGHT-WORD SQUARE
Chris Long & Computer (1992)

```
Q U A D R I A D
U N T R A N C E
A T L A N T I C
D R A I S I N E
R A N S O M E D
I N T I M A T E
A C I N E T A N
D E C E D E N T
```

Tunste made the first double eight-word square, published in *Daily Inter-Ocean,* Oct. 15, 1901.

The "Q" Eight-Word Square, computer-made by Chris Long, is the only one of its size.

The Connected Double Eight-Word Square, which he also discovered, is the only one composed entirely of words in Merriam-Webster's dictionaries. He created both the "Q" and the connected word squares in 1992.

CONNECTED DOUBLE EIGHT-WORD SQUARES
Chris Long & Computer (1992)

```
C A I M A C A M E S D A M E S
A G M I N A T E X P I R A N T
I M P L A N T S P R A T T L E
M I L K M A I D I A M E T E R
A N A M I R T A R T E S I A N
C A N A R I U M A T T I N G S
A T T I T U D E N L E A G U E
M E S D A M E S T E R N S E T
```

Here are two more eight-word squares found by Chris Long's computer search in 1992. Richard Sabey created the final eight-word square with computer aid and words from *Webster's Third New International*

Dictionary, unabridged (1971). Sabey's word square was published in *WW*, Aug. 1995.

MORE EIGHT-WORD SQUARES

Chris Long & Computer (1992)

```
B I G A M I S T
I M A G I N E R
G A M E S O M E
A G E N E S I S
M I S E D I T S
I N O S I T O L
S E M I T O N E
T R E S S L E T
```

Chris Long & Computer (1992)

```
B E C L A S P S
E P H E M E R A
C H A P E R O N
L E P O R I N E
A M E R I C A N
S E R I C A T E
P R O N A T E S
S A N E N E S S
```

Richard Sabey (1995)

```
N E A T H E R D
E N G R A V E R
A G M I N A T E
T R I N D L E S
H A N D G U N S
E V A L U A T E
R E T E N T O R
D R E S S E R S
```

THE NINE-WORD SQUARE— Quaint Wonders Here

Arthur F. Holt made the first nine-word square, which appeared as puzzle #10,000 in the Chicago *Sunday Inter-Ocean*, Dec. 28, 1897. Better nine-word squares by Holt and others were published soon thereafter. The *Ardmore Puzzler*, Nov. 15, 1904, featured ten of Holt's nine-word squares. Hercules composed the anagram THE NINE-WORD SQUARE—"quaint wonders here," which says it all.

Clues to the second nine-word square shown on p. 181 were given in *TE*, Sept. 1992. It was computer-generated by Chris Long, who published it, his first word square, under the NPL pseudonym Cubist. It is composed of unhyphenated lowercase dictionary words, all but one of which (*trabeatae*), are in the *OED*.

An interesting aspect of Chris Long's "Easeresse" nine-word square, published in *TE*, June 1993, is the number of common words it contains. The words *echolalia, altimeter, ileitises,* and *dissevers* are from *Merriam-Webster's Collegiate Dictionary*, 10th edition (1993). *Vespacide, sheetless,* and *poeticise* are from the second edition, unabridged *Webster's New International Dictionary* (1960), and *calcevive* and *easeresse* are from the *OED*.

FIRST NINE-WORD SQUARE
Arthur Holt (1897)

```
Q U A R E L E S T
U P P E R E S T E
A P P O I N T E R
R E O M E T E R S
E R I E V I L L E
L E N T I L L I N
E S T E L L I N E
S T E R L I N G S
T E R S E N E S S
```

COMPUTER-MADE NINE-WORD SQUARES
Chris Long & Computer (1992)

```
B O R T S C H E S
O V E R T R U S T
R E P A R E N C E
T R A B E A T A E
S T R E S T E L L
C R E A T U R A L
H U N T E R I T E
E S C A L A T E S
S T E E L L E S S
```

Chris Long & Computer (1992)

```
V E S P A C I D E
E C H O L A L I A
S H E E T L E S S
P O E T I C I S E
A L T I M E T E R
C A L C E V I V E
I L E I T I S E S
D I S S E V E R S
E A S E R E S S E
```

More Nines

The nine-word square based on *mergences* was created by Eric Albert and his computer. It was the first nine-word square composed entirely of words from one source, Webster's second unabridged dictionary. Most formists believed that such a square would be impossible. It could be said that its only (minor) flaws are the capitalized word *Sturnidae* and the obsolete word *circumfer*. *WW, Nov. 1991,* featured an interesting article by Mr. Albert, a computer scientist and noted crossword constructor, on how he developed his program to find the square in June 1989.

Here are two more squares made by Chris Long with his trusty computer. Every word in the "Reedlesse" square is in the *OED*. This was the second nine-word square made of words from a single source, published in *TE*, Sept. 1993.

Although the "Serenesse"-based word square from *TE*, Feb. 1993, contains a hyphenated word, it also has two *X*s, two *Z*s, and three *K*s—letters difficult to use in any word square or form. Remarkably, six words in this nine-word square contain at least one of these difficult letters. All words can be found in Webster's second unabridged dictionary, except *karatekas*, from *Chambers Dictionary* (1994), which means "karate experts," and *epoxidize* from the unabridged *Webster's Third New International Dictionary* (1971) and the *OED*. All three are excellent examples of nine-word squares.

SINGLE-SOURCE NINES
Eric Albert & Computer (1991)

```
N E C E S S I S M
E X I S T E N C E
C I R C U M F E R
E S C A R P I N G
S T U R N I D A E
S E M P I T E R N
I N F I D E L I C
S C E N A R I Z E
M E R G E N C E S
```

STILL NINE WORDS
Chris Long & Computer (1992)

```
W O R C E S T E R
O V E R L A R G E
R E C O I N A G E
C R O S S T I E D
E L I S I O N A L
S A N T O N A T E
T R A I N A G E S
E G G E A T E R S
R E E D L E S S E
```

```
K A R A T E K A S
A P O C O P A T E
R O S E C O L O R
A C E T O X I M E
T O C O K I N I N
E P O X I D I Z E
K A L I N I T E S
A T O M I Z E R S
S E R E N E S S E
```

TEN-WORD SQUARES

A. F. Holt built the first ten-word square, shown here in slightly modified form, published in *TE,* Dec. 1921. It was composed entirely of tautonyms and based on a technique conceived by Tunste a year earlier. In the original square, the word *orangutang* was originally *arangarang* and the word *tangatanga* was originally *rangaranga.* Gyles Brandreth in *Joy of Lex* (1980) discusses definitions and sources.

TAUTONYMIC "TEN"
A. F. Holt (1921)

```
O R A N G U T A N G
R A N G A R A N G A
A N D O L A N D O L
N G O T A N G O T A
G A L A N G A L A N
U R A N G U T A N G
T A N G A T A N G A
A N D O L A N D O L
N G O T A N G O T A
G A L A N G A L A N
```

Top Ten & Double Nine

Word Ways has published ten-word squares without tautonyms. Jeff Grant created ten-word squares, with each containing at least one word not listed in a standard reference. Recent work by Eric Albert, Chris Long, and Jeff Grant suggests that an all-dictionary ten-word square might eventually be composed, but, according to Palmer Peterson, "the chance of a genuine" double nine-word square is "nil." Chris Long has written articles on square-building in *WW,* Feb. 1993 and May 1993 issues.

WORD-SQUARE NOVELTIES

A Matter of Chronology

Clues to "A Chronological Square" were originally given in verse with fictional events on the dates. It was made by Ernest Ager and published in *AP*, Sept. 15, 1905. The version shown here is from Dmitri Borgmann's *Language on Vacation* (1965).

A CHRONOLOGICAL SQUARE
Ernest Ager (1905)

Decoding the Dates

3850 B.C. The dawn of Egyptian civilization.	M M M D C C C L
2860 B.C. Cheops the pyramid-builder reigns.	M M D C C C L X
1870 B.C. The 12th Dynasty is in power.	M D C C C L X X
880 B.C. Assyria recovers its preeminence.	D C C C L X X X
385 B.C. Aristotle will be born next year.	C C C L X X X V
286 B.C. Demetrius surrenders to Seleucus.	C C L X X X V I
187 B.C. Antiochus III is dead, alas!	C L X X X V I I
88 B.C. Sulla marches on Rome.	L X X X V I I I

Not Just Square

Here are more word-square novelties. The Poser composed a "Cryptogrammatic" in *Wild Oats*, May 10, 1876. Old Joe created the "Square within a Square" in *Danbury News*, Apr. 29, 1876, and O. Possum the "Acrostic Square with Enclosed Diamond" in the *Saturday Evening Post*, 1879.

CRYPTOGRAMMATIC
The Poser (1876)

```
1 2 3 2 1    M A D A M
2 4 5 6 2    A R E N A
3 5 7 8 6    D E I G N
2 6 8 9 0    A N G L O
1 2 6 0 4    M A N O R
```

SQUARE WITHIN A SQUARE
Old Joe (1876)

```
F I R S T
I R A T E
R A C E R
S T E A M
T E R M S
```

ACROSTIC SQUARE WITH ENCLOSED DIAMOND
O. Possum (1879)

```
W I T C H
I S O L A
T O P A Z
C L A R E
H A Z E L
```

22 FORM PUZZLES

THE COMPLETE PUZZLER

Form puzzles draw on the multiple skills of anagrammatist, palindromist, and crossword puzzler. And perhaps one must be as patient as an engineer in their construction, carefully bridging words and admitting no gaps between. Puzzlers everywhere have benefited from the talents of 19th and 20th century puzzlemeisters Bolis, Skeeziks, Sherlock Holmes, and others who have excelled as master builders of form puzzles. In the late 20th century, a new breed of puzzlers has built complex form and other word puzzles with the aid of a computer.

Here are some highlights of puzzle history, from early word squares, that suggest the magic squares of mathematicians, to the sturdy-legged final conceit of Sherlock Holmes's "Armless Man." Many form puzzles have been given titles for easy reference. The puzzler's name, usually a pseudonym, and the date are given when known. To discover the puzzler behind the pseudonym, consult the index Puzzlers & Their Pseudonyms.

Early Broadsides, Journals & Magazines

The first American journal devoted to the art of the puzzle was the *Nutcrackers' Monthly*, edited and published by W. L. Small of Auburn, Maine, from Jan. 1875 to Aug. 1876. According to Theodore Meyer, in the 30 years that followed, 127 puzzle broadsides and journals appeared in the United States and Canada. More than half were published in Philadelphia. Most were monthlies with an average life span of two issues. Although many were produced by teenage amateurs, nearly all were of professional quality.

Many form puzzles and other oddities collected in this book have been selected from those rare publications. Most were found in newspapers and magazines published since the mid-19th century.

MASTER BUILDERS

Skeeziks (1852-1935)

Perhaps the most famous "unknown" puzzler in the golden age of puzzledom was William L. Ougheltree (1852-1935) of Rondout, Tarrytown, and New York. He wrote under many pen names, but submitted most of his work under the pseudonyms Mrs. Harris and Skeeziks.

Ougheltree was one of the most versatile puzzlers in his time and, undoubtedly, the most original. He invented at least fifteen puzzles and was the author of the classic anagram WASHINGTON CROSSING THE DELAWARE—"He saw his ragged Continentals row," used as an example by *Collier's Encyclopedia* for many years. He was well known for his form puzzles, which depend upon a deft arrangement of letters in words.

Skeeziks built the first seven-letter word square, published in *Wild Oats* magazine's puzzle column "Oats to Sift" on June 27, 1877. He introduced the "checkerboard" word square in the Aug. 29, 1877 issue. A *sarn*, in provincial English, means "stepping-stone" or "pavement."

CHECKERBOARD WORD SQUARE
Skeeziks (1877)

```
M A S T
S C A R
A L A R
H O V E
  S E R E
O R E S
  S E N T
E A S T
```

Ougheltree's career in puzzling spanned nearly 40 years, beginning before the American Civil War and extending into the late 1890s. Little is known about his activities outside *the-dom*, or *The Dom*, which meant puzzledom, EPL style, members of the EPL, or amateurdom. He was a consultant for *Webster's International Dictionary* in 1890 and its supplement, published the following year. Skeeziks may have derived *The Dom* from *thedom* (*theedom*, *thedam*), a word now obsolete, found in Geoffrey Chaucer's *Canterbury Tales*, "The Shipman's Tale" (1386), and other medieval sources, meaning "thriving" or "prosperity."

Arty Fishel, Puzzle Dean (1865-1906)

Theodore G. Meyer, aka Arty Fishel, has been considered the dean or father of organized puzzledom. From 1895 to 1906 he edited what was then the most prominent puzzle column in America, "Puzzledom," in *Golden Days for Boys & Girls*, a Philadelphia weekly magazine. He has also written over 1,000 encyclopedic articles on the subject. In *A Key to Puzzledom* (1906), published by William Delaney for the EPL, Meyer stated that the earliest American puzzle column appeared in 1802 in the *Farmer's Almanack*, published in Boston.

Bolis (1866-1887)

Born in New York, New York, George B. Haywood lived in Rutherford, New Jersey, from age five. The young puzzlemeister died of tuberculosis in 1887, while he was serving his second term as EPL editor. He had just turned 21 years old. He was popularly known by his pseudonym Bolis (earlier Bolus).

Although Haywood was best known for verse puzzles, like Skeeziks, he was equally adept at most, if not all puzzle types, both as a composer and solver. He built the first twelve-word inverted half-square, published in the column "Puzzledom" in *Golden Days* magazine, Mar. 22, 1884. A revision appeared 22 years later in the book *A Key to Puzzledom* (1906). The Bolis "Hexdecagon" is from the column "Puzzle Calls" in the *Newark Sunday Call*, Apr. 3, 1887.

TWELVE-WORD INVERTED HALF-SQUARE
Bolis (1884)

```
                  C
                R A
              H E R
            M A G E
          M A B E L
        C O N I N E
        C I N G L E S
      M O N T O I R S
    M A N G O S T A N
    H A B I L I T A T E
  R E G E N E R A T E S
C A R E L E S S N E S S
```

REVISED TWELVE-WORD INVERTED HALF-SQUARE
Bolis (1906)

```
                  H
                D O
              H E M
            M A G E
          M A B E L
        C O N I N E
        C I N G L E S
      M O N T O I R S
    M A N G O S T A N
    H A B I L I T A T E
  D E G E N E R A T E S
H O M E L E S S N E S S
```

HEXDECAGON
Bolis (1887)

```
          R I G
          A C E
          D O N
        C I S T I
  R A D I C A L N E S S
  I C O S A H E D R O N
  G E N T L E M A N L Y
        I N D A L
          E R N
          S O L
          S N Y
```

Sherlock Holmes, the Amazing (1902-1979)

Palmer Peterson, aka Sherlock Holmes, constructed nearly a quarter of the more than a thousand nine-word squares published in the United States, and he constructed at least 25 double eight-word squares. This puzzler, a Norwegian bachelor farmer, completed only eight years of formal schooling, but this was by no means the end of his education. He had an enormous vocabulary. In his 50th year as a formist in 1970, he stated that he had compiled well over one million words of up to seventeen letters. He continued collecting words and building forms until his death at age 77 in 1979. Except for occasional visits with friends in different parts of the United States, he spent his entire life on his farm near Worthing, South Dakota.

GETTING INTO SHAPE

Here are words bent into shape in diverse form puzzles. Each letter serves as a brick vital to the construction of a newfound word architecture. Word squares might have been the first stable houses of the word puzzle trade, but these form puzzles are delightful curiosities that please the eyes and the mind. Observe their nuances.

Non Plus in the *Chicago Daily Tribune*, Nov. 30, 1878, created the "Square & Diamond Inside." Rom Dos built the "Reversible Inverted Half-Square" from *TE*, June 1993, and the "Connected Reversible Inverted Half-Squares" from *TE*, Apr. 1995. Tom A. Hawk composed the "Double Half-Square," found in *Newark Sunday Call*, May 12, 1889. My "The Top" appeared in *WF*, June 1995. King Cotton made the "Progressive Half-Square," published in *Waverley*, Nov. 6, 1879. R. O. Chester published "Diagonal Square" in *Inter-Ocean*, Feb. 10, 1895; it reads across and left-to-right diagonally. A diagonal reversible square by Ed Ward was published in Oct. 1886 and later in the book *A Key to Puzzledom* (1906), but it contained suffixes, prefixes, little-known names, and obsolete words. The "Left & Right Lattice" by Fanacro was published in *TE*, June 1975.

SQUARE & DIAMOND INSIDE

Non Plus (1878)

```
O B E S E
B R A W L
E A V E S
S W E D E
E L S E S
```

REVERSIBLE INVERTED HALF-SQUARE

Rom Dos (1993)

```
N A M E T A G
L A M I N A
D I M I T
T I M E
D A M
L A
N
```

DOUBLE HALF-SQUARE
Tom A. Hawk (1889)

```
        P
      M A
    C A R
  H A R E
C U M I N
L A M E N T
M I N E R A L
R O S T R A T E
M A L L E A T E S
L E T T E R L E S S
```

PROGRESSIVE HALF-SQUARE
King Cotton (1897)

```
O
O R
O R A
O R A N
O R A N G
O R A N G E
O R A N G E R
O R A N G E R Y
```

CONNECTED REVERSIBLE INVERTED HALF-SQUARES
Rom Dos (1995)

```
F A C E D I M I T
M A D E D I T
P A C O D
M A L
F
```

DIAGONAL SQUARE
R. O. Chester (1895)

```
P E R O G U E
S A L I N A S
P A R A D E D
P A L A T E S
D E R I D E S
P A R O T I D
M A N T L E S
```

THE TOP
O. V. Michaelsen (1995)

```
        A C T
        B O A
        S N L
        E V E
        N E B
        T R E
        A S A
P R O T A R S U S
  E D I T I O N
    D O I N E
      N O G
        N
```

LEFT & RIGHT LATTICE
Fanacro (1975)

```
I S O S C E L E S
S A R A H       T
O R A L E       R
S A L V E       E
C H E E R L E S S
E       L I M A S
L       E M O T E
E       S A T Y R
S T R E S S E R S


T E A M S T E R S
E       H A V O C
A       O K A P I
M       R E D E S
S H O R T N E S S
T A K E N       O
E V A D E       R
R O P E S       E
S C I S S O R E D
```

First Halves

C. T. Hat created the first regular half-square, published *Our Boys & Girls* in 1873. The shape is a mirror image of the "Reversible Inverted Half-Square," The puzzler Icicle made the first inverted half-square, in the shape of the "Double Half-Square" shown here. Icicle's version appeared in *Danbury News*, Nov. 20, 1875.

Sequential Word Squares

In the *National Tribune,* Jan. 3, 1895, editor of the column "Mystery," R. O. Chester, stated that the puzzler Nypho wanted to compose seven sonnets paired with squares containing the word *sonnets* in each of the seven positions. Majolica referred to these as "sequential squares." The third square in the example here contains the proper name Ararat (or Arafat). Notice how the word *atoner* can be read across all six sequential word squares.

I developed the first, third, and last word squares, but the second by Will A. Mette (June 4, 1882), fourth by Robert Dow (May 7, 1876), and fifth by Dandy Lion (Sept. 11, 1881) appeared in the (Newark) *Sunday Call.*

SEQUENTIAL SQUARES
O. V. Michaelsen (1992) & Others (1876-1882)

ATONER	TABARD	ARARAT
TAMALE	ATONER	RETARE
OMASUM	BOGGLE	ATONER
NASUTE	ANGLES	RANDOM
ELUTED	RELETS	AEROLA
REMEDY	DRESSY	TERMAS
PLEASE	ASTRAL	PANADA
LISTEN	STRATA	AMULET
ESCORT	TRIPOD	NUMERO
ATONER	RAPINE	ALEVIN
SERENE	ATONER	DERIDE
ENTREE	LADERS	ATONER

 *A combination and a form indeed.* —**William Shakespeare**

The first sequential word squares were seven-word squares made by Sphinx and published in Feb. 1895. Others soon appeared under the pseudonyms H. S. Nut, Tom A. Hawk, Poly, Phil Down, and Arty Ess. These were followed by eight-word sequential squares from A. F. Holt, Mentor, Tunste, and Majolica.

Foreign-Word Squares

Balmar in "On the Square" in *TEE*, Nov. 15, 1905, explains: "While on the subject of squares, it may not be amiss to quote one in French by Skeeziks and one in Spanish by the writer Balmar (Frank T. Koons)." The first appeared in *Thedom*, May 1894; the second square is from *TEE*, June 1902. Balmar continues: "It may be said that word squares are of ancient origin. A two-letter (Latin) specimen, said to have been discovered in the year one A.D." is this:

        AN
        NO(DOMINI)

The Icelandic and Italian word squares shown here were found in Dmitri Borgmann's *Language on Vacation* (1965).

Shown here is the first Spanish seven-word square. Other forms by the puzzler Skeeziks in *Thedom*, May 1894, included the first three Spanish five-word squares, one of which was double. Skeeziks also created the first French five-word square; two seven-word diamonds, one in French and one in Italian; and two English five-

word squares, a double and a double reversible.

FRENCH
Skeeziks (1894)

R A M P A N T
A M A R R E R
M A R O T T E
P R O J E T S
A R T E R E S
N E T T E T E
T R E S S E R

SPANISH
Balmar (1902)

C A R A C O L
A D A M A R A
R A M A D A S
A M A N A R A
C A D A V E R
O R A R E I S
L A S A R S E

ICELANDIC
Dmitri Borgmann (1965)

T A M A S T A
A D A L V A R
M A K L E G T
A L L I L L A
S V E L L I D
T A G L I N U
A R T A D U R

ITALIAN
Dmitri Borgmann (1965)

S T A C C A T A
T O R E A D O R
A R I S T O N E
C E S S E R A N
C A T E N A T A
A D O R A T O R
T O N A T O R I
A R E N A R I O

Chris Long built these Dutch, German, Italian, Norwegian, and French word squares (below) by computer in 1992. Each foreign-language word square is composed of common, unhyphenated words; no proper nouns are used. The French word *éternels*, in the French word square, is the only accented word. Note the diagonal row of *E*s in the German word square.

Chris Long's Foreign-Word Squares

DUTCH

```
Z A K L A M P
A C R I B I E
K R I J S E N
L I J M E R S
A B S E N T E
M I E R T J E
P E N S E E L
```

GERMAN

```
W A E L Z T E
A B H A U E N
E H R T E S T
L A T E N T E
Z U E N D E N
T E S T E S T
E N T E N T E
```

ITALIAN

```
A C C O S T O
C I A S C U N
C A M P A T O
O S P I T E R
S C A T O L A
T U T E L E R
O N O R A R E
```

NORWEGIAN

```
K A S K A D E
A P P A R A T
S P I N E T T
K A N T A T E
A R E A L E R
D A T T E R A
E T T E R A T
```

FRENCH

```
M A R B R I E R
A M A R A N T E
R A B A T T E S
B R A S I E R S
R A T I O N N A
I N T E N S E S
E T E R N E L S
R E S S A S S A
```

DIAMONDS, a Puzzler's Best Friend

Another variation on the word square is the diamond-shaped puzzle. In regular diamonds, like these first two, each word may be read horizontally and vertically. By changing some of the words in these double elevens, the horizontal and vertical words may differ.

The first diamond, by Towhead, was published in the *Chicago Daily Tribune*, June 21, 1879. The second is by Tom A. Hawk and published in *Newark Call*, Sept. 4, 1881. The puzzler Daunter composed the third diamond shown here. It was the first double eleven-line diamond to be published, found in *Wild Oats*, June 13, 1878.

DIAMONDS
Towhead (1879)

```
        M
      M A P
    P A N E D
  P E N I C I L
M A N I P U L A R
M A N I P U L A T E D
  P E C U L A T E D
    D I L A T E D
      L A T E D
        R E D
          D
```

Tom A. Hawk (1881)

```
          P
        M A P
      H O N E D
    H E L I C E S
  M O L E C U L A R
P A N I C U L A T E D
  P E C U L A T E D
    D E L A T O R
      S A T E R
        R E D
          D
```

Daunter (1878)

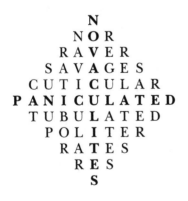

```
        N
      N O R
    R A V E R
  S A V A G E S
C U T I C U L A R
P A N I C U L A T E D
  T U B U L A T E D
    P O L I T E R
      R A T E S
        R E S
          S
```

The first diamond ("Annie") by an unknown puzzler is the earliest on record; it is from the "Round Table" in Frank Leslie's *Boys & Girls Weekly*, May 25, 1870. Rusticus made the second diamond ("Hat & Hands"), a double five-line diamond, found in *Our Boys & Girls*, June 1873. The reversible double five-line diamond ("Ten Miles") was in "The Riddle Box" column, edited by noted children's writer Mary Mapes Dodge, in *St. Nicholas*, Nov. 1874. The original puzzles were untitled.

```
      A                   H
    A N D               H A T
  A N N I E           M O N E Y
    D I D               E D A
      E                   S


                S
              T E N
            M I L E S
              P I T
                M
```

Deacon made the first seven-line diamond ("Theatre") for *Our Boys & Girls*, July 9, 1870. The first double seven-line diamond ("Homer & Robin") was created by Rusticus and appeared in the magazine Feb. 1874.

Deacon (1870)   ### Rusticus (1874)

```
      T                   G
    A H A               S E T
  A R E N A           H O M E R
T H E A T R E     F E L S P A R
  A N T I C           R O B I N
    A R C               N O D
      E                   K
```

Dressed to the Nines

The puzzler Sphinx created the first nine-line diamond ("September") for *Our Boys & Girls*, Mar. 1874. Hyperion built the first double nine-line diamond ("Saturated") for *St. Nicholas*, Sept. 1875.

Sphinx (1874)

```
        S
      P E T
    H O P E S
  P O R T R A Y
S E P T E M B E R
  T E R M E R S
    S A B R E
      Y E S
        R
```

Hyperion (1875)

```
        S
      L A R
    M A T E D
  T I T U L A R
C A M E R A T E D
  P I R A T E D
    C A T E S
      L E D
        D
```

News at Eleven

And puzzler George Ross, who called himself Happy Thought, created the first eleven-line diamond ("Pacificator") published in *Wild Oats*, Aug. 15, 1877. Asbestos published the eleven-line diamond ("Castigation") in *Independent*, Mar. 29, 1894, and E. Q. published his eleven-line diamond ("Manufactory") in *Independent*, Dec. 20, 1894.

DIAMONDS
Happy Thought (1877)

```
          P
        P A R
      R A C E S
    R E C I T E D
  P A C I F I C A L
P A C I F I C A T O R
  R E T I C U L E S
    S E C A L E S
      D A T E S
        L O S
          R
```

Asbestos (1894)

```
          C
        P A R
      C A S E D
    C A S T L E S
  P A S S I O N A L
C A S T I G A T I O N
  R E L O A D I N G
    D E N T I S T
      S A I N T
        L O G
          N
```

E. Q. (1894)

```
          M
        M A D
      M A N E D
    M I N U T E S
  M A N I F E S T O
M A N U F A C T O R Y
  D E T E C T I V E
    D E S T I N E
      S T O V E
        O R E
          Y
```

Lucky Thirteens

The puzzler Odoacer created the first thirteen-line diamond ("Boner"), published in *Mystic Knight*, Sept. 1880. It had been denounced for containing the Latinized Roman surname Macatus and the word *boner*, which had not been recognized as an acceptable English word until decades later.

Touted as the perfect thirteen-line diamond, "Contravention" was created by The General, puzzler Michael Lee, for *Baltimore Sunday News*, Apr. 23, 1882.

Prudence built the first double thirteen-line diamond ("Dangleberries"), printed in *American Farmer*, Dec. 1, 1894. Here are some definitions Prudence, puzzler E. A. Hill, gave for some of its words. *Amiet* is the name of a little-known French physician from Paris; *jungletea* is the Assam name for bun fullup, plants of the *Camellia* genus; *boreberries*, the fruit of the *Sambucus nigra*; and *candlefat*, fat from which candles are made.

The General (1882)

```
            C
          C O D
        C O N E D
      K E N T L E S
    C E N T R I C A L
  C O N T R A T E N O R
C O N T R A V E N T I O N
  D E L I T E S C E N T
    D E C E N C I E S
      S A N T E E S
        L O I N S
          R O T
            N
```

Prudence (1894)

```
            C
          C A B
        J A N O D
      H U N D R E D
    C A N D L E F A T
  T A N G L E B E R R Y
D A N G L E B E R R I E S
  W I N E B E R R I E S
    D E T E R R E N T
      T E A R I N G
        A M I E T
          S E S
            S
```

Odacer (1880)

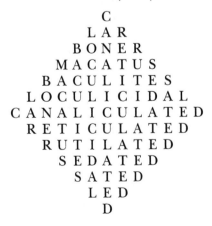

```
            C
          L A R
        B O N E R
      M A C A T U S
    B A C U L I T E S
  L O C U L I C I D A L
C A N A L I C U L A T E D
  R E T I C U L A T E D
    R U T I L A T E D
      S E D A T E D
        S A T E D
          L E D
            D
```

Finally Fifteen

Holt created the first fifteen-line diamond, published in *Ardmore Puzzler*, Dec. 15, 1901. Nypho composed the first double fifteen-line diamond and the regular seventeen-line diamond, containing the center words *realisticallier* and *rantasticallier*, published in *The Formist*, July 1918, and with the center word *manneristicallier*, published in *Forms*, May 1918.

MORE FORMS & AMUSEMENTS

Fancy diamonds, crosses, and other shapes of form puzzles date from the 1870s and 1880s. Here is a small collection of nice historic examples. Will o' the Wisp made the "Connected Diamonds," published in the *Philadelphia Free Press*, Oct. 13, 1886. Pen Ledcil created the "Diamond Cross," found in *Newark Call*, Apr. 9, 1882. The playful "Enneagon" made by Maya had been first conceived by St. Julian in 1899; this version was published in *TE*, Oct. 1995.

CONNECTED DIAMONDS
Will o' the Wisp (1886)

```
          P                   C
        E R A               E L D
      G L E B E           F L E E S
    E L U S I V E       E L E V A T E
P R E S I D E N T C L E V E L A N D
    A B I D E R S       D E A L E R S
      E V E R Y           S T A R E
        E N S               E N S
          T                   D
```

DIAMOND CROSS
Pen Ledcil (1882)

```
            S                   E
          C O G               H O D
        B O A R D           H E L E D
      C O M P A R E       H E M I N A S
  S O A P S T O N E O L I P I L E S
      G R A T I N G A D E N I Z E N
        D R O N E E R E D A L E S
          E N G R A T E R S E N
            E A R T H P E A S
          A N D E E P E S T E A
        U R G E D R E S S E A R S
      A R G O L I S A T E N D R A C
  E N G O T I N E S E A D R A G O N
        D E L I V E R   A R R A Y E D
          D I N E S       S A G E S
            S E R           C O D
              S               N
```

ENNEAGON
St. Julian (1889) & Maya (1995)

```
        S
      R A P
      R A D A R
  S A D D L E B A G S
  P A L A T A B L E
  R E T A I L E R
      B A I L E E S
      A B L E
      G L E E
      S E R S
```

Here is a "Heptagon" by Miss L. (Lucile) Irwin from *National Tribune*, Mar. 5, 1892. The form had been invented Oct. 29, 1881 by H. S. Nut for the *National Tribune.* The "Inverted Heptagon" by Alexander appeared in the newspaper's Apr. 28, 1892 issue.

The "Old Style Diamond Cross" is composed of seven seven-line diamonds and eleven five-line double diamonds (slightly modified). Beau K., puzzler Joseph Badger, Jr., created this masterwork in *Wild Oats*, Jan. 24, 1877. The "Connected Diamonds with a Square Center," also in *Wild Oats*, May 16, 1877, is by puzzler Old Joe.

HEPTAGON
Miss L. Irwin (1892)

INVERTED HEPTAGON
Alexander (1892)

OLD STYLE DIAMOND CROSS
Beau K. (1877)

```
                C
               C A M
              C A L E B
             S I L U R U S
              D E M I T
               R E T
              M O T O R
               P I N
   J           P I C U L            T
  S U P   V   P   M A R   J   B   C U B
  S A P O R A G A G I L E S O P O T A M E D
R E V I S A L E P A L A D I N A H U M B L E D
 T O T E M U M A D A M A R A P E N E L L Y
  R E D   E   W   N U N   H   A   L E E
  R               M U S I C               R
                   R E P
                  C A R U M
                   B U G
                  H U M U S
                   L O T
                  C A R A T
                   C U P
         C       B A S A L   R
        G A S   P E R   L E X
        B O R E D O S E D A N E S
       C A R A V A N A D I C E B O X
        R E V E L E M A N E W E L
         D E N   S U N   S A C
          L       M         L
```

CONNECTED DIAMONDS
WITH A SQUARE CENTER
Old Joe (1877)

```
                    R
                   R I B
                  R I V E R
                   B E Y
                    R
        O     V E S T A      S
      A C T   E N T E R    A H A
      O C E A N S T E A M S H I P S
      T A X   T E A S E    A P T
      N       A R M E D      S
                    B
                   B O A
                  B O A T S
                   A T E
                    S
```

PYRAMIDS

Earliest Constructions

Here are some of the earliest word pyramids. A puzzler who called himself Bleak House created the first "Old Style Pyramid," published in *Our Boys & Girls,* Apr. 1874.

C. T. Hat, puzzler W. S. Lord, created the "First Regular Pyramid," which he had called a "half-diamond." In a regular pyramid, which is inherently double, words can be read horizontally and vertically. The example here by C. T. Hat appeared in *Our Boys & Girls,* Nov. 1874.

OLD STYLE PYRAMID
Bleak House (1874)

```
        T
       H E R
     E R A S E
   M I S S I O N
 E N T R E A T E D
```

FIRST REGULAR PYRAMID
C. T. Hat (1874)

```
        D
       E R E
     S L A V E
   C O M M E N D
```

More Pyramids

Puzzler Col. Ossus made the first thirteen-letter inverted pyramid, which appeared in *Golden Days,* Apr. 7, 1883.

The famous puzzle sleuth Sherlock Holmes, aka Palmer Peterson, created a thirteen-letter regular pyramid, published in *TE,* Feb. 1975, as well as the truncated pyramid, which contains phrases, published in *TE,* Aug. 1963.

INVERTED PYRAMID
Col. Ossus (1883)

```
M A G I S T R A T I C A L
M A C H A I R O D U S
  R E I N C I T E D
    D E V I C E S
      L A N E S
        T I N
          C
```

REGULAR THIRTEEN-LETTER PYRAMID
Sherlock Holmes (1975)

```
            G
          P R A
        C O U B A
      M O N T A N A
    L O U I S I A N A
  C O N N E C T I C U T
M A S S A C H U S E T T S
```

TRUNCATED PYRAMID
Sherlock Holmes (1963)

```
          O M
        C U O Q
      T A T R O S
    G E M S T A T E
  B O W I E S T A T E
C Y C L O N E S T A T E
P A N H A N D L E S T A T E
```

These two pyramids contain phrases. The first ("Paradise Regained") is another Sherlock Holmes creation for *TE*, March 1977, and the second ("San Francisco"), a truncated and inverted pyramid, is by the puzzle sorcerer Merlin, published in *The Former*, Jan. 1989.

PHRASE PYRAMID
Sherlock Holmes (1977)

```
          L A
         P U L T
        R A C K A D
       S I R I A S I S
      P A P A L S T A T E
     P A R A D I S E L O S T
    C A R O L I N A P O P L A R
  P A R A D I S E R E G A I N E D
```

TRUNCATED INVERTED PYRAMID
Merlin (1989)

```
 S A N F R A N C I S C O
  C A L I F O R N I A
   B A S E M E N T
    G E N I E S
     R I N K
      L A
```

Sherlock's Pyramid Power

By combining these two half-squares, Sherlock Holmes formed a fifteen-letter "Siamese" pyramid, printed in *TE*, May 1961.

TWO HALVES
Sherlock Holmes (1961)

```
        Z            Z
       M E          E D
      W E R        R I D
     M O I N      N E A U
    F A R M E    E N G R O
   P U R S E S  S T R I N G
  S E R P E N T  T E A T E R S
 B A S T A R D I  I N D I G O E S
```

WHOLE "SIAMESE" PYRAMID
Sherlock Holmes (1961)

```
              Z
            M E D
          W E R I D
        M O I N E A U
      F A R M E N G R O
    P U R S E S T R I N G
  S E R P E N T E A T E R S
B A S T A R D I N D I G O E S
```

These next two pyramids ("Goitered Antelopes" and "Prairie Antelopes") are from Sherlock Holmes's series of eight, found in *TE,* Dec. 1947. Each has eight words, read downward, with double letter endings. Many puzzle masters consider the "Goitered Antelopes" pyramid the best pyramid, if not the best form, ever made.

ANTELOPE PYRAMIDS
Sherlock Holmes (1947)

```
              L
            S O B
          F E U R S
        P A R R I E D
      H I E R I S S O S
    T U R N I N G T R E E
  P R E R A P H A E L I T E
C H I N E S E A N T E L O P E
GOI T E R E D A N T E L O P E S


            M U
          P U N E
        P E S T L S
      K E N S E L I N
    H U T T E R I T E S
  M A S S A L I O T I C A
I N D I A N A N T E L O P E
P R A I R I E A N T E L O P E S
```

FORMAL FEATS

Pygmy Hourglass

Palmer Peterson, under his usual Sherlock Holmes cloak, also created the "Pygmy Hourglass," published in *TE,* Jan. 1954. Holmes named the form after the pseudonym of its inventor, Fred A. Tapley, whose original hourglass appeared in *Golden Days,* Jan. 9, 1886. This impressive example contains what are probably the longest terms ever used in a form, *cisterna intercruralis* and *anterior nasal arteries.* The words in this hourglass, a double form, can be read across and diagonally downward, left to right.

PYGMY HOURGLASS
Sherlock Holmes (1954)

```
C A S T A N H A N U T S
I N T E R D E B A T E
  S T E R E O B A T E
    T E R R A L I N E
    E R E A R I N G
      R I O L I T E
      N O M I N E
        A R E N G
          I N R E
          N A S
          T S
          B E A
        F I R L
      C E C C A
      C A T A R R
    C A R T R U T
    C E L A M I R E
  P A R A V A N A R
  N A M A S A G A L I
W A D I T E L E T I E
H O P E L E S S N E S S
```

Rating: Three Stars

The "Titulet" star created by Aspiro and printed Aug. 21, 1886 in the Boston magazine *American Exchange & Mart* reads across and diagonally downward, and left to right. The "Natural" star appeared in "The Mystic World" column, edited by Will A. Mette of the *Saturday Globe*, Dec. 1900. The double diagonal ("Pastors"), also in a Star-of-David shape, was the first of its kind, created by O. Range. It reads diagonally from right to left and from left to right, but not across. It was included in the column "Cylo-

Puzzledom," edited by Arty Fishel, in the Philadelphia *Cycle Guide*, Dec. 26, 1894.

THREE STARS
Aspiro (1886)

```
        T
      I F
  T I T U L E T
  F U T I L E
  L I V E R
  E L E V E N
T E R E D O S
    N O
    S
```

(1900)

```
      F
    H O
N A T U R A L
A R I S E N
T I N T S
H U S T L E
F O R E S E E
  A N
  L
```

O. Range (1894)

```
      P
    A A
S E S M S E S
H T P P T H
O E U E O
R R R R R
S E T N T E S
  E E
  N
```

Royal Crown & Hexagon

The "Crown," created by C. A. M. Den, reads across and diagonally, left to right. This form puzzle appeared in *Newark Sunday Call*, Dec. 18, 1887. The puzzler Aspiro introduced the form in the Dec. 13, 1885 issue of the column. The "Hexagon" by Phil Down was printed in "Puzzlemaze" in the *Philadelphia Press*, Mar. 23, 1887.

CROWN
C. A. M. Den (1887)

```
        B
       P A
      T A R
  D E T E R R E D
  A V E R T E D
  C E A S E D
  E R R E D
```

HEXAGON
Phil Down (1887)

```
R                 S
A B             B A
P E P         P E R
I N A M O R A T O
D E C O R A T E S
    S T R A K E S
    S A T E S
      L E D
        S
```

Hexdecagons

Skeeziks invented the hexdecagon ("Dapifer"), published in the Columbus, Ohio, *City & Country* magazine, June 1886. And Bolis published the second hexdecagon shown here ("Potassa") in *Newark Puzzler*, July 1887; the magazine's puzzle editor, Adonis, considered this puzzle "simon-pure" and "a good combination."

The first was also published in *Thedom*, June 1886.

HEXDECAGONS
Skeeziks (1886)

```
            N
           L A
      D A P I F E R
       C R I M E A
       A P O C O P E
       R E T O R T
       P O L A R I C
       L I T E R A T I
   N I C A R A G U A
   A M O R O S O S
       F O R A G E R
       E R A S E R
       E P I G E N E
       A T T O R N
       R E C U R E D
           I S
            A
```

Bolis (1887)

```
           B
          I O
      P O T A S S A
       C A R R O M
       O M E N T A L
       A U R A T E
       T E S T A T E
       I R R I T A N T
   B A N T E R I N G
   O R A T O R I O
       S T A R I N G
       O T A R I A
       S A T I N E T
       M E N I A L
   A L E N G T H
          T O
           G
```

More Form Puzzles

Here are examples of diverse form puzzles; most date from the late 19th century. The "Pentagon" form, *Milwaukee Sentinel,* Dec. 23, 1886, was called an oblique or Georgia pentagon by its creator Pink, aka Mrs. Frank E. Foster. The word *Sabines* refers to members of an ancient Italian tribe.

Mrs. Harris, more familiar to us as Skeeziks or William Ougheltree, created the "Diamond-Shaped Icosahedron," printed in *Newark Sunday Call,* Apr. 24, 1886. It reads across and down. The word *aum* (also *aam*) is a Dutch measure of liquids, and *OG* is the abbreviation for "Officer of the Guard."

The "Bolis Hexagon" appeared in *Golden Argosy,* Aug. 29, 1883. The puzzler Bolis, aka George Haywood, constructed it to read across and diagonally, left to right. The word *cardamine* is an herb of the mustard family, *loment* means "the seed pod of indehiscent legumes" and *sirname* is an old spelling of *surname.*

The "Staten Island Cross" by Tryon, aka Alice Ross Butler, was published in the *Newark Advertiser,* Oct. 10, 1903. The "Double Square Cross," also created by Tryon, was published in the newspaper's Oct. 31, 1903 issue. The word *engem* means "adorn with a gem or gems"; it is obsolete.

PENTAGON
Pink (1886)

```
        C
      S A D
    C A P E R
    S A B I N E S
  C A P I T U L A R
  D E N U D A T E D
    R E L A T I V E
      S A T I N E T
        R E V E R E
        D E T E R
```

DIAMOND-SHAPED
ICOSAHEDRON
Mrs. Harris (1886)

```
          S
        P   I
      A   U   M
        A   N
      A     L     E
    P   A   R   D   O   N
  S U L T A N A
    I   N D I G O
    M     A       D
        O   G
      E   N   D
        N   O
          A
```

BOLIS HEXAGON
Bolis (1883)

```
  C O O L S
  M A R R O W
  S I R N A M E
  M I S D A T E D
  C A R D A M I N E
  O R N A M E N T
  O R A T I N G
  L O M E N T
  S W E D E
```

STATEN ISLAND CROSS
Tryon (1903)

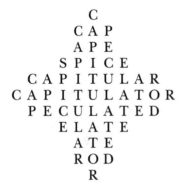

```
        C
      C A P
      A P E
    S P I C E
C A P I T U L A R
C A P I T U L A T O R
  P E C U L A T E D
    E L A T E
      A T E
      R O D
        R
```

DOUBLE SQUARE CROSS
Tryon (1903)

```
        D
        E
    L A P E L
    I N A N E
D I V E R G E N T
    E N T E R
    S T I M Y
        N
        G
```

the lapwing bird, which is also called the tirwhit and pewit; and *Eneid*, a variant spelling of the *Aeneid*, is a reference to Virgil's Latin epic poem.

DECAGON
Iron Mask (1892)

```
      M
    F I R
  B A S E D
F A N C I E D
M I S C A L L E D
R E I L L U M E
  D E L U G E D
    D E M E R I T E D
    D E D I C A T E S
        T A L I P E S
        E T I O L A T E
        D E P L O R E R S
          S E A R C E R
          S T E E P
          E R R
            S
```

NEWARK ICOSAHEDRON
Jo Hootey (1890)

```
  B A   G
P R A T E R
B E A T E R S
R A V I N E
  A R E N A
  A V E R T S
A T E L E N E
T I R W I T
  E N E I D
  E N T I C E
G R A N D E E
R E S T E D
S   E   E
```

Here is a "Decagon" by the puzzler Iron Mask, aka Stanley Giddings, from the *Philadelphia Press*, Oct. 12, 1892. The word *talipes* means "clubfoot," and the word *etiolate* means "to make pale or feeble."

The "Newark Icosahedron," slightly modified here, was constructed by puzzler Jo Hootey and printed in *Newark Sunday Call*, July 27, 1890. The word *atelene* means "imperfect; lacking regular forms in the genus"; *tirwit* is

Triple Acrostic

The puzzler Comet created the "Triple Acrostic" shown here, with the original clues (1-11), published in *Newark Puzzler*, Nov. 1883. The three long words of the answer also fit three categories cited for the primal (*metaphorical*), central (*explanatory*), and final (*reproduces*) terms established by the puzzler. Some puzzlers call this form a rectangle, and many prefer the long words of the answer (PARABOLICAL, ELUCIDATORY, REGENERATES) to read horizontally, stacked on top of each other.

COMET'S TRIPLE ACROSTIC (1883)

1. for each	P E R
2. a malt beverage	A L E
3. a thick fabric for covering part of a floor	R U G
4. a playing card	A C E
5. a box	B I N
6. a lyric poem	O D E
7. a household deity (Roman religion)	L A R
8. a town in Spain	I T A
9. a small house	C O T
10. a measure of surface	A R E
11. a river in western Belgium and northern France	L Y S

Star Crossed

The "Skeeziks Star," the puzzler's first, appeared in *Golden Days*, May 5, 1886, and the "Maltese Cross" by Will o' the Wisp appeared in *Philadelphia Press*, Jan. 18, 1888.

SKEEZIKS STAR
Skeeziks (1886)

```
   P       O
  A C   T S
P A R A M A T T A
  C A T A R R H
    M A O R I
  T A R R A C E
O S T R I C H E S
  T H   E E
  A       S
```

MALTESE CROSS
Will o' the Wisp (1888)

```
      C A R E W
        B E D
C   L O V E R   S
A B O M I N A T E
R E V I C T I O N
E D E N T A T E D
W   R A I T H   S
        T O E
      S E N D S
```

The puzzler Old Joe created the first rhomboid form puzzle, published in *Danbury News* in 1875. Other rhomboids followed. The first rhomboid shown here ("Collateral") was more difficult to build than the second rhomboid ("Bass Strait") shown here. These two are unusually large examples. Both were constructed by puzzler Sherlock Holmes and published in *TE*; the first Feb. 1950 and the second Jan. 1946. Some forms, like rhomboids and pyramids, are inherently double.

RHOMBOIDS

Sherlock Holmes (1950)

```
C O L L A T E R A L
  N E U R O S O M E S
    D E C K T E N N I S
      S E K E R I N G E S
        S E M I S I N G L E
          R E V I L E M E N T
            S E D I M E N T A L
              R E T E N D E R E D
                S E N T E N T I A E
                  M O T I O N I S T S
                    S T A R T E R O F F
```

Sherlock Holmes (1946)

```
        B A S S S T R A I T
        P I L C H E R I N G
      F A C I L I T I E S
    M A R A K A N E N G
  C O N C R E T E R S
G A R T H I N E R S
L O R R A I N E R S
T A N D I S E A S E
M O T I O N I S T S
H E R O D S G A T E
```

Transdeletions

In a *transdeletion,* which is not considered a form puzzle, one letter is omitted from each descending word and the remaining letters are transposed to make another word. These puzzles are judged by size and how well the letters are shuffled at each step. Kent Aldershof was the chief author of the "Predominates" transdeletion shown here.

Kyle Corbin made the longest full transdeletion, printed in *WW,* May 1988: "anticeremonialist, nonmaterialities, ornamentalities, interlaminates, maternalities, matrilineate, trilaminate, terminalia, latimeria, material, taliera, retail, alter, rate, tea, at, a."

Mabel Poete invented the transdeletion, a term coined by Novus Homo in 1895. She introduced a *deleted transposition* in *Study,* Apr. 1, 1894. The clues were in rhymed verse, and the solution was "inland seas, sea island, assailed, sad isle, sailed, slade, lads, sad, as, S." The dropped letters in Mabel Poete's puzzle can be transposed to form the words *inland sea.*

According to the *OED,* a *strine,* from Kent Aldershof's 1992 "Predominates" transdeletion puzzle, means "Australian, an Australian, or the English language spoken by Australians"; the term has been traced to Afferbeck Lauder, the pseudonym of Alistair Morrison.

TRANSDELETIONS
Kent Aldershof (1992)

```
P R E D O M I N A T E S
D E S P E R A T I O N
I N T E R P O S E D
E N T R O P I E S
P R O T E I N S
S T O N I E R
S T R I N E
R E S I N
R I S E
S I R
I S
I
```

```
T R I N E S        S E R I N
R I T E S          I R E S
T I R E            E R S
R E T              R E
E R                E
E
```

```
R I S E N          S I R E N
S I R E            R I S E
R E S              R E S
E R                E R
E                  E
```

Kyle Corbin (1988)

```
A N T I C E R E M O N I A L I S T
N O N M A T E R I A L I T I E S
O R N A M E N T A L I T I E S
I N T E R L A M I N A T E S
M A T E R N A L I T I E S
M A T R I L I N E A T E
T R I L A M I N A T E
T E R M I N A L I A
L A T I M E R I A
M A T E R I A L
T A L I E R A
R E T A I L
A L T E R
R A T E
T E A
A T
A
```

St. Julian invented the oblique rectangle, which first appeared in the *Saginaw Evening Journal*, June 15, 1886. The example shown here ("Oblique Rectangle") by the puzzler Lateo, appeared in the *Newark Advertiser*, Aug. 18, 1906. The "Conundrum Club Octagon" has nine diagonal rows of the same letters. It was constructed by Harley Quin, printed in *Waverley*, June 24, 1899. The "Octagon" shown here was invented by Albion for "Our Puzzle Box" in *The Canaan Reporter*, Apr. 30, 1886. Puzzler Delphine constructed the "New Style Octagon," printed in *Golden Days*, Jan. 2, 1886. The "Compound Octagon," created by Graham, appeared in "Nuts to Crack," *Nutcrackers' Monthly*, Oct. 1879. Park made the "New Style Diamond," printed in *Newark Evening Star*, May 11, 1907. The new style diamond was invented by the puzzler Beech Nut, aka Brainerd P. Emery; his first was printed in "Gordian Knots," *East Boston Advocate*, May 23, 1885.

OBLIQUE RECTANGLE
Lateo (1906)

```
        T
      O R B
    O R I O N
  T R I F L E R
    B O L S T E R
      N E T T L E S
        R E L I C T S
        R E C E I P T
          S T I B I A L
            S P I N N E Y
              T A N K A
                L E A
                  Y
```

CONUNDRUM CLUB OCTAGON
Harley Quin (1899)

```
I S L A M
S H A M E
L A M E D
A M E R I C A N
M E D I C I N E
      C I N E S
      A N E N T
      N E S T S
```

OCTAGON
Albion (1886)

```
  R A P S
 M A R R E R
R A T I O N A L
A R I L L A T E
P R O L A T E S
S E N A T O R S
 R A T E R S
  L E S S
```

NEW STYLE OCTAGON
Delphine (1886)

```
  C O R
 S C A B
V A L E T
S P A R E D
C A P I T O L
C A B I R I
P L I V I L E
A R I M A N
R E T I R E D
B E R A T E
 T O L E S
  D I N E
  L E D
```

COMPOUND OCTAGON
Graham (1879)

```
  C A R         R E D
 C A D E S     C A P E L
C A L A M A R A D I C A L
A D A L I N E P I D O T E
R E M I P E D E C O Y E D
 S A N E R     L A T E R
  R E D         L E D
 M E L E E     G E M E L
R E F U S A L E V E R E T
E L U S I V E M E L I N E
D E S I R E D E R I V E D
 E A V E S     L E N E S
  L E D         T E D
```

NEW STYLE DIAMOND
Park (1907)

```
        R
       B E
      B O W
     R E N T
    B A S I C
   B E S T O W
  R O S T R U M
   E N T I R E
    W I R E D
     T O R N
      C U D
       W E
        M
```

Double Hollow Diamond

This "Double Hollow Diamond" created by Palmer Peterson and printed in *WW*, May 1971, is unique, since all earlier hollow diamonds were compound forms, made up of a standard pyramid, an inverted pyramid, and two right and two left rhomboids. In this one, however, all "downs" (like the words *waste detector* and *recapitulates*) are undivided words or phrases. According to Ross Eckler (written under his pseudonym FaRo), one of many contributors to *In Memoriam: Sherlock Holmes* (1980), produced by the NPL: "This form must rank with the finest of all time, for despite its size, every word, except *vanites*," found in *Webster's New International Dictionary*, first unabridged edition, "was taken from" *Webster's New International Dictionary*, second unabridged edition.

The standard word authorities used by members of the EPL and NPL have been Funk & Wagnalls *Standard Dictionary* (until 1901) and *Webster's New International Dictionary* (since 1923).

DOUBLE HOLLOW DIAMOND
Palmer Peterson (1971)

```
                    P
                  T A S
                W E R P S
              C A R V E N E
            T O R N A R I A N
          P E L M A T O G R A M
        W A N D E R I N G S T A R
      M A S T E R Y   S L A T T E R
    C A S T O R S       E N L A C E D
    F A C T O R S       D E R A T E D
    F I S H E R Y       D A P I C O S
  C O S S I D S           S I N A G O G
S A L T I N E             T A N S I E S
  P L U M A T E           M U L A T T O
    E L E M E N T         M U L I T A S
    E R E C T O R         B E C A T E R
      E N T E L A M     V A N I T E S
        T O R A N A S   S O R A G E S
          R E N A L A R T E R I E S
            R E R A D I A T I O N
              S I G N A T I O N
                A M E L I A S
                  A S T O N
                    S O N
                      S
```

Ultimate Form Puzzle

Sherlock Holmes's amazing work "The Armless Man" was first published in *TE*, Apr. 1943. It consists of two squares, two rhomboids, and four pyramids. Note that the *S* at the center is shared by a pyramid and two rhomboids. This form has been justly termed "outstanding," "remarkable," and requiring "great ingenuity . . . and a pertinacity that very few have," Ross Eckler notes in *In Memoriam: "Sherlock Holmes"* (1980).

THE ARMLESS MAN
Sherlock Holmes (1943)

```
            A S P A R A M I D
            S T O N E C O L E
            P O P A F A L L S
            A N A C A R D I A
            R E F A N N I N G
            A C A R N A N I A
            M O L D I N E S S
             I L L I N I S S A
            D E S A G A S A N
               A R E P A
               T E A R Y
               A C L I S
        P A R I E T A L L O B U L E S
        U P E L L E T I E R I N E S E
        R A P I L E E N G I N E S I N
        P R A M A D I D A T E S A N S
        L A R A S E N A T O R A N C E
        E L A R A D E N E R E N G E L
        J U G G L E D U S A L T I R E
        A M O R A D O S Y L U A N E S
        C I N E M A S I T A M P A N S
        O N I V A L U N E S E E R E N
        B I T E N A N C R A S E I S E
        A T E S A R T E N T E S E S S
        E E S O R D I C I T I E S E S
        A S U P R E M E N E S S E S E
        S E A S I D E R A D I S H E S
       A O T E A R O A   C A S C A N T A
         A N T I A R I N     N S E N T A R U
        V I A T E C T A       I N D E X I N G
        P O R T U N U S       E U R I S T I C
       B I R L I N N S         B A G T A B L E
      F L O R A N G E           L O O P L I N E
   P O U N A W E A               E N S A I N T S
```

KEY TO ABBREVIATIONS

Here are some shortened book titles; abbreviations for periodicals; notes about popular puzzle columns, editors, and organizations; and other important sources for this book. Many other books, articles, magazines, newspapers, and broadsides were consulted. These "short lists" will help you identify attributed puzzlemakers and enjoy word puzzle history. Also discover the identity of the puzzler behind the pseudonym in the section Puzzlers & Their Pseudonyms.

SHORTENED BOOK TITLES

Alphabet Avenue   David Morice, *Alphabet Avenue: Life in the Fast Lane* (1997)

"Anagrammasia"   Amaranth (Newton B. Lovejoy), "Anagrammasia," unpublished book manuscript (1926) shared by NPL members

Anagrams & Word Puzzles   Astra Cielo (Milton Goldsmith), *Anagrams & Word Puzzles* (1930)

An Almanac   Willard R. Espy, *An Almanac of Words at Play* (1975)

Another Almanac   Willard R. Espy, *Another Almanac of Words at Play* (1980)

A Key to Puzzledom   William W. Delaney, et al., *A Key to Puzzledom; or Complete Handbook of the Enigmatic Art* (1906), published by William W. Delaney for EPL

Bailey's Dictionary   Nathan Bailey, *Bailey's Universal Etymological Dictionary; An Interpreter of Hard Words* (1721)

Beyond Language   Dmitri A. Borgmann, *Beyond Language: Adventures in Word & Thought* (1967)

Biblia Anagrammatica   Walter Begley, *Biblia Anagrammatica* (1904)

Boy's Own Book   William Clarke, *The Boy's Own Book* (1828)

Curious Crosswords   Dmitri A. Borgmann, *Curious Crosswords* (1970)

Daffodil   John Pool, *Lid off a Daffodil* (1982)

Devil's Dictionary   Ambrose Gwinett Bierce, *The Devil's Dictionary* (1911)

Dynamos   Jon Agee, *So Many Dynamos! (& Other Palindromes)* (1994)

1893 Puzzlers' Directory   Ernest W. Ager, *The "1893" Puzzlers' Directory*

Enigma Puzzlers' Directory   *The Enigma Puzzlers' Directory* (1927); directories issued annually by the National Puzzlers' League

From A to Zotamorf   Stephen J. Chism, *From A to Zotamorf: The Dictionary of Palindromes; Word Ways* monograph series no. 4 (1992)

Gleanings (1860)   Charles Carroll Bombaugh, *Gleanings from the Harvest Fields of Literature, Science & Art* (1860) This was the first book of word recreations published in the United States. Since 1860, there have been many revisions and new editions, some with title changes, notably 1867, 1870, 1875, and 1890; it was also reissued and updated as *Oddities & Curiosities* (1961), edited with annotations by Martin Gardner.

Gleanings (1867)   Charles Carroll Bombaugh, *Gleanings from the Harvest Fields of Literature*, 3rd edition (1867)

Go Hang   Jon Agee, *Go Hang a Salami—I'm a Lasagna Hog* (1991)

Golden Days Puzzlers' Directory   Mystic (Randolph C. Lewis), *The Golden Days Puzzlers' Directory* (1886)

Handy-Book   William Sheppard Walsh, *The Handy-Book of Literary Curiosities* (1892; 1904)

Historical Charades   J. C. Maitland, *Historical Charades* (1847)

I Love Me, vol. I   Michael Donner, *I Love Me, Vol. I, S. Wordrow's Palindrome Encyclopedia* (1996)

Language on Vacation   Dmitri A. Borgmann, *Language on Vacation: An Olio of Orthographical Oddities* (1965)

Longman   Rik J. Edwards, *Longman Anagram Dictionary* (1985)

Making the Alphabet Dance   Ross Eckler, *Making the Alphabet Dance; Recreational Wordplay* (1996)

Masquerade   *The Masquerade*, six volumes (1797-1806); chapter "Transpositions," edited by George Wilkie

Merry's Puzzles   John Newton, *Robert Merry's Second Book of Puzzles* (ca. 1860)

Modern Sphinx   *The Modern Sphinx* (1873)

More Joy of Lex   Gyles Brandreth, *More Joy of Lex* (1982)

New Anagrammasia   Ross Eckler, *The New Anagrammasia; Word Ways* monograph no. 2 (1991); revised edition of Amaranth's (Newton B. Lovejoy) "Anagrammasia"

New Sphinx   *The New Sphinx* (1806)

O&C   see *Oddities & Curiosities*

Oddities & Curiosities   Martin Gardner, *Oddities & Curiosities of Words & Literature* (1961)   This is an updated version of Charles Carroll Bombaugh, *Gleanings for the Curious from the Harvest Fields of Literature*, 3rd edition (1890).

OED   *The Oxford English Dictionary* (1971) and supplements   All *OED* text references are to the 1971 edition.

Of Anagrams   Henry Benjamin Wheatley, *Of Anagrams* (1862)

On Vacation   see *Language on Vacation*

Oxford Guide   Tony Augarde, *The Oxford Guide to Word Games* (1984)

Palindromes   G. R. Clarke, *Palindromes* (1887)

P&A   Howard W. Bergerson, *Palindromes & Anagrams* (1973)

Palindromicon   Jeff Grant, *The Palindromicon; Word Ways* monograph no. 3 (1992)

Parlour Pastime   Uncle George, *Parlour Pastime for the Young* (1857)

Pictured Puzzles & Wordplay   Arthur Cyril Pearson, *Pictured Puzzles & Wordplay* (1908)

Portable Curmudgeon   Jon Winokur, *The Portable Curmudgeon* (1987)

PP&W   see *Pictured Puzzles & Wordplay*

Puzzleana   *Puzzleana*, 13th edition (1990); publications in the library of Will Shortz

Puzzledom in a Nutshell   Henry E. Juergens and James A. Woolf, *Puzzledom in a Nutshell*, chapter "Names, Noms de Plume & Addresses of Puzzlers" (1877)

Puzzles & Oddities M. A. A. D., *Puzzles & Oddities* (1876)

Rats Live Joaquin Kuhn and Maura Kuhn, *Rats Live on No Evil Star: The Backwords Puzzle Book* (1981)

Real Puzzles John Q. Boyer, Rufus T. Strohm, and George H. Pryor, *Real Puzzles: Handbook of the Enigmatic Art* (1925)

Remains William Camden, *Remains* (1605)

S&L Treasury Samuel Maunder, *Science & Literature Treasury* (1825)

20th Cent. Book Arthur Cyril Pearson, *The Twentieth-Century Book of Puzzles* (1915)

20th Cent. Standard Arthur Cyril Pearson, *The Twentieth-Century Standard Puzzle Book* (1907)

Witt's Recreations *Witt's Recreations* (1807)

PERIODICALS & POPULAR PUZZLE COLUMNS

American Agriculturist *American Agriculturist*; column "New Puzzles to Solve," 1857-1871

American Exchange & Mart *The American Exchange & Mart (& Household Journal)*; Boston and New York; 1886-1887

American Farmer *American Farmer*, Washington, D.C., and Baltimore; column "The Enigma," edited by R. O. Chester (Charles H. Coons), 1894-1897

American N&Q *American Notes & Queries*; Philadelphia journal; edited by William Sheppard Walsh and H. C. Walsh

AP *The Ardmore Puzzler*, Ardmore, Pennsylvania; column "Merion Maze," edited by Remardo (Edwin Smith), 1899-1909

Atlantic Unbound *Atlantic Unbound*, computer on-line *The Atlantic Monthly;* column "Word Games," edited by Emily Cox and Henry Rathvon

Athenaeum *The Athenaeum*; London; weekly journal

Ballou's Monthly *Ballou's Monthly Magazine*, Boston; column "Ruthven's Puzzle Page," edited by Ruthven (Edwin R. Briggs), 1872-1891

Baltimore Item *The Baltimore Item*; newspaper column "Marginalia," edited by Hal Hazard (James R. Price), 1880-1881

Baltimore Sunday News *Baltimore Sunday News*; column "Salmagundi," edited by Maud Lynn (Harry C. Vansant), 1881-1883

B&O *Baltimore & Ohio Magazine*; column "In the Realm of the Riddle," edited by Miss Fitts (Eugene H. Pryor), 1922-1932

Bath Gazette *Bath Gazette*, Bath, England

Central NJ Times *Central New Jersey Times*; Plainfield, New Jersey; column "Guess Work," edited by Eureka (George P. Taggart), 1886-1887

Chicago Daily Tribune *Chicago Daily Tribune*; column "Puzzlers' Corner," edited by Old Man of the C., 1877-1880

Cycle Guide *Cycle Guide*; Philadelphia; column "Cyclo-Puzzledom," edited by Arty Fishel (Theodore G. Meyer), 1894-1895

Danbury News *Danbury News*; Danbury, Connecticut; column "Witch Knots," edited by Ruthven (Edwin R. Briggs), 1873-1882

Eastern Enigma see *TEE*

Ecclesiastical Gazette *Ecclesiastical Gazette*; London; journal, 1886

Enigma see *TE*

Eurekan *The Eurekan*; San Francisco; broadside, 1893-1894, 1902-1904

Evening Telegraph   *Daily Evening Telegraph*;
Philadelphia; column "Telegraph
Twisters," edited by D. C. Ver (George B.
King), 1904-1907

Everyman   *Everyman*; London weekly
magazine; column "Prose & Verse
Competitions"

Farmer's Almanac   *The Old Farmer's
Almanac*; annuals

Farmer's Almanack   *The Farmer's Almanack*;
Boston; founded 1792; printed earliest
American puzzle column, 1802; now
called *The Old Farmer's Almanac*

Farmer's Wife   *The Farmer's Wife*; St. Paul,
Minnesota; column "In Mystic Mood,"
edited by Kappa Kappa (Clara C.
Wouters) and Fred Domino (H. Grady
Peery), 1905-1912

F-SP   *The Four-Star Puzzler*; New York;
1981-1983

Games   *Games*; Ambler, Pennsylvania, and
New York

Games & Puzzles   *Games & Puzzles*;
London, and Luton, England; 1972-1981

GD   see *Golden Days*

Gentleman   *The Gentleman*; New York; column "Puzzleland," edited by C. Saw
(Lewis Truckenbrodt), 1897-1899

Golden Days   *Golden Days for Boys &
Girls*; Philadelphia weekly; column
"Puzzledom," edited by Mystic (Randolph
C. Lewis) and others 1880-1895, and by
Arty Fishel (Theodore G. Meyer), 1896-
1906

Harper's Young People   *Harper's Young
People*; New York; column "Puzzles from
Young Contributors," edited by Koe
(Louis Koelle), 1880-1891

Henry Republican   *The Henry Republican*;
Henry, Illinois; "Our Puzzle Column,"
1881-1887

Home Monthly   *The Home Monthly*;
Pittsburgh, Pennsylvania; column
"Quizzisms," edited by The Poser (Henry
E. Juergens), 1897-1898

Independent   *The Independent*; New York
weekly; column "Odd Knots," edited by
Erlon R. Chadbourn, 1894-1896

Inter-Ocean   *Daily Inter-Ocean, Sunday
Inter-Ocean,* or *Weekly Inter-Ocean;* Chicago;
column "Complications," edited by Erlon
R. Chadbourn, 1881-1914

London Evening Standard   *The London
Evening Standard*; column edited by
Arthur Cyril Pearson, 1905-1907

London News Chronicle   *London News
Chronicle*; column "Behind the Headlines,"
edited by Timothy Shy (D. B. Windham
Lewis)

Macmillan's   *Macmillan's Magazine*; article
"Anagrams & All Their Kin"

Mensa Bulletin   *Mensa Bulletin*; Fort
Worth, Texas; official organ of Mensa; column "Wordplay," edited by Bob Kusnetz

Mensa International Journal   *Mensa
International Journal*; London; edited by
Kim Walker-Daniels; column "Puzzle
Matters," edited by O. V. Michaelsen,
1993-1994

Modern Sphinx   *The Modern Sphinx;* Santa
Clara, California; puzzle journal, first
series, 1879

NA   *The Newark Advertiser* and *The Newark
Daily Advertiser;* Newark, New Jersey; col-
umn "The Newark Puzzler," edited by
Abel Em (A. Barent Le Massena), 1904-
1907, as official organ of the Newark
Puzzle Club

N&Q   *Notes & Queries*; London

Newark Call   *The Newark Call,* a daily, and
The Newark Sunday Call; Newark, New
Jersey; column "Puzzle Calls" and others,
1875-1891; edited by Will A. Mette
(William V. Belknap), 1881–1886

New Monthly Magazine   *The New Monthly Magazine,* "On Palindromes," 1821

New Statesman   *The New Statesman;* London weekly journal; column "Weekend Competition"

Newark Puzzler   *The Newark Puzzler,* Newark, New Jersey; edited by Adonis (Herman E. L. Beyer), first series 1882-1885

NT   *The National Tribune,* Washington, D.C.; column "Mystery," edited by Youandi (Charles H. Coons and Eugene J. Hazard), 1886-1897

Nutcrackers' Monthly   *Nutcrackers' Monthly;* Auburn, Maine; column "Nuts to Crack," edited by W. L. Small, 1875-1876

NY Recorder   *New York Recorder,* column "Pastimes," edited by Phil O. Sopher (Oswald C. Drew), 1893

NY Times Magazine   *The New York Times Magazine,* column "On Language," edited by William Safire

O'London's   *John O'London's Weekly;* London; column "Literary Competitions," edited by Tantalus (William T. Williams), 1928-1945

Oracle   *The Oracle;* Newburgh, New York; Newburyport, Pennsylvania; and Pittsburgh; edited by Beech Nut (Brainerd P. Emery), 1896-1899, 1905-1910

Our Boys & Girls   *Our Boys & Girls,* also called *Oliver Optic's Magazine,* Boston; column "Headwork," edited by Oliver Optic (William Taylor Adams), 1867-1875

Our Young Folks   *Our Young Folks* magazine; Boston; columns "Our Letter Box" and "Round the Evening Lamp," edited by Lucy Larcom, 1865-1873

Owl   *The Owl; Wednesday Journal of Politics & Society;* London; 1867

Palindromist   *The Palindromist,* San Francisco; quarterly edited by Mark Saltveit, 1996-present

Pearson's Weekly   *Pearson's Weekly;* London; edited by Arthur Cyril Pearson

Pittsburgh Post   *The Pittsburgh Post;* Sunday column "Enigmatic Oddities," edited by Erlon R. Chadbourn, 1900-1910

Puzzletown Oracle   *The Puzzletown Oracle;* Newburgh, New York monthly amateur puzzle broadside, forerunner of *The Oracle* and successor of *Thedom,* all edited by Beech Nut (Brainerd P. Emery), 1896

Saturday Evening Post   *Saturday Evening Post,* column "Cerebrations," edited by Wilkins Micawber (E. C. Rideout), 1879-1880

Science Digest   *Science Digest;* New York; column "Puzzles, Paradoxes, Pitfalls," edited by Dr. Crypton (Paul Hoffman), 1980s

Scientific American   *Scientific American;* column "Mathematical Games," edited by Martin Gardner, 1960s-1980s

Somerset Messenger   *Somerset Messenger;* Somerville, New Jersey; column "Cabala," edited by Calvin (H. C. Vanderveer), 1895-1899

St. Nicholas   *St. Nicholas;* New York; monthly juvenile magazine; column "The Riddle Box," edited by Mary Mapes Dodge

Strand   *The Strand Magazine,* London; column "Perplexities," edited by Henry E. Dudeney, 1910-1931

Study   *The Study;* Philadelphia; bi-monthly amateur magazine and broadside, edited by Anise Lang (Agnes Rosenkrans), 1889-1890

Sunday Standard   *The Sunday Standard;* Newark, New Jersey; column "Our Puzzles," edited by Erlon R. Chadbourn, 1894

TE *The Enigma*; official organ of the National Puzzlers' League; column "Penetralia," 1920-present; edited by Arty Ess (Rufus T. Strohm), 1923-1953; currently edited by Lunch Boy (Francis Heaney)

TEE *The Eastern Enigma*; official organ of the Eastern Puzzlers' League, 1883-1910; column "Penetralia," 1900-1902, 1910-1920; magazine retitled in 1920 *The Enigma*, organ of the National Puzzlers' League

Thedom *Thedom*; Newburgh, New York; amateur puzzle broadside; edited by Beech Nut (Brainerd P. Emery), 1889-1895

The Former *The Former*, Atlanta; newsletter edited by Qaqaq (Trip Payne) and Jo the Loiterer (Julian P. Ochrymowych), 1988-1990

TS *The Sphinx*, Savannah, Georgia; column "New Puzzles," edited by Tunste (Paul M. Bryan), 1901

Wall Street Journal *The Wall Street Journal*

Washington Post *The Washington Post*; column "Our Puzzle Department," edited by Carl/ Charles Decker, 1882-1885

Waverley *Waverley Magazine*, Boston; column "Mystic Argosy," edited by Primrose (John Q. Boyer), 1897-1905

WF *Word Fun*; Lockhart, Texas; Mensa SIG newsletter edited by Ken Elrod, 1989-present; column edited by Kent L. Aldershof

Wild Oats *Wild Oats*; New York; weekly journal, column "Oats to Sift," edited by Effen (Thomas A. Finley), 1876-1879

Windsor Magazine *Windsor Magazine*, London; column edited by Arthur Cyril Pearson, c. 1905

WW *Word Ways: The Journal of Recreational Linguistics*; Morristown, New Jersey; edited by A. Ross Eckler; formerly edited by Dmitri A. Borgmann and Howard W. Bergerson; column "Kickshaws," edited by David Morice and others

WWW *Word-Wide Web,* computer site, various "pages": Brian Hall's "Public Domain Palindrome Page," 1995; John Jensen, "Official Palindrome Page," 1995; Neil (Fred) Picciotto's "Gigantic List of Palindromes," Dec. 1, 1995; Jouko I. Valta's "International Palindromes" page, Dec. 1995

YC *The Youth's Companion*; Boston; column "Nuts to Crack," edited by Uncle Tangler (Carlton B. Case) and others, 1871-1929

ORGANIZED PUZZLERS

The Eastern Puzzlers' League (EPL), established in New York, New York, July 4, 1883, published the magazine *The Eastern Enigma* from Oct. 1883 until 1910 at irregular intervals. In Jan. 1920, the magazine name was changed to *The Enigma* and the organization name to the National Puzzlers' League (NPL). In *The Enigma*, issue no. 1000, July 1987, puzzler Merlin (Murray R. Pearce) discusses the history of *TE* and *TEE*.

While other, smaller, puzzlers' organizations exist, the NPL and its predecessor the EPL are the most active and are well represented here. The league is the world's oldest puzzlers' association.

PUZZLERS & THEIR PSEUDONYMS

Pseudonyms are in italics for easy discovery. Some real names are unknown; those in doubt are followed by a question mark. Some locations are unknown, and, of course, cities or towns of puzzlers may change.

A. Barent Le Massena   Newark, New Jersey; aka *Abel Em*

Abel Em   A. Barent Le Massena; Newark, New Jersey

Ab Struse   David Shulman; New York, New York

A. Chem   Helen M.(Mrs. Coleman) Miller; Virginia Beach, Virginia

Adonis   Herman E. L. Beyer; Newark, New Jersey

A. E. Anderson   Watertown, Wisconsin; aka *Lew Ward*

Agnes Rosenkrans   Oconomowoc, Wisconsin; aka *Anise Lang*

Ahmed   George M. Woodcock; Buffalo, New York

Ai   Arthur Schulman; Charlottesville, Virginia

Air Raid   H. H. Bailey; London, England

A. J. Meister   Philadelphia, Pennsylvania; aka *Will Dexter*

Alan Frank   Arlington, Virginia; aka *Alf*

Albert H. Homburg   Baltimore, Maryland; aka *Atlas*

Albert M. De Armit   Storm Lake, Iowa; aka *C. U. Rious*

Albert Pennell   West Gray, Maine; aka *Alexander*

Albion   Edwin F. Edgett; Boston, Massachusetts

Alec Sander   E. J. Rodden; Philadelphia, Pennsylvania

Alexander   Albert Pennell; West Gray, Maine

Alf   Alan Frank; Arlington, Virginia

Alfred Snyder   Philadelphia, Pennsylvania; aka *King Cotton*

Al Gebra   Robert Hooke; Pittsburgh, Pennsylvania

Alice   Sally Picciotto; New Haven, Connecticut

Alice Ross Butler   Port Richmond, New York; aka *Tryon*

Allez   Zella I. Price; Ferndale, Michigan

Alouette   J. W. Moore; Pareblossom, California

A. L. S.   Annie Lanman Smith; Urbana, Ohio

Alvah S. Pendleton   Nicolaus, California; aka *Percy Vere*

Amaranth   Newton B. Lovejoy; Pittsburgh, Pennsylvania

André Pujon   Riom, France

Anglo Saxon   John C. Ball; Philadelphia, Pennsylvania

Anise Lang   Agnes Rosenkrans; Oconomowoc, Wisconsin

Annie Lanman Smith   Urbana, Ohio; aka *A. L. S.*

Ann S. Thetics   William George Jordan; Philadelphia, Pennsylvania

Anonyme   William Grossman; New York, New York

A. Prestin Mellish   Providence, Rhode Island; aka *Dreamer*

Arcanus   J(acob). E. Reizenstein; Iowa City, Iowa

Archimedes   Dr. Harry Langman; Brooklyn, New York

A. R. Graser   Philadelphia, Pennsylvania; aka *King Carnival*

Arthur Cyril Pearson   London, England

Arthur F. Holt   Lynn, Massachusetts

Arthur K. Harris   Rumson, New Jersey; aka *Hart King*

Arthur Schulman   Charlottesville, Virginia; aka *Ai*

Arthur Wynne   location unknown

Arty Ess   Rufus T(racey). Strohm; Scranton, Pennsylvania

Arty Fishel   Theodore G. Meyer; Philadelphia, Pennsylvania

Asbestos   real name unknown

Aspiro   Mark Durant; Dubois, Illinois

Astra Cielo   Milton Goldsmith

Atlantic   Mark Oshin; Portland, Oregon

Atlantis   V. E. Beckley; Lima, Ohio

Atlas   Albert H. Homburg; Baltimore, Maryland

Awl Wrong   Patrick J(ohn). Flavin; Dorchester, Massachusetts

Balmar   Frank T. Koons; Baltimore, Maryland

Barnyard   Edward W. Barnard; Fall River, Massachusetts

Beachcomber   D(ominic). B(evan). Wyndham Lewis; London, England

Beau K.   Joseph Badger, Jr.; St. Joseph, Missouri

Beech Nut   Brainerd P. Emery; Newburgh, New York

Benjamin C. Pearson   location unknown

Benjamin F. Bush   Courtney, Missouri; aka *Ben J. Min*

Benjamin Haworth-Booth   Hornsea, England

Ben J. Min   Benjamin F(rancis). Bush; Courtney, Missouri

Betsy Mirarchi   location unknown

Beverly Y. Morris   Oakland, California; aka *Frank Lynn*

Bill O'Malley   location unknown

Blackstone   Paul E. Thompson; Allstead, New Hampshire

Bleak House   real name unknown

B. Lumley   England; aka *Hermes?*

Bolis   George B(olis?). Haywood; Rutherford, New Jersey

Boo   Miss V. M. Reynolds; Bournemouth, England

Boo-Jee-Kay   Rosemary Kelso; Wilmington, Delaware

Brainerd P. Emery   Newburgh, New York; aka *Beech Nut*

Brian Hall   location unknown

C. A. H. Greene   New York, New York

Calvin   H(enry). C(alvin). Vanderveer; Whitehouse, New Jersey

C. A. M. Den   real name unknown; Camden, New Jersey

Camillus   real name unknown; Chicago, Illinois

Carlton B. Case   Boston, Massachusetts; aka *Uncle Tangler*

Carrol Mayors   Roswell, New Mexico; aka *Neophyte*

Carter Bennett   Kilgore, Texas

Castet   G. C. Nichols; Berlin, West Germany

C. E. Chalfant   Media, Pennsylvania; aka *Rusticus*

Cephas   Peter H. Thomson; Minden, Nebraska

C. F. McCormick Binghampton, New York; aka *Pygmalion*

Charles A. Kizer Dalton, Ohio; aka *Tom A. Hawk*

Charles Decker (Carl); Washington, D.C.

Charles E. Fowler New Haven, Connecticut; aka *O. Possum*

Charles E. Holding Silver Spring, Maryland; aka *Mephisto*

Charles H. Coons Pittsburgh, Pennsylvania; aka *R. O. Chester* and *Youandi*

Charles Lutwidge Dodgson England; aka *Lewis Carroll*

Charles N. Crowder Baltimore, Maryland; aka *L. M. N. Terry*

Charles T. St. Louis, Missouri

Charlie B. real name unknown

Chin Chin real name unknown

Chris Long Bridgewater, New Jersey; aka *Cubist*

Christopher McManus Silver Spring, Maryland

Clara C. Wouters Hawley, Minnesota; aka *Kappa Kappa*

C. Lawrence Ford Bath, England

Cloves Frank W. Elwell; Philadelphia, Pennsylvania

Col. Ossus George Frell; Brooklyn, New York

Comet George I. Dibble; Santa Clara, California

Corn Cob Laura A. Bosch; Bowling Green, Virginia

Cornel G. Ormsby West Sacramento, California

Correl Kendall Boston, Massachusetts; aka *Sphinx*

Coxy real name unknown; Newark, New Jersey

C. P. Phin England

Crossman, Jr. first name unknown; location unknown

Cryptox William S. Hoffman; State College, Pennsylvania

C. Saw Lewis Truckenbrodt (changed in 1916 to Trent); New York, New York

C. T. Burroughs Brooklyn, New York; aka *Moonshine*

C. T. Hat W. S. Lord; Springfield, Massachusetts

Cubist Chris Long; Bridgewater, New Jersey

C. U. Rious Albert M. De Armit; Storm Lake, Iowa

Damonomad George C. Lamb; Burton, Ohio

Dana Richards Indianapolis, Indiana; aka *George Groth*

Dandy Lion real name unknown; Manayuk, Pennsylvania

Daniel F. Savage Hopkinsville, Kentucky; aka *Delian*

Daniel S. Taylor Hyde Park, Massachusetts; aka *Dona Telore*

Darryl H. Francis Sutton, England; aka *Lyrrad*

Daunter James A. Woolf; Pittsburgh, Pennsylvania

Dauntless Harry P. Leonard; New York, New York

Dave Morice Iowa City, Iowa; aka *Walter Fretlaw*

David Ellis Dickerson Tucson, Arizona; aka *Deacon*

David J. Ray location unknown

David L. Silverman West Los Angeles, California; aka *Stilicho*

David Shulman New York, New York; aka *Ab Struse*

David Stone location unknown

D. B. Wyndham Lewis London, England; aka *Timothy Shy* and *Beachcomber*

D. C. Ver   George B. King; Philadelphia, Pennsylvania

Deacon   David Ellis Dickerson; Tucson, Arizona

Deacon   real name unknown; Boston, Massachusetts; 1870 puzzle

Delian   Daniel F. Savage; Hopkinsville, Kentucky

Delphine   Henry B. Ocabock; Auburn, New York

Dmitri A(lfred). Borgmann   Dayton, Washington; aka *El Uqsor*

Dona Telore   Daniel S. Taylor; Hyde Park, Massachusetts

Double H   Henry Hook; East Rutherford, New Jersey

Douglas Fink   Norwalk, Connecticut; aka *Sphinx* and *Non Sequitur*

Dr. Crypton   Paul Hoffman

Dreamer   A. Prestin Mellish; Providence, Rhode Island

Dr. Lamb   Ireland

D. Scott Marley   Albany, California; aka *Hudu*

Dwight R. Gill   location unknown

E. A. Hill   Mystic, Connecticut; aka *Prudence*

E. C. Rideout   Philadelphia, Pennsylvania; aka *Wilkins Micawber*

Edgar Allan Poe   New York, New York

Ed Ward   J. E(dward). Hardenbergh; New York, New York

Edward R. Wolpow   Brookline, Massachusetts; aka *Newrow*

Edward Scher   location unknown

Edward W. Barnard   Fall River, Massachusetts; aka *Barnyard*

Edwin Drood   Nathan Lang; Warren, Ohio

Edwin F. Edgett   Boston, Massachusetts; aka *Albion*

Edwin Fitzpatrick   Howard W. Bergerson; Sweet Home, Oregon

Edwin R. Briggs   West Bethel, Maine; aka *Ruthven*

Edwin Smith   Ardmore, Pennsylvania; aka *Remardo*

E. E. Hollingworth   Brooklyn, New York; aka *St. Julian*

Effen   Thomas A. Finley; Alton, Illinois

E. H. Campbell   Pittsburgh, Pennsylvania; aka *Neophyte*

E. J. McIlvane   Washington, D.C.; aka *Enavlicm*

E. J. Rodden   Philadelphia, Pennsylvania; aka *Alec Sander*

Eleanor Audeley   Ireland

Ellen Auriti   location unknown

Ellsworth   Norman E. Nelson; Fort Worth, Texas

El Uqsor   Dmitri A(lfred). Borgmann; Oak Park, Illinois

Emily P. Arulpragasam   location unknown

Emily Cox and **Henry Rathvon**   Hershey, Pennsylvania; aka *Hex*

Emmo W.   M(elvin). O. Wellman; Lansing, Michigan

Enavlicm   E. J. McIlvane; Washington, D.C.

E. Pinnock   Thatcham, England

E. Q.   E. Quigley; location unknown

E. Quigley   location unknown; aka *E. Q.*

Eric Albert   Auburndale, Massachusetts; aka *Eric*

Eric   Eric Albert; Auburndale, Massachusetts

ErichWR   location unknown

Erik Bodin   Norfolk, Virginia; aka *Viking*

Erlon R. Chadbourn   Lewiston, Maine

Ernest   Ernest W. Ager; Navesink, New Jersey

Ernest W. Ager   Navesink, New Jersey; aka *Ernest*

E. S. Crow   Capt. William B(irney). Kirk; Lima, Ohio

Ess Ell   Irene Fullarton; Silver Lake, New Jersey

Eugene J. Hazard   Washington, D.C.; aka *Youandi*

Eugene J. Ulrich   Enid, Oklahoma; aka *Ulk*

Eureka   George P. Taggart; Oakland, California

Evelyn Mills   Long Beach, California; aka *Mrs. Ev*

Evening Star   John E. Walsh; Bridgeton, New Jersey

Everett Ewing   Norfolk, Virginia; aka *Hi Kerr*

Evergreen   Frank G. Mills; Wauwatosa, Wisconsin

E. W. Dutcher   Fulton, Illinois; aka *Towhead*

Fanacro   Walter Shedlofsky; St. Louis, Missouri

FaRo   (Dr. A.) Ross Eckler; Morristown, New Jersey

F. E. Nash   Fort Wayne, Indiana; aka *Hexagony*

Francis Heaney   New York, New York; aka *Lunch Boy*

Francis Lenton   location unknown

François Marie Arouet   France; aka *Voltaire*

Francolin   Frank M. Walling; Meadville, Pennsylvania

Frank G. Mills   Wauwatosa, Wisconsin; aka *Evergreen*

Frank L. Foss   West Mentor, Ohio; aka *Frans Folks*

Frank Lynn   B(everly). Y. Morris; Oakland, California

Frank M. Walling   Meadville, Pennsylvania; aka *Francolin*

Frank T. Koons   Baltimore, Maryland; aka *Balmar*

Frank W. Elwell   Philadelphia, Pennsylvania; aka *Cloves*

Frans Folks   Frank L. Foss; West Mentor, Ohio

Fred A. Tapley   Haverhill, Massachusetts; aka *Pygmy*

Fred Domino   H. Grady Peery; Corinth, Mississippi

Frederick A. Morton   Newark, New Jersey; aka *Park*

Fred J. Abrahams   New York, New York

Fred James   London, England

Fred Klein   Ann Arbor, Michigan

Fred P. Story   Ennis, Texas; aka *Y. Knott*

G. C. Nichols   Berlin, West Germany; aka *Castet*

Gemini   William R. Hooper; Brooklyn, New York

George A. Snow   Lakewood, Ohio; aka *H. S. Nut*

George B. Haywood   Rutherford, New Jersey; aka *Bolis*

George B. King   Philadelphia, Pennsylvania; aka *D. C. Ver*

George B. Tiffany   Gibson, Pennsylvania; aka *Odoacer*

George Chaiyar   New York, New York

George C. Lamb   Burton, Ohio; aka *Damonomad*

George Frell   Brooklyn, New York; aka *Col. Ossus*

George Groth   Dana Richards; Indianapolis, Indiana

George Herbert   England

George H. Pryor   Baltimore, Maryland; aka *Miss Fitts*

George I. Dibble   Santa Clara, California; aka *Comet*

George M. Woodcock   Buffalo, New York; aka *Ahmed*

George P. Taggart   Oakland, California; aka *Eureka*

George Puttenham   England

George Ross   Port Richmond, New York; aka *Happy Thought*

Gertrude Rowe   location unknown

Gil Blas   Mason P. Weller; Washington, D.C.

G. J. Blundell   England

Graham   Levi G(raham). De Lee; West Meriden, Connecticut

Graham Reynolds   location unknown

G. R. Clarke   Glasgow, Scotland

Guillielmus Rex   William V. Belknap; Newark, New Jersey

Guy Jacobson   Bridgewater, New Jersey; aka *Xemu*

Hal Hazard   James R. Price; Baltimore, Maryland

Hal Ober   location unknown

Happy Thought   George Ross; Port Richmond, New York

Harlan J. Murphy   Yazoo City, Mississippi; aka *Spud*

Harriet Eleanor Phillimon   England; aka *H. E. P.?*

H(arry). C(lay). Vansant   Baltimore, Maryland; aka *Maud Lynn* and *Verdant Green*

Harry Langman   Brooklyn, New York; aka *Archimedes*

Harry Ober   Boston, Massachusetts; aka *Hoho*

Harry P. Leonard   New York, New York; aka *Dauntless*

Hart King   Arthur K. Harris; Rumson, New Jersey

H. C. Laughlin   Belle Centre, Pennsylvania; aka *H. C. L.*

H. C. L.   H. C. Laughlin; Belle Centre, Pennsylvania

Helen M. Miller   Virginia Beach, Virginia; aka *A. Chem*

Henry B. Ocabock   Auburn, New York; aka *Delphine*

Henry Burrell   Freeport, Illinois; aka *Happy Thought*

Henry Calvin Vanderveer   Whitehouse, New Jersey; aka *Calvin*

Henry Campkin   England

Henry C. Wiltbank   New York, New York; aka *Nypho*

Henry E. Everding   Newark, New Jersey; aka *Simon Ease*

H(enry). E. Juergens   Pittsburgh, Pennsylvania; aka *The Poser*

Henry H. Breen   England

Henry Hook   East Rutherford, New Jersey; aka *Double H*

Henry Rathvon and **Emily Cox**   Hershey, Pennsylvania; aka *Hex*

H. E. P.   Harriet Eleanor Phillimon?; England

Hercules   Howard B. McPherrin; Denver, Colorado

Herman E. L. Beyer   Newark, New Jersey; aka *Adonis*

Hermes   B. Lumley?

Hexagony   F. E. Nash; Fort Wayne, Indiana

Hex   Emily Cox and Henry Rathvon; Hershey, Pennsylvania

H. Grady Peery   Corinth, Mississippi; aka *Fred Domino*

H. H. Bailey   London, England; aka *Air Raid*

H. H. Glyde   Pretoria, South Africa

Hi Kerr   Everett Ewing; Norfolk, Virginia

Hitty Maginn   real name unknown; St. Louis, Missouri

H. J. Wismar   Sherman Oaks, California; aka *Pacifico*

Hoho   Harry Ober; Boston, Massachusetts

Hoodwink James Lloyd Hood; Bastrop, Texas

Hoosier Theodore A. Funk; Detroit, Michigan

Horace G. Crevling Newark, New Jersey; aka *Pen Ledcil*

Howard B. McPherrin Denver, Colorado; aka *Hercules*

Howard Richler Côte-Saint-Luc, Quebec; aka *Retrosorter*

Howard W. Bergerson Sweet Home, Oregon; aka *Edwin Fitzpatrick*

H. S. Nut George A. Snow; Lakewood, Ohio

Hudu D. Scott Marley; Albany, California

Hugh Hazelrigg location unknown

Hyperion real name unknown

Icicle J. G(eorge). Augustin; New Orleans, Louisiana

Imperial real name unknown; Toledo, Ohio

Irene Fullarton Silver Lake, New Jersey; aka *Ess Ell*

Iron Mask Stanley A. Giddings; Batavia, New York

J. A. Haddock Philadelphia, Pennsylvania; aka *Old Joe*

Jamaica John J. McAlinney; Pittsburgh, Pennsylvania

J(ames). A. Lindon Weybridge, England

James A. Woolf Pittsburgh, Pennsylvania; aka *Daunter*

James B. Kirk Lima, Ohio; aka *Jim Jam*

James C. P. location unknown

James I. Rambo San Francisco, California; aka *Tut*

James Lloyd Hood Bastrop, Texas; aka *Hoodwink*

James R. Price Baltimore, Maryland; aka *Hal Hazard*

Jane Prins location unknown

Jarep Richard J. Pigott; New York, New York

Jason J(ames). J(ason). Bradley; New York, New York

J. C. Maitland location unknown

Jean Mary Baardsen Beaufort, North Carolina; aka *Maya*

J. E. C. Snyder Hoboken, New Jersey; aka *Lateo*

Jed Martinez Margate, Florida; aka *Te-Zir-Man*

Jeff Grant Hastings, New Zealand

J. E. Hardenbergh New York, New York; aka *Ed Ward*

Jemand McCulloch B. Wilson; Wilmington, North Carolina

J. E. Reizenstein Iowa City, Iowa; aka *Arcanus*

Jessie McPherrin Denver, Colorado

J. Fred Windolph Norwich, New York; aka *Phil Down*

J. F. Shine Bromley, England

J. G. Augustin New Orleans, Louisiana; aka *Icicle*

J. G. Hassocks England

J. H. Armington Leesburg, Indiana; aka *Novus Homo*

Jim Beloff Los Angeles, California

Jim Jam James B. Kirk; Lima, Ohio

J. J. Bradley New York, New York; aka *Jason*

Joaquin Kuhn Fenelon Falls, Ontario

John B. Walsh Bridgeton, New Jersey; aka *Evening Star*

John C. Ball Philadelphia, Pennsylvania; aka *Anglo Saxon*

John E. Connett Minneapolis, Minnesota; aka *Rosco X. Ocsor*

John Hesemann location unknown

John Jensen location unknown

John J. McAlinney Pittsburgh, Pennsylvania; aka *Jamaica*

John J. Toohey Harrison, New Jersey; aka *Jo Hootey*

John Leavy location unknown

John L. Hervey Chicago, Illinois; aka *Majolica*

John Meade location unknown

John M. Meyer Walton, New York; aka *Smith, Tim S.*

John Nesbit New York, New York; aka *O. N. E. One*

John Newton location unknown; aka *Robert Merry*

John Pool location unknown

John Q. Boyer Baltimore, Maryland; aka *Primrose*

John Taylor England; called the Water Poet, but not a pseudonym

Jo Hootey John J. Toohey; Harrison, New Jersey

Jon Agee New York, New York

Josefa Heifetz Byrne location unknown

Joseph Badger, Jr. St. Joseph, Missouri; aka *Beau K.*

Joseph J. Adamski Jenison, Michigan; aka *Mercury*

Joshua Sylvester location unknown

Jo the Loiterer Julian P. Ochrymowych; Basking Ridge, New Jersey

Jouko I. Valta location unknown

Judith E(isenstein). Bagai Portland, Oregon; aka *Sibyl*

Julian P. Ochrymowych Basking Ridge, New Jersey; aka *Jo the Loiterer*

J. W. Moore Pareblossom, California; aka *Alouette*

J. Yeoman South Shields, England

Kamel Kathryn Ludlam; St. Petersburg, Florida

Kappa Kappa Clara C. Wouters; Hawley, Minnesota

Kathryn Ludlam St. Petersburg, Florida; aka *Kamel*

Kea Roger Phillips; London, England

Ken Elrod Lockhart, Texas

Kenneth William A(ntoine). Moore, Jr.; Morton Park, Illinois

Kent L. Aldershof Ridgewood, New Jersey

K. F. Ross New York, New York

King Carnival A. R. Graser; Philadelphia, Pennsylvania

King Cotton Alfred Snyder; Philadelphia, Pennsylvania

Koe Louis Koelle; New York, New York

Lane Ambler Ove Ofteness; Whiting, New Jersey

Larry Loris B. Curtis; Mason, Michigan

Lateo Dr. J. E. C. Snyder; Hoboken, New Jersey

L. C. real name unknown

Le Dare Leslie D. Rees; Denver, Colorado

Lee Sallows Nijmegen, Netherlands

Leigh Mercer London, England; aka *Roger G. M'Gregor*

Len Elliott location unknown

Leslie D. Rees Denver, Colorado; aka *Le Dare* and *Virginia Dare*

Leslie E. Card Urbana, Illinois

Levi G. De Lee West Meriden, Connecticut; aka *Graham*

Lewis Carroll Charles Lutwidge Dodgson; England

Lewis Truckenbrodt (Trent) (Truckenbrodt changed to Trent in 1916); New York, New York; aka *C. Saw*

Lewis Zander Harrison New York, New York; aka *L. Z. H.*

Lew Ward A. E. Anderson; Watertown, Wisconsin

Linda Bosson New York, New York; aka *Mona Lisa*

Livedevil William Lutwiniak; Jersey City, New Jersey

L. M. N. Terry   Charles N(ewton). Crowder; Baltimore, Maryland

Lois M(arin). Fischer   Whiting, New Jersey; aka *Ms. Dos*

Lord Baltimore   Simon J. Block; Baltimore, Maryland

Loris B. Curtis   Mason, Michigan; aka *Larry*

Louisa H. Sheriden   England

Louis Koelle   New York, New York; aka *Koe*

L. P. Flash   real name unknown

Lubin   real name unknown; England

Lucille Irwin   Washington, D.C.; aka *Lucille*

Lucy Larcom   Boston, Massachusetts

Lucille   Lucille Irwin; Washington, D.C.

Lunch Boy   Francis Heaney; New York, New York

Lycophron   Thrace

Lyrrad   Darryl H. Francis; Sutton, England

L. Z. H.   Lewis Zander Harrison; New York, New York

M. A. A. D.   Real name unknown

Mabel P.   Mabel Poete; Waccamaw, South Carolina

Mabel Poete   Waccamaw, South Carolina; aka *Mabel P.*

Madda Boutem   Mrs. John L. Lee; Newport, Michigan

Majolica   John L. Hervey; Chicago, Illinois

Malcolm Tent   Ove Ofteness; Whiting, New Jersey

Mangie   Margerie Friedman; Buffalo, New York

Margaretta   Margaretta Strohm; Trenton, New Jersey

Margaretta Strohm   formerly Margaretta Burkholder; Trenton, New Jersey; aka *Margaretta*

MargB   real name unknown

Margerie Friedman   Buffalo, New York; aka *Mangie*

Mark Durant   Dubois, Illinois; aka *Aspiro*

Mark Oshin   Portland, Oregon; aka *Atlantic*

Mark Saltveit   San Francisco, California

Martin Gardner   Hendersonville, North Carolina

Mary C. Snyder   Springfield, Illinois; aka *M. C. S.*

Mary E. Holmes   Plymouth, Massachusetts; aka *May Le Hosmer*

Mary J. Hazard   née Youngquist; Rochester, New York; aka *Nightowl*

Mary Mapes Dodge   New York, New York

Mason P. Weller   Washington, D.C.; aka *Gil Blas*

Matilda   real name unknown

Matthew J. Hackett   New York, New York; aka *Mattie Jay*

Matthew J. Sheedy   New York, New York; aka *Rose Budd*

Matthew K. Franklin   location unknown

Mattie Jay   Matthew J. Hackett; New York, New York

Maud Lynn   H(arry). C(lay). Vansant; Baltimore, Maryland

Maura Kuhn   location unknown

Maxey Brooke   Sweeny, Texas

Maya   Jean Mary Baardsen; Beaufort, North Carolina

May H. Reed   Pasadena, California; aka *Quirk*

May Le Hosmer   Mary E. Holmes; Plymouth, Massachusetts

McCulloch B. Wilson   Wilmington, North Carolina; aka *Jemand*

M. C. S.   Mary C. Snyder; Springfield, Illinois

M. Douglas McIlroy   Bernardsville, New Jersey

Medius   real name unknown; Farmington, Connecticut

Melvin O. Wellman   Lansing, Michigan; aka *Emmo W.*

Mentor   Wayne M. Goodman; Chicago, Illinois

Mephisto   Charles E. Holding; Silver Spring, Maryland

Mercury   Joseph J. Adamski; Jenison, Michigan

Merlin   Murray R. Pearce; Bismarck, North Dakota

Michael Donner   aka *S. Wordrow*

Michael Lee   New York, New York; aka *The General*

Michael Taub   Philadelphia, Pennsylvania

Micky Mackenzie   Grand Rapids, Michigan

Mike Griffin   location unknown

Mike Morton   Waipahu, Hawaii

Milton Goldsmith   location unknown; aka *Astra Cielo*

Minnie Mum   Mrs. Paul Smith; Maplewood, New Jersey

Miss H. Selway   Belfast, Ireland

Miss L. Booth   Cloverdale, Virginia; aka *Palea*

Miss R. E. Speight   Nuneaten, England

Miss T. Ree   Mrs. H. P. Taggert; Plainfield, New Jersey

Miss V. M. Reynolds   Bournemouth, England; aka *Boo*

Molemi   Morton L(eslie). Mitchell; St. Louis, Missouri

Mona Lisa   Linda Bosson; New York, New York

Moonshine   C. T. Burroughs; Brooklyn, New York

Morton G. Lloyd   Philadelphia, Pennsylvania; aka *O. Range*

Morton L. Mitchell   St. Louis, Missouri; aka *Molemi*

M. O. Wellman   Lansing, Michigan; aka *Emmo W.*

Mrs. B. Woodward   London, England

Mrs. Dean   Tipperary, Ireland

Mrs. E. H. Fatkin   Leeds, England

Mrs. E. J. Tillman   Cambridge, Minnesota; aka *Svensk Grandy-bo*

Mrs. Ev   Evelyn (Mrs. Frank G.) Mills; Long Beach, California

Mrs. Frank E. Foster   Iowa Falls, Iowa; aka *Pink*

Mrs. Harris   William L. Ougheltree; New York, New York

Mrs. Henry Eagleton   Norfolk, Virginia; aka *Su San*

Mrs. H. P. Leonard   New York, New York; aka *Seer*

Mrs. H. P. Taggert   Plainfield, New Jersey; aka *Miss T. Ree*

Mrs. James F. Morton   Paterson, New Jersey; aka *Plantina*

Mrs. John L. Lee   Newport, Michigan; aka *Madda Boutem*

Mrs. M. A. M. Macalister   Cambridge, England

Mrs. M. K. Barnes   Cape Town, South Africa

Mrs. Paul Smith   Maplewood, New Jersey; aka *Minnie Mum*

Mrs. S. F. Bardwell   Whitney Crossings, New York; aka *Spica*

Ms. Dos   Lois M(arin). Fischer; Whiting, New Jersey

Murray R. Pearce   Bismarck, North Dakota; aka *Merlin*

M. Victor Goodrich   Rock Falls, Illinois; aka *Swamp Angel*

Natalie Heiman   location unknown

Nathan Lang   Warren, Ohio; aka *Edwin Drood* and *Uncle Nat*

Neil (Fred) Picciotto   location unknown

Nellie Jay   Nellie Jones; Elgin, Illinois

Nellie Jones   Elgin, Illinois; aka *Nellie Jay*

Neophyte   Carrol Mayors; Roswell, New Mexico; 1977 puzzle

Neophyte   E. H. Campbell; Pittsburgh, Pennsylvania; 1896 and 1906 puzzles

Newrow   Edward R. Wolpow; Brookline, Massachusetts

Newton B. Lovejoy   Pittsburgh, Pennsylvania; aka *Amaranth*

Niagara   real name unknown

Nibbs   R. L. Dow; Hartford, Connecticut

Nicholas Fairbairn   Scotland

Nightowl   Mary J(osephine). Hazard, née Youngquist; Rochester, New York

N. Jineer   Olive W(etzel). Dennis; Baltimore, Maryland

Noah R. Deneau   location unknown

Noble Holderread   Milford, Indiana; aka *Sakr-El-Bahr*

Non Plus   real name unknown; Chicago, Illinois

Non Sequitur   Douglas Fink; Norwalk, Connecticut

Norman E. Nelson   Fort Worth, Texas; aka *Ellsworth*

Novus Homo   J. H. Armington; Leesburg, Indiana

Nugarum Amator   England

Nyas   William S. Clarke; Washington, D.C.

Nypho   H(enry). C. Wiltbank; New York, New York

O. C. Drew   Brooklyn, New York; aka *Phil O. Sopher*

Odoacer   George B. Tiffany; Gibson, Pennsylvania

Old Joe   J(oseph). A. Haddock; Philadelphia, Pennsylvania

Old Man of the C.   real name unknown; Chicago, Illinois

Olive W. Dennis   Baltimore, Maryland; aka *N. Jineer*

O. M.   Ove Ofteness; Whiting, New Jersey

O. N. E. One   John Nesbit; New York, New York

O. O.   real name unknown

O. Possum   Charles E. Fowler; New Haven, Connecticut

O. Range   Morton G. Lloyd; Philadelphia, Pennsylvania

Ove Ofteness   Whiting, New Jersey; aka *Lane Ambler, Malcolm Tent, O. M., O. V. Michaelsen,* and *Rom Dos*

O. V. Michaelsen   Ove Ofteness; Whiting, New Jersey

Pacifico   H. J. Wismar; Sherman Oaks, California

Palea   Miss L. Booth; Cloverdale, Virginia

Palmer C. Peterson   Worthing, South Dakota; aka *Sherlock Holmes*

Park   Frederick A. Morton; Newark, New Jersey

Patrick J(ohn). Flavin   Dorchester, Massachusetts; aka *Awl Wrong*

Patrick Robbins   location unknown

Paul E. Thompson   Cleveland Heights, Ohio; aka *Blackstone*

Paul Hoffman   location unknown; aka *Dr. Crypton*

Paul M. Bryan   Washington, D.C.; aka *Tunste*

Pedestrian   real name unknown

Pen Ledcil   Horace G. Crevling; Newark, New Jersey

Percy Vere   Alvah S. Pendleton; Nicolaus, California

Peter Hilton   location unknown

Peter H. Thomson   Minden, Nebraska; aka *Cephas*

Peter L. Stein   location unknown

Peter Newby   Chesterfield, England

Peter N. Horne   Seattle, Washington

Phil Down   J. Fred Windolph; Norwich, New York

Philip M(ichael). Cohen   West Chester, Pennsylvania; aka *Treesong*

Philip Morse   location unknown

Phil O. Sopher   O(swald). C. Drew; Brooklyn, New York

PikMee   real name unknown

Pink   Mrs. Frank E. Foster; Iowa Falls, Iowa

Plantina   Mrs. James F. Morton; Paterson, New Jersey

Polly   real name unknown

Poly   William H. Quick, Jr.; Brooklyn, New York

Primrose   John Q. Boyer; Baltimore, Maryland

Prudence   E. A. Hill; Mystic, Connecticut

Pygmalion   C. F. McCormick; Binghampton, New York

Pygmy   Fred A. Tapley; Haverhill, Massachusetts

Pythagoras   Greece

Q   William Lawrence; Mount Vernon, New York

Qaqaq   Trip Payne; Atlanta, Georgia

Quirk   May H. Reed; Pasadena, California

R   real name unknown

R. Are   real name unknown

Remardo   Edwin Smith; Ardmore, Pennsylvania

Retrosorter   Howard Richler; Côte-Saint-Luc, Quebec

R. G.   Robert Gillespie?; Brooklyn, New York

Richard Blackbourne   England

Richard Edes Harrison   location unknown

Richard J. Pigott   New York, New York; aka *Jarep*

Richard Lederer   San Diego, California

Rizpah   real name unknown; Baltimore, Maryland

R. L. Dow   Hartford, Connecticut; aka *Nibbs*

Robert G. Evans   Holland, Michigan; aka *Wrong Font*

Robert Gillespie   Brooklyn, New York; aka *R.. G.?*

Robert Hooke   Pittsburgh, Pennsylvania; aka *Al Gebra*

Robert Merry   John Newton; location unknown

Robert P. King   Erie, Pennsylvania; aka *Sans Souci*

Robert S. Dow   Newark, New Jersey

Robert Siegel   location unknown

Robert Ustrich   Los Angeles, California; aka *Sol, Jr.*

R. O. Chester   Charles H. Coons; Pittsburgh, Pennsylvania

Roger G. M'Gregor   Leigh Mercer; London, England

Roger Phillips   London, England; aka *Kea*

Rom Dos   Ove Ofteness; Whiting, New Jersey

Ron Howes   location unknown

Rosalie Moscovitch   Côte-Saint-Luc, Quebec; aka *Wabbit*

Rosco X. Ocsor   John E. Connett; Minneapolis, Minnesota

Rose Budd   Matthew J. Sheedy; New York, New York

Rosemary Kelso   Wilmington, Delaware; aka *Boo-Jee-Kay*

Ross Eckler   Morristown, New Jersey; aka *FaRo*

R. T. S. Rufus T(racey). Strohm; Scranton, Pennsylvania

Rufus T. Strohm Scranton, Pennsylvania; aka *Arty Ess* and *R. T. S.*

Rusticus C. E(dgar). Chalfant; Media, Pennsylvania

Ruth Ruth Germann; Newark, New Jersey

Ruth Germann Newark, New Jersey; aka *Ruth*

Ruth Herbert Palo Alto, California; aka *Ruthless*

Ruthless Ruth Herbert; Palo Alto, California

Ruthven Edwin R. Briggs; West Bethel, Maine

Sakr-El-Bahr Noble Holderread; Milford, Indiana

Sally Picciotto New Haven, Connecticut; aka *Alice* and *Sally*

Sally Sally Picciotto; New Haven, Connecticut

Samuel Maunder England

Sam Weller Torry Kirk; Lima, Ohio

Sans Souci Robert P. King; Erie, Pennsylvania

Seer Mrs. H. P. Leonard; New York, New York

S. E. G. real name unknown

Sherlock Holmes Palmer C. Peterson; Worthing, South Dakota

Sibyl Judith E(isenstein). Bagai; Portland, Oregon

Simon Ease H(enry). E(dgar). Everding; Newark, New Jersey

Simon J. Block Baltimore, Maryland; aka *Lord Baltimore*

Skeeziks William L. Ougheltree; New York, New York

S. L. B. real name unknown

Smith, Tim S. John M. Meyer; Walton, New York

Sol, Jr. Robert Ustrich; Los Angeles, California

Sotades Maroneia, Crete, Greece

Sphinx Correl Kendall; Boston, Massachusetts; late 1800s

Sphinx Douglas Fink; Norwalk, Connecticut; 1980s-1990s

Spica Mrs. S. F. Bardwell; Whitney Crossings, New York

Spud Harlan J. Murphy; Yazoo City, Mississippi

Stanley A. Giddings Batavia, New York; aka *Iron Mask*

Stephan R. Marlow location unknown

Stephen J. Chism Fayetteville, Arkansas

Stephen Sondheim location unknown

Stilicho David L. Silverman, West Los Angeles, California

St. Julian E(dward). E(verett). Hollingworth; Brooklyn, New York

Stocles Thomas F. Wood; St. Louis, Missouri

Susan C. Ridgeway location unknown

Susan Leslie location unknown

Su San Mrs. Henry Eagleton; Norfolk, Virginia

Susan Thorpe Buckinghamshire, England

Svensk Grandy-bo Mrs. E. J. Tillman; Cambridge, Minnesota

Swamp Angel M. Victor Goodrich; Rock Falls, Illinois

S. Wordrow Michael Donner

S. W. Parker London, England

Sydney Abbey Ottawa, Ontario

Talon Tom Allen; Iowa City, Iowa

Tantalus William T(om). Williams; London, England

Te-Zir-Man Jed Martinez; Margate, Florida

T. H. real name unknown; Moscow, Idaho

The Duke real name unknown

The General Michael Lee; New York, New York

Theodore A. Funk Detroit, Michigan; aka *Hoosier*

Theodore G. Meyer Philadelphia, Pennsylvania; aka *Arty Fishel*

The Poser H(enry). E. Juergens; Pittsburgh, Pennsylvania

Thomas Billon France

Thomas A. Finley Alton, Illinois; aka *Effen*

Thomas F. Wood St. Louis, Missouri; aka *Stocles*

Timothy J. Wheeler Shelbyville, Indiana; aka *Tweaser*

Timothy Shy D(ominic). B(evan). Wyndham Lewis; London, England

Tom A. Hawk Charles A. Kizer; Dalton, Ohio

Tom Allen Iowa City, Iowa; aka *Talon*

Tom Deneau location unknown

Tom Nobel location unknown

Tom Pulliam Somerset, New Jersey

Torry Kirk Lima, Ohio; aka *Traddles* and *Sam Weller*

Towhead E(dward). W(illiam). Dutcher; Fulton, Illinois

T. P. O'Brien location unknown

Traddles Torry Kirk; Lima, Ohio

Treesong Philip M(ichael). Cohen; West Chester, Pennsylvania

Trip Payne Atlanta, Georgia; aka *Qaqaq*

Tryon Alice Ross Butler; Port Richmond, New York

Tunste Paul M. Bryan; Washington, D.C.

Tut James I(rwin). Rambo; San Francisco, California

Tweaser Timothy J. Wheeler; Shelbyville, Indiana

Ulk Eugene J. Ulrich; Grand Chain, Illinois

Uncle George real name unknown

Uncle Nat Nathan Lang; Warren, Ohio

Uncle Tangler Carlton B. Case; Boston, Massachusetts

V. E. Beckley Lima, Ohio; aka *Atlantis*

Verdant Green H(arry). C(lay). Vansant; Baltimore, Maryland

Viking Erik Bodin; Norfolk, Virginia

Virginia Dare Leslie D. Rees; Denver, Colorado

V. M. Reynolds Bournemouth, England

Voltaire François Marie Arouet; France

Wabbit Rosalie Moscovitch; Côte-Saint-Luc, Quebec

Walter Fretlaw Dave Morice; Iowa City, Iowa

Walter Gwyn England

Walter Shedlofsky St. Louis, Missouri; aka *Fanacro*

Wayne M. Goodman Chicago, Illinois; aka *Mentor*

Wede Willard R. Espy; New York, New York

W. G. Scribner Lincoln, Nebraska; aka *W. G. S.?* and *Willy Wisp?*

W. G. S. W. G. Scribner?

Will A. Mette William V. Belknap; Newark, New Jersey

Willard R. Espy New York, New York; aka *Wede*

Will Dexter A. J. Meister; Philadelphia, Pennsylvania

William A. Moore, Jr. Morton Park, Illinois; aka *Kenneth*

William B. Kirk Lima, Ohio; aka *E. S. Crow*

Will(iam) (F.) Shortz Pleasantville, New York; aka *Willz*

William George Jordan Philadelphia, Pennsylvania; aka *Ann S. Thetics*

William Grossman New York, New York; aka *Anonyme*

William Holden Charteris, England

William H. Pollock New York, New York; aka *Will o' the Wisp*

William H. Quick, Jr. Brooklyn, New York; aka *Poly*

William Lawrence Mount Vernon, New York; aka *Q*

William L. Ougheltree New York; New York; aka *Skeeziks* and *Mrs. Harris*

William L. Sacrey Philadelphia, Pennsylvania; aka *Yercas*

William Lutwiniak Jersey City, New Jersey; aka *Livedevil*

William Oldys England

William R. Hooper Brooklyn, New York; aka *Gemini*

William S. Clarke Washington, D.C.; aka *Nyas*

William S. Hoffman State College, Pennsylvania; aka *Cryptox*

William T. Williams London, England; aka *Tantalus*

William V. Belknap Newark, New Jersey; aka *Will A. Mette* and *Guillielmus Rex*

William W. Delaney location unknown

Will o' the Wisp William H. Pollock; New York, New York

Willy Wisp W. G. Scribner?; Lincoln, Nebraska?

Willz Will(iam) (F.) Shortz; Pleasantville, New York

Wilkins Micawber E. C. Rideout; Philadelphia, Pennsylvania

Winfred S. Emmons Waco, Texas

Wrong Font Robert G. Evans; Holland, Michigan

W. S. Lord Springfield, Massachusetts; aka *C. T. Hat*

W. Williams Haverfordwest, Wales

Xemu Guy Jacobson; Bridgewater, New Jersey

X. Spellary real name unknown

Yercas Dr. William L. Sacrey; Philadelphia, Pennsylvania

Y. Knott Dr. Fred P. Story; Ennis, Texas

Youandi Charles H. Coons; Pittsburgh, Pennsylvania; and Eugene J. Hazard; Washington, D.C.

Zella I. Price Ferndale, Michigan; aka *Allez*

INDEX

ABOUT THE AUTHOR

O. V. Michaelsen is a former puzzle columnist for the *Mensa International Journal.* His articles on wordplay have appeared in many publications, including *Word Ways* magazine and *Collier's Encyclopedia.* He is also a singer, songwriter, and guitarist of contemporary folk, rock, and country music. A collection of his songs will soon be available on compact disc. For questions about his album or comments about word puzzles, O. V. Michaelsen may be reached at his E-mail address: ovmichaelsen@juno.com